# IPTV and Internet Video

# IPTV and Internet Video: New Markets in Television Broadcasting

Wes Simpson & Howard Greenfield

National Association of
BROADCASTERS

AMSTERDAM • BOSTON • HEIDELBERG • LONDON
NEW YORK • OXFORD • PARIS • SAN DIEGO
SAN FRANCISCO • SINGAPORE • SYDNEY • TOKYO
Focal Press Is an Imprint of Elsevier

Focal
Press

Senior Acquisitions Editor:    Angelina Ward
Publishing Services Manager:    George Morrison
Senior Project Manager:    Brandy Lilly
Assistant Editor:    Doug Shults
Marketing Manager:    Christine Degon Veroulis
Cover Design:    Eric Decicco

Focal Press is an imprint of Elsevier
30 Corporate Drive, Suite 400, Burlington, MA 01803, USA
Linacre House, Jordan Hill, Oxford OX2 8DP, UK

**Library of Congress Cataloging-in-Publication Data**
Application submitted

**British Library Cataloguing-in-Publication Data**
A catalogue record for this book is available from the British Library.

ISBN 13: 978-0-240-80954-0
ISBN 10: 0-240-80954-8

For information on all Focal Press publications
visit our website at www.books.elsevier.com

07 08 09 10 11    10 9 8 7 6 5 4 3 2 1

Typeset by Charon Tec Ltd (A Macmillan Company)
www.charontec.com
Printed in the United States of America

# Contents

# Dedication

Thanks to my loving wife, Laurie, and our fantastic children, Taylor and Cameron, for giving me your support and gentle encouragement to embark on this fascinating journey.

—Wes Simpson

Dedicated to my parents, Sam and Rose Greenfield, for lifting me on their shoulders and keeping me in their great hearts.

—Howard Greenfield

# Acknowledgments

The authors would like to acknowledge the many industry experts and thought leaders whose open, generous dialogues—and vision—have provided insights that contribute so significantly to our work. This book benefits from their ideas and from the influence of their efforts upon tomorrow's technology, business, and culture.

We also salute a great many other kind individuals close to our work and dreams for their help and support in pulling it all together to accomplish this awesome task: Angelina Ward, Beth Millett, Joanne Tracy, Mark Weiss, Olaf Nielsen, Keith Galitz, Gene de Vore, Justin Radke, Pierre Costa, John Trimper, Paul Atwell, Graeme Packman, Cesar Bachelet, Jon Haass, Dan Gillmor, John Markoff, Françoise Groben, Barbara Bouchet, Ephraim Schwartz, Susan Daffron, Jean Anderson, Bill Veltrop, Steve Schneider and Clare Henjum.

# About the Authors

**Wes Simpson** is president and founder of Telecom Product Consulting, an independent consulting firm that focuses on helping companies develop and market video and telecommunications products. He is a frequent speaker and analyst for the video transport marketplace; in the past three years alone he has spoken at IBC, NAB, BroadcastAsia, SMPTE, VidTrans and a number of other conferences. Wes is author of the well-received book "Video Over IP, A Practical User's Guide to Technologies and Applications" published by Focal Press in 2006.

Wes has more than 25 years experience in the design, development and marketing of products for telecommunication applications. Before founding Telecom Product Consulting, he was COO of VBrick Systems, Inc., a manufacturer of MPEG video equipment. Earlier, at ADC Telecommunications, Wes was the director of product management for the DV6000, a market leading video transport system. He previously held a variety of marketing and engineering positions in the telecommunications industry. Wes was a founding member of the Video Services Forum, and was a member of its Board of Directors from 1997 to 2001. He holds a BSEE from Clarkson University and an MBA from the University of Rochester.

**Howard Greenfield** is president of Go Associates, a global consulting firm that helps companies bring technology to the marketplace. He is a digital media and business development strategist as well as an accomplished columnist, widely published around the world. Howard has held senior management and consulting positions with Sun Microsystems, Informix Software, British Telecom and Apple Computer. He was the creator and leader of Sun's first Media Lab and completed graduate studies at Stanford University.

For the last two decades, Howard has been a successful technology developer, manager, educator and writer. In addition to front-line collaborative development ventures with Xerox PARC, Ericsson and the American Film Institute, he has held leadership roles involving early stage start-up companies and established corporations, three of which were subsequently acquired by Ariba, IBM and Microsoft.

Howard has presented and moderated at conferences throughout Silicon Valley, Europe, and Asia. He has served on government and cultural advisory boards that include the State of California, UK Trade & Invest, CNET and others. He also worked in the Apple Classroom of Tomorrow research and development, and is currently a board member of BlueVoice.org, an Internet media non-profit dedicated to protecting ocean life and habitats.

The authors welcome any comments, questions, or insights from readers. Please feel free to send e-mail to Wes at wes.simpson@gmail.com and Howard at howard@go-associates.com.

# Introduction

The world is changing very fast. Big will not beat small anymore. It will be the fast beating the slow.

—Rupert Murdoch

The traditional business model for broadcasters, which has worked reasonably well for the past few decades, is starting to break down. Increasingly, consumers are demanding (and starting to receive) their video content in ways that were impractical even a few years ago. Consider the following:

- **Television Has Moved to the Web.** Viewers around the world tuned in to watch the 2006 FIFA World Cup in record numbers using their PCs and other Internet connected devices. InFront Sports reported more than 125 million downloads[1] from the fifaworldcup.com Web site of two-minute video clips with game summaries. While this number pales in comparison with the estimated 32 billion viewers of live broadcast coverage, the number of clip downloads increased by a huge factor between 2002 and 2006.

- **It's All Personal: PVR Timeshifting and Ad-Zapping.** The use of personal video recorders in the U.S. has skyrocketed over the past few years, with a variety of stand-alone solutions as well as those integrated into set top boxes from satellite and cable television providers. Worldwide sales in 2005 totaled 19 million units, and 11 percent of U.S. households have units.[2] Broadcast advertisers have grown increasingly upset by the practice of commercial skipping and the

---

1. fifaworldcup.yahoo.com/06/en/060713/1/8s8z.html
2. In-Stat, June 5, 2006,www.instat.com/press.asp?Sku=IN0603110ME&ID=1680

loss of their ability to control the timing when viewers watch ads for specific events, such as movie openings or store sales.

- **Media Has Gone Mobile.** In Asia, mobile phones are just beginning to be used to deliver both broadcast and on-demand video services. Reports show that by 2010, there will be 68 million mobile TV users in Asia,[3] or 55 percent of the worldwide total of 120 million. Also, new standards for mobile file and stream delivery are often based on IP technology, indicating an increase in market penetration in coming years.

- **Everyone Wants to Be a Producer.** Meanwhile, a wide range of user generated video content continues to drive viewers to sites like youtube.com which generated more than 100 million downloads per day in 2006. Clearly, at least for certain types of content, viewers are perfectly happy to watch video on normal PC displays.

- **Podcasting Is Official.** Over 500,000 listeners downloaded podcasts of Ricky Gervais' free weekly show in early 2006, and the term "podcasting" has officially become part of the language.

- **You Are Now Free to Placeshift.** Devices from Sling Media, Apple and many others are now allowing consumers to move content among several different viewing devices, such as PCs, home television sets and portable media players.

What had been only whisperings about the promise of new digital media networks for the last 25 years is now becoming an audible roar on the horizon, and a commercial revolution is building. How will traditional broadcasters compete with the surge of disruptive technology ahead? One way is by understanding and harnessing some of the key technologies that support these competitive video outlets. Both IPTV and Internet Video depend on IP technology, something not lost on the broadcasting industry.

Television broadcasters have long been intensive IP technology users. A walk around any modern video production facility will reveal all types of devices that use IP technology, from digital editing stations to file servers to playout control systems. It is also highly unusual nowadays to find a broadcast executive who doesn't use some type of IP enabled device, such as a laptop computer, portable e-mail device or voice over IP telephone.

---

3. *Business Week*, June 20, 2006,
   www.businessweek.com/globalbiz/content/jun2006/gb20060620_115324.htm?chan=tc

However, until recently, it has not been feasible to deliver broadcast-quality video over IP networks to consumers. Today, with the growth of high speed networks to consumers and the adoption of IP technology by carriers around the world, video delivery over IP networks is not only feasible, it is becoming the only way to reach some categories of viewers. The key for both established and aspiring video content distributors will be to understand how IP technology will affect the ways viewers watch and pay for video content.

In this book, we explore both the technologies of video delivery and the business aspects, as IP increasingly makes a bold mark across production, delivery and business practices. IP technology creates a wide array of new ways to deliver content to consumers, particularly when compared to traditional linear broadcasting supported by advertising. From a business perspective, IP video opens up many avenues for generating revenue, including customer payments in many forms and opportunities for sponsorships and advertising. The ease of implementing new technologies on an IP platform means that different business models can be supported. It's a combined creative challenge and window of opportunity.

# Who Should Read This Book

This book is focused on providing readers a good, direct understanding of the technologies and business issues surrounding IPTV and Internet Video. Care is taken to present major concepts clearly while staying above the specific details of individual implementations. Case studies are used to provide real-world examples of this technology being used to deliver actual services to paying customers.

Executives, managers and technologists will benefit from this information. Executives will find a guide to many different technology and business options that can be used to attain strategic goals for many different kinds of organizations, ranging from large established media and telecommunications providers to small startups.

Managers will find a variety of technologies and business models that can be used to achieve their organizations' strategic video delivery business goals. Technologists will find overviews of a number of different tools and techniques that can be used to construct video delivery systems, allowing them to quickly identify areas for further research and paths to implementation.

Many different industry segments are about to be significantly affected by the coming wave of IPTV and Internet Video delivery systems.

- Existing broadcasters will be introduced to a variety of techniques that can be used to deliver content and new ways to enhance viewer experiences.

- Telecommunications network operators will discover a range of services and delivery models that will enable their companies to benefit from existing plant and infrastructure investments, as well as providing a guide to new possibilities for network migration.

- Media providers and content owners will see a range of choices that can be used to deliver content to viewers in both local markets and around the globe, and will see different business models for maximizing the value of their assets.

- IT architects and software developers will get a high-level view of ways that applications, middleware and server systems are being integrated into media delivery, creating new, hybrid network operations.

- Investors will gain a deeper understanding of the technologies and business practices that impact this wildly diverse marketplace and generate new investment models. The increased ability to identify specific sectors that warrant their support will drive clearer investment decisions.

# Features of This Book

This book has been designed to make it easy for readers to find a wide variety of information quickly and efficiently. The following three features complement the main focus of each chapter to provide even more insight for decision makers.

## The Corner Office View

Placed near the beginning of each chapter is a brief "Corner Office View" section. Each of these sidebars offers direct quotations from influential industry executives pioneering the future who offer meaningful perspective on the industry and its new direction.

## Reality Checks

Because this book is aimed at decision makers who need to understand both the benefits and drawbacks of this new technology, we have added a section at the end of each chapter to serve as a Reality Check. Sometimes, this section will be devoted to application studies or market data that pertain to the subject of the chapter. Other times, we will focus on issues or concerns that may serve to limit the widespread deployment of a technology. Either way, we hope to highlight issues that will help readers to get a better understanding of the wild and wonderful world of IP video.

# Glossary

Understanding the jargon used in this industry is essential to gaining a good appreciation of the important issues facing executives. This book includes an extended glossary, with more than 150 technical terms defined in crisp, clear language.

# Organization of this Book

Each chapter is designed to address an important issue for broadcasters and service providers. Readers are encouraged to choose whatever chapters interest them in any order, with the caveat that some of the more fundamental topics are described in the early chapters. In some cases, the latter chapters will refer to information presented in early chapters.

### Chapter 1: What is IP, and Why Use it for Video?

This chapter analyzes the basic motivations for using IP networks to deliver video services. We also take a look at the market trends driving the rapid growth in this market.

### Chapter 2: IPTV vs. Internet Video

This chapter focuses on the differences between "IPTV" and "Internet Video," terms that are often used in very similar contexts by experts. IPTV offers multiple channels of programming distributed to viewers who use a set top box and a television. Internet Video consists of thousands or millions of individual video files viewed using a PC.

### Chapter 3: Business Models

Many different business models are being tried for both IPTV and Internet Video. We cover equipment costs, programming costs and viewer payment methods. We conclude with an in-depth look at a real IPTV system that is meeting its financial goals ahead of plan.

### Chapter 4: Network Overviews

This chapter covers the basic architecture of both IPTV and Internet Video systems. All of the key elements of both types of systems are described, including hardware and software functions.

### Chapter 5: IP—The Internet Protocol

IP is essential for IPTV and Internet Video. We provide a good introduction to IP and some popular types of devices that support it. Multicasting, a key concept for IPTV, is also explained.

## Chapter 6: Video Compression

Video compression is a requirement for essentially all IPTV and Internet Video systems. We begin with a discussion of the basics and then describe the most popular compression systems—the MPEG family, Microsoft Windows Media, and others.

## Chapter 7: Maintaining Video Quality and Security

This chapter focuses on video quality and security. Video and network impairments are described, along with what system designers have done to minimize or compensate for those errors. Several techniques for both conditional access and digital rights management are described.

## Chapter 8: Video Servers

Servers are often used for IPTV and Internet Video systems. Several technologies are described, including a focus on servers used for VOD, advertising and live streaming, which are all key for IPTV and Internet Video systems.

## Chapter 9: The Importance of Bandwidth

Many different services compete for a limited amount of IP bandwidth. We examine an emerging ecosystem of DSL technology and home networks and give an example of network bandwidth calculation.

## Chapter 10: Set Top Boxes

The set top box (STB) is a crucial component of any IPTV network. It must receive video packets, decompress them and display images in real time. The STB and middleware systems must also handle all of the user interaction for an IPTV system

## Chapter 11: Internet Video Technologies

A variety of different technologies can be used for Internet Video services, including true streaming, download, and progressive download and play. We look at each of these technologies and the associated protocols and media players.

## Chapter 12: The Future of IP Video

This chapter looks at a range of possible futures for both IPTV and Internet Video. Business drivers, advanced technology and mobile media devices are all discussed. We wrap up with a look through the eyes of business leaders, soothsayers and technical wizards as they try to discern the future from a variety of perspectives.

# Summary

Throughout this book, you will find discussions about the future and about some of the forces re-shaping video as a medium. Including this perspective has been intentional. IP has nearly unlimited creative potential for re-inventing the way common tasks are accomplished and how entire global architectures are implemented. Without a constantly improving Internet functionality, this book could never have been written. As the Web becomes more powerful and IP applications more elegant, perhaps the next edition of this book won't even be printed on paper. Perhaps it will be released as part of a new online channel, with interactive segments and multimedia showcases featuring the systems, people and processes.

It's clear the future is going to be different from the broadcast and communications environment of today. We hope the reader will enjoy the insights and benefit from the expertise we've strived to provide. Moreover, we trust this book will provide a key to understanding the vast range of opportunities that will involve us all as technology and business developers, and as an audience in a new world of media.

# 1 What is IP, and Why Use it for Video?

Nothing is really real unless it happens on television.
—Daniel J. Boorstin (American social historian and educator)

Before we try to answer this question, it's appropriate to consider what may be obvious – that video transport over *Internet Protocol* (IP) networks is not only here today, but is poised to become a dominant form of video service delivery for the next 20 years. As it unfolds, new media communications services that only the imagination can anticipate will arise along with it. We are at the dawn of an era that some hail as possibly the most fascinating phase in broadcasting history.

We will discuss the reasons more in this chapter, and the spread of IP will form a subtext throughout the rest of this book. However, there is little doubt that a large and vigorous market is developing though a confluence of improved compression, faster data links, more sophisticated software and evolving viewer habits. So, let's explore these trends, see how they impact network, technology, and business decisions today and, in the final chapter, see where these trends may lead us in the decades ahead.

Digital video is a precisely timed, continuous stream of constant bit rate information, which commonly works on networks where each signal is carried over a network that is purpose-built for video. In contrast, IP networks carry many different kinds of data from a huge variety of sources on a common channel, including e-mail, Web pages, instant messaging, *voice over IP* (VoIP) and many other types of data. With all of this data flowing together, the Internet is, at best, a loosely timed collection of information that is broken up into discrete packets. Clearly, IP and video don't make an ideal marriage of technologies.

In spite of this fundamental incompatibility, the market for IPTV and Internet Video is exploding. Why? Well, the answer to that question boils down to five basic arguments:

- Because broadband IP networks reach so many households in developed countries, video service providers can use these networks to launch video services without having to build their own networks.

- IP can simplify the task of launching new video services, such as interactive programming, *video on demand* (VOD) and targeted, viewer-specific advertising.

- The cost of IP networking continues to decline due to the massive volume of equipment produced each year and the existence of worldwide standards.

- IP networks can be found in every country in the world, and the number of users with high-speed Internet connections continues to grow at a rapid pace.

- IP is a perfect technology for many other applications, including data transactions (such as e-mail or banking), local area networking, file sharing, Web surfing and many others.

In this chapter, we will begin with a brief summary of the market trends for IPTV and Internet Video. We will then discuss in greater depth the five forces mentioned above that are driving the migration of video into IP, followed by a look at some issues that need to be addressed by any system trying to send video over an IP network. We'll conclude with a case study of a successful IPTV network installation.

## The Corner Office View

"IPTV is a huge growth initiative. It's huge for us, it's huge for our partners. Count the number of TVs, and you don't have to get a lot of money per TV per year to start feeling kind of excited about the size of the opportunity."

— Steve Ballmer, CEO, Microsoft, speaking to analysts in July 2006[1]

---

1. IPTV International, Volume 2, Issue 2

# The Internet Protocol

IP provides a mechanism for directing packet flows between devices connected on a network. IP is a common protocol used throughout the Internet and any of the millions of other networks that use IP. Without IP, chaos would reign because there would be no way for one device to send data specifically to another.

At its heart, IP is a standard method for formatting and addressing data packets in a large, multi-function network such as the Internet. A packet is a variable length unit of information (a collection of bytes) in a well-defined format that can be sent across an IP network. Typically, a message such as e-mail or a video signal will be broken up into multiple IP packets. IP can be used on many different network technologies, such as Ethernet LANs, long haul fiber optic and telephony networks, and wireless Wi-Fi links.

A number of different video services operate on IP networks, as we shall see in this book. Applications range all the way from low resolution, low frame rate applications like Webcams to high definition television and medical images. IP technology is incredibly widespread, and a huge variety of video technologies can use IP networks.

# The Market for IP Video

So many different video applications can be implemented over IP networks that it can be hard to quantify them, and any attempt to do so will be quickly outdated. Nevertheless, a few facts and figures may be interesting:

- AT&T has begun rollout of Project Lightspeed, an IPTV network intended to be available to 19 million homes in the company's service area by the end of 2008. The company is planning an investment of $4.6 billion to make this a reality.[2]

- France Telecom had 421,000 ADSL Digital Television (IPTV) subscribers in France as of September 30, 2006. This is an increase of 38 percent over the 306,000 IPTV subscribers reported as of June 30, 2006.[3] Figure 1.1 shows the subscriber growth over two years, with a cumulative annual growth rate of more than 150 percent.

---

2. AT&T Corporate press release, May 8, 2006

3. France Telecom press releases, July 27 and October 26, 2006

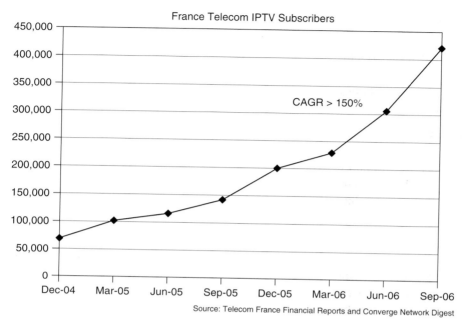

Source: Telecom France Financial Reports and Converge Network Digest

**FIGURE 1.1**  *France Telecom's IPTV Subscriber Growth 2004–2006*

- Google agreed to acquire YouTube, a leading Web site that allows users to view and upload original videos, for $1.65 billion in October 2006. At the time, YouTube was delivering more than 100 million video views every day and receiving 65,000 video uploads daily.[4]

- MRG, a market research firm, predicts that the number of global IPTV subscribers will grow from 8.0 million in 2006 to 50.7 million in 2010, a compound annual growth rate of 58 percent.[5] See the Reality Check section at the end of this chapter for more detailed information from this study.

The number of applications for video transport over IP networks is large and constantly growing. In this book, we will be focusing on IPTV and Internet Video, both of which are defined in detail in Chapter 2. However, there are a number of

---

4. Google/YouTube joint press release, October 9, 2006

5. IPTV Global Forecast—2006 to 2010, Semiannual IPTV Global Forecast, October 2006. Published by Multimedia Research Group, Inc., www.mrgco.com

other applications that use video transport over IP networks that deserve to be mentioned:

- Videoconferencing has moved out of the realm of dedicated rooms with specialized telecom data circuits into the world of desktop PCs interfacing with IP networks. These systems are characterized by low delay, low bit-rate systems that are suitable for "talking head" video but not much else.

- Webcams have become very popular, particularly for low cost, real-time communication. These systems typically run at very low frame rates (10 or fewer frames per second) and employ very inexpensive digital cameras. These systems can even be configured to work on dial-up connections, although this converts the "video" image into a series of still images with very low resolution.

- Many video surveillance devices intended for use in security applications have migrated to IP technology. There are a number of reasons for this transition, but one of the most compelling is the ability to use existing or easy-to-install Ethernet data cabling in place of coaxial video cables. In these networks, IP protocols and Ethernet cabling is simply used as a means to provide point-to-point connectivity between cameras, video recorders and displays.

- In the world of professional video production, IP networks are used for a variety of purposes (as is the case in many other modern businesses.) IP networks are used to provide connections between video editing workstations and file servers in a production studio. IP networks are used to transmit high quality video files and live feeds from remote venues back to production facilities. And IP networks are used to move video files containing raw footage, finished programming and advertisements to and from virtually every studio, post house and broadcaster in business today.

Not all of the above applications relate directly to the focus of this book, but all of them contribute to the rapidly growing, multi-billion dollar market that constitutes video over IP today.

# Arguments in Favor of IP Video

There are a number of reasons companies and individuals decide to transport video signals over IP networks. Three of the most popular revolve around the flexibility of IP networks, their low cost and the incredible coverage that IP networks provide within an organization and around the world. Let's examine each of these arguments in more detail.

# IP Network Flexibility

The number of applications of IP networks is truly staggering. The Internet Assigned Numbers Authority (IANA), which maintains the master address book for the Internet, has several thousand well-known and registered ports for different applications that use the IP protocol.[6] Some of the most common ones include port 80 for the Hypertext Transfer Protocol (http) that is used by the World Wide Web and ports 25 for Simple Mail Transfer Protocol (smtp) and 110 for Post Office Protocol – Version 3 (pop3) that are used for e-mail.

Counting the number of IP ports is just measuring the tip of the iceberg of IP applications, because many other programs use the protocols that have these port assignments. For example, there are literally dozens of different e-mail programs that work on a variety of different operating systems (Windows, Mac-OS, Linux, etc.) which all communicate by means of the ports defined for smtp and pop3.

Many different devices support IP. In addition to desktop and laptop PCs, servers and mainframes with a variety of different software operating systems can be configured to use IP. In addition, many other devices in the video world have Ethernet ports to allow all sorts of functions, ranging from simple status monitoring and control all the way up to HD video transport.

IP is also very flexible because it is not tied to a specific physical communication technology. IP links have been successfully established over a wide variety of different physical links. One very popular technology for IP transport is Ethernet, which is the dominant network technology in local area networks. Many other technologies can support IP, including dial-up modems, wireless links (such as Wi-Fi), and SONET and ATM telecom links. IP will even work across connections where several network technologies are combined, such as a wireless home access link that connects to a CATV system offering cable modem services, which in turn sends customer data to the Internet by means of a fiber optic backbone.

For broadcasters, this flexibility is important, but it is also a challenge. It is important because it gives broadcasters a choice among a large number of technologies and business models that can be used to deliver content in new formats. It is a challenge because it is impossible to choose a single solution for delivering video over IP networks that will suit all potential viewers.

---

6. A list of these ports was located at www.iana.org/assignments/port-numbers in August 2006

# IP Cost Advantages

Economics is where things start to get interesting, because IP technology has a very low hardware cost. Virtually all new PCs and laptops come equipped with Ethernet ports. A quick scan of the Web shows that Gigabit Ethernet interface cards (which operate at 1,000 Mbps) can be purchased for as little as $15, and they get cheaper all the time. Other infrastructure, such as Ethernet switches, can be purchased for as little as $10 per port. For other networking technologies, such as ATM, SONET or even SDI video routers, costs are typically 10 to 100 times more expensive.

Basic IP software is also very inexpensive or often free. All major computer operating systems include built-in IP software "stacks" that support many different IP services without added cost to the user. This is important not only in commercial applications, but also for home users who might want to access Internet Video services while retrieving their e-mail. This is not to say that all IP video software is inexpensive—far from it. The software necessary to put together a functioning IPTV delivery platform that is scalable to hundreds of video channels and thousands of viewers can easily reach into the millions of dollars.

The low costs of IP networks are of great benefit to broadcasters for two reasons. First, low cost means that much of the network infrastructure needed to connect a video source to a viewer has already been purchased and installed by potential viewers; that which hasn't can affordably be purchased by the broadcaster. Second, as viewer expectations for quality and availability of content grow, putting upward pressure on network bandwidths, broadcasters can safely assume that the IP networks will continue to expand in capacity (which has proven to be a safe assumption for every year over the past three decades.)

# IP Ubiquity

IP networks are truly pervasive in the post-millennial world. Both Antarctica and Greenland have over 8,000 Internet hosts each; the United States has 195 million.[7] Private IP networks exist in hundreds of millions of homes and businesses around the world—IP is the default technology today when people want to connect two computers together in order to share a printer or an Internet connection. For the traveler, Internet connectivity is available in hotels, airports, coffee shops and via *3G* mobile phone data networks in many large cities around the globe.

---

7.  From the CIA Factbook located at www.cia.gov/cia/publications/factbook/fields/2184.html in August 2006

High-speed data access lines are continuing to be installed at a rapid rate in most developed countries. In the U.S., data collected by the Federal Communications Commission's Wireline Competition Bureau show that by the end of 2005, close to 40 percent of the nation's 109 million households had high-speed access lines in service. This number has been growing by between 3 and 5 million homes every six months for the past three years and shows no sign of abating. Figure 1.2 shows the trend for the past five years.

For broadcasters, the global reach of the Internet is both good and bad. It's good in the sense that anyone in the world with a suitable network connection is part of the potential audience for the broadcaster. (For example, it is perfectly possible to see the local Doppler radar for Connecticut from a hotel room in Tokyo.) It's bad in the sense that the role of the local broadcaster can be fiscally undermined by the disintermediation capability of the Internet. (Viewers in a locality have no need to watch a Hollywood movie by way of their local broadcaster's Web site when they can just as easily get the content directly from the studio's film library.)

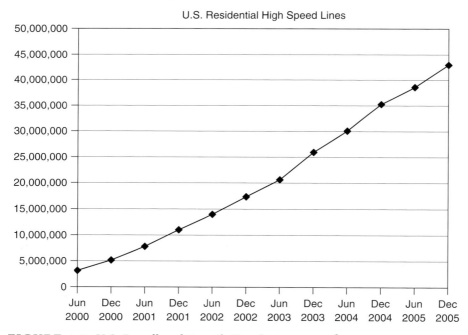

**FIGURE 1.2** *U.S. Broadband Growth Trends, 2000–2005*[8]

---

8. From reports published by the FCC's Wireline Competition Bureau, www.fcc.gov/wcb/iatd/stats.html

# Arguments Against IP Video

While there are powerful forces driving the use of IP networks for video transport, it is important to understand some of the potential drawbacks of this new technology. The first argument is primarily economic and revolves around the history of many things on the Internet being free of charge. The second is technical and centers on the difficulty of taking smooth, constant bit rate video signals and adapting them for transmission over IP networks. The third argument focuses on the dilemma of combining video signals that have very high demands for network resources on links that must carry other traffic and determining which uses will get priority. Let's look at each on of these in more detail.

## Bad Attitudes About Payment

In some ways, the Internet is still dealing with some bad habits that were established in early days, when content was available for free to anyone who was able to connect. This spirit lives on today in a variety of ways, particularly in the widespread use of illegal file sharing for valuable music and video content.

Any broadcaster hoping to sell content over the Internet needs to be aware of these traditions and expectations and develop a policy to deal with them. One popular method is to deliver the content for free, but to include advertising on the Web site or inserted into the content itself. Another method is to charge fees on a subscription or pay-per-view basis. Both of these options will be discussed more in Chapter 3.

Obtaining legal access to content can also be a challenge. Many content owners have separate licensing terms for different forms of distribution. For example, a movie studio will have different terms and different licensees for each type of release: theatrical, pay-per-view, subscription television, DVD, commercial television and others. Creating a functional team inside a network-based carrier's organization to obtain these licenses can be an expensive and time-consuming process.

Jon Taplin, former CEO of Intertainer, now adjunct professor of communications at the University of Southern California, once related a pertinent anecdote about a conversation he had at a dinner party near the time of the first incarnation of Napster.[9] The conversation was with a father who had just surprised his teenage daughter with three music CDs that, through close family research, he knew she would love to have. Her response on receiving the gift was, "Dad! You bought these for me? Why didn't you tell me? We could have just downloaded them off the Internet!"

---

9. From www.go-associates.com/files/DigitalPiracy.pdf

As the public's perceptions of the Internet mature, and as content owners continue to win high-profile convictions against illegal file sharing, theft of services may become less of an issue. However, it is inevitable that some content will be stolen by some users some of the time. Also, as technology advances, the skills of encryption crackers will increase, forcing improvements to be made to encryption algorithms that modern *digital rights management* (DRM) are based on. It is incumbent upon content owners to ensure that all of their valuable content is protected with the latest available DRM technology.

## Established Viewing Habits

Introducing new viewing habits into large populations of viewers can be difficult and time-consuming. Basic IPTV services closely mirror broadcast television and CATV, but so do viewer expectations about these services. Viewers will expect (and rightly so) that these basic services on IPTV offer a similar level of video quality and system performance to preexisting forms of delivery. More advanced services—such as video on demand and interactive programming—may require viewers to develop new patterns.

While these habits aren't impossible to change (look at the increasing penetration of digital video recorders), there can be a long and expensive learning curve. Plus, IP system operators must be conscious about competitors who create new services that can work over their existing broadcast and CATV facilities. New service providers need to take these factors into account, particularly when creating business plans for exciting new services that may be highly profitable but also require a change in viewing habits.

## Network Jitters

Whenever continuous signals like video are cut up into packets for transport over an IP network, difficulties can arise. These mainly stem from the need for the packets to arrive in a timely manner, in the same order they were sent. When this doesn't happen, it places a tremendous burden on the receiving device to properly realign the packets while at the same time doing all of the processing necessary to produce the decoded video output. Some of these variations can be accommodated through the use of memory buffers in the receiving device, but these add delay to the end-to-end video connection.

Broadcasters need to realize that these potential impairments exist, and that there are methods for dealing with problems as they occur. Some of these solutions (such as increasing network bandwidth or replacing network routers) may not only be expensive but also impractical for networks that rely on the Internet.

# A Matter of Priority

One of the great benefits of IP networks is the number of different applications that are supported. However, one of the burdens this flexibility places on network administrators is the need to prioritize the applications. Without a priority system, time-critical packets can run into delays caused by congestion of packets from many different flows, which can happen surprisingly often on IP networks.

Unfortunately, the existing mechanisms for handling priority packets on private networks are limited at best. These schemes are also useless on the public Internet, because priority routing is not implemented there. To understand why, consider the dilemma of deciding which packets in the public Internet should receive priority. Each user will, of course, think their packets are more important than those of other users. Without some type of global prioritizing or pricing scheme for different classes of packet service, efforts to add priority filtering to the Internet will be impossible.

Inside private networks, priority systems can be used, but there are still difficulties. Again, the problem arises from determining which types of signals will get priority. The argument for giving video signals priority over other signals is clear, because video signals do not perform well if their packets are delayed or dropped. However, video signals are one of the largest users of bandwidth on most networks and can take up a significant portion of the available capacity. Hence, the dilemma about choosing suitable priority levels can occur on almost any type of IP network.

# Pioneer Syndrome

The old cliché about pioneers getting arrows in their backs can certainly be applied to IPTV pathfinders. Because of the complexity and relative immaturity of several of the technologies involved, innovators in IPTV can run into difficulties in a number of areas. One particular area of potential trouble is system integration, where technologies from different suppliers need to be knitted together into a seamless whole. A second area of potential trouble occurs when the network is scaled up to full deployment, where the number of subscribers moves from a few hundred relatively friendly customers to many thousands of paying customers. Large, technically proficient suppliers and system operators have run into problems like these in the past. Companies wishing to install IPTV systems need to recognize that much of this technology is relatively new and unproven and that problems can and will occur.

# Reality Check

For this chapter's Reality Checks, we first explore an impressively large forecast that has been published for this market. While the amount of growth projected in this forecast is quite large, it certainly isn't the highest growth projection that we have seen. In the second reality check, we take a look at the IPTV market in France, which must be called a success by any measure.

## Market Forecast

By any standard, the market for IPTV services has grown rapidly for the past few years, and industry observers expect that trend to continue. As can be clearly seen on the following charts, the pace of IPTV subscriber growth continues to accelerate. Figure 1.3 shows a forecast of the growth in the number of subscribers worldwide for IPTV from 2006 to 2010. Figure 1.4 shows a forecast of the growth in the amount of service revenue worldwide for IPTV from 2006 to 2010.

## IPTV in France

At the IBC in Amsterdam in September 2006, IPTV was a hot topic, and for good reason: service providers were rapidly rolling out IPTV services to consumers all over the planet. Not every venture produces a winner, but there have been a number of successful deployments, and more are on the way. Graeme Packman, of Understanding & Solutions, a UK-based consulting firm, gave a very interesting presentation on IPTV during IBC and provided additional data used here.[10]

One country where IPTV seemed to be taking hold is in France. Between 2004 and 2006, more than 400,000 subscribers signed up for IPTV service from Orange (France Telecom). Alternative ISP Free provided an IPTV service with more than 80 channels in a package that included Internet access and telephony. About two-thirds of Free's 1.9 million broadband subscribers were eligible for this package. Other IPTV providers included alternative operator Neuf Cegetel, which had recently acquired AOL France, Telecom Italia subsidiary Alice and T-Online (Deutsche Telekom) subsidiary Club Internet.

France had an estimated 25 million television households, with approximately 3 million CATV subscribers and 4 million satellite subscribers (in addition to the

---

10. From a presentation entitled "IPTV—Overview and Keys to Success," September 10, 2006, at IBC, Amsterdam, and subsequent interviews. For more information, please visit www.uands.com

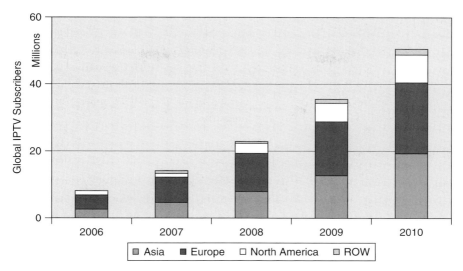

**FIGURE 1.3**    *IPTV Subscriber Growth Forecast 2006–2010.*
*Source: © MRG Inc. 2006*

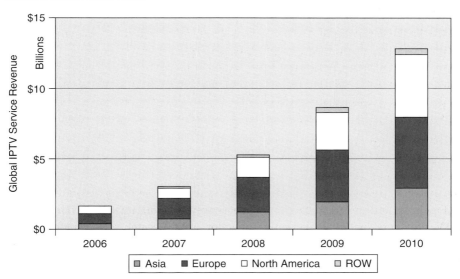

**FIGURE 1.4**    *IPTV Service Revenue Growth Forecast 2006–2010.*
*Source: © MRG Inc. 2006*

---

[11]Multimedia Research Group, Inc., publishes market analyses of new technologies for the communications industries and provides market intelligence and strategy consulting for its client companies.

1.6 million subscribers with IPTV service available). According to Point-Topic, another UK consultancy,[11] France had 11.7 million broadband subscribers as of June 2006, so there were a significant number of potential IPTV subscribers.

The success of IPTV in France occurred for a number of reasons, some of which were specific to the French market and some that may also have been true for other locations:

- **Pricing.** Due to a very competitive market, the prices for IPTV services were very low. Orange/France Telecom's basic IPTV service with more than 40 channels cost 16 Euros per month. Free's basic triple-play package—which included high speed ADSL2+ Internet access, free voice calls to fixed lines in more than 20 countries and IPTV—cost 30 Euros per month. At this low price, many Free customers were happy purchasing the package just to get Internet and telephone service and didn't utilize the television services. Incumbent Orange started to bundle its basic IPTV service, which includes more than 30 channels, free of charge with some of its broadband access offerings.

- **Weak competition.** As mentioned above, the main alternatives to IPTV were CATV and satellite, both of which achieved penetration far below levels in other countries. In the case of CATV, up to 2005 there were several cable operators who had not converted the analog base to digital as rapidly as in the UK, and most of these systems were without VOD capability. In the case of satellite TV, penetration was hurt by strict local planning rules that make it impossible for many potential subscribers to mount antennas on their homes. As a result, for many potential viewers, IPTV was possibly the only way to get digital TV services.

- **Wide range of content.** The channel offerings of the two largest IPTV suppliers were quite extensive. In addition to channels from all over France, both services offered basic-tier international programming from a number of other countries in Europe and the Middle East. In addition, Orange/France Telecom offered more than 200 premium channels. Both operators also partnered with media group Canal+ to offer premium content.

- **New services (HD and VOD).** While not as important as the reasons mentioned above, both high definition (HD) content and VOD services may have acted to drive subscribers to IPTV. The HD broadcast market in France was much less developed than the U.S. market at the time. IPTV service providers were positioning themselves to capture HD business by deploying HD-capable *set top*

---

11. Data supplied by private correspondence with Point-Topic www.point-topic.com

*boxes* (STBs) early-on. In France, VOD services were also not common, and IPTV providers were, in practicality, the first providers to offer VOD.

Other countries in Europe offered a different picture for IPTV. For example, the UK, a country with roughly the same number of television households as France, had twice as many digital satellite subscribers (more than 7 million). NTL/Telewest operated CATV systems that passed half the homes in the UK and had 3.3 million subscribers. Overall, the penetration of digital TV services in the UK was almost 70 percent of viewers, a much higher ratio than in France or many other countries in Europe. As a result of these and other factors, the penetration of IPTV in the UK was much lower – only 30,000 subscribers as of 2005, according to an article in *The Register*. UK levels were expected to stay below levels in France for several years following 2006.

# Summary

By now, it should be clear that IPTV is a force to be reckoned with today and for the foreseeable future, as powerful market drivers push companies and consumers to adopt this technology. Even though there are a number of issues that must be addressed before IPTV can reach its full potential, these issues are surmountable and are not very different in scope or magnitude from the difficulties that face any new technology.

In this chapter, we covered the basic motivations for using IP networks to deliver video services, including the flexibility, ubiquity and cost advantages that have persuaded many carriers to begin offering these services. We took a look at the market trends that are driving the rapid growth in this market. We then examined several factors pushing the spread of this technology. We concluded with a look at some issues that work against IPTV—although none of these appear to be anything more than the teething pains of a new technology.

# 2 IPTV versus Internet Video

This is definitely the Wild West in some ways; it's in the very early stages, and people are still learning.

—Adam Berrey, VP of marketing and strategy, Brightcove,
in *The Washington Post*

Both IPTV and Internet Video use IP technology for video delivery, but that's where the similarities end. IPTV has similarities to traditional CATV, satellite and broadcast television, where continuous channels of programming are delivered to consumers for viewing on traditional television sets. In contrast, Internet Video delivers discrete pieces of content selected by individual viewers for viewing on a display connected to a personal computer. In terms of the range of content and amount of control, IPTV is like listening to music from a radio broadcast, whereas Internet Video is like listening to music on a personal MP3 player.

Both technologies have a role to play in video delivery. In Chapter 3, we will discuss ways that either IPTV or Internet Video can be used to create successful video delivery businesses. Many broadcasters will find themselves offering programming by means of one or both of these technologies; they are not mutually exclusive. Both forms of delivery can be useful for reaching different markets—or even a single group of consumers—who may want to view content in different ways at different times of the day. Broadcasters should become familiar with both IPTV and Internet Video technologies in order to position themselves to benefit as both markets mature.

This chapter is made up of two sections. In the first section, we will discuss the principal characteristics of an IPTV system. In the second section, we will discuss the different characteristics of an Internet Video System. At the end of the chapter, we will summarize the main differences in a table. In the Reality Check, we'll see how, even now, the differences between these two categories are starting to melt away.

# The Corner Office View

Let's start with what IPTV is not. Specifically, it is not TV that is broadcast over the Internet. While the "IP" in its name stands for Internet Protocol, that doesn't mean people will log onto their favorite Web page to access television programming. The IP refers to a method of sending information over a secure, tightly managed network that results in a superior entertainment experience.

In particular, IPTV allows the service provider to deliver only those channels that the consumer wants at any given time—unlike traditional television broadcasting, where every channel is delivered to every home on the network. For the first time, it will be economical to deliver a college basketball game to everyone who wants to see it, for example, rather than just a particular local community.

— Mike Quigley, president and chief operating officer of Alcatel, writing in *Business Week*, May 20, 2005

# Characteristics of IPTV

IPTV is primarily used to offer services that duplicate or exceed the features and functions of a CATV or direct broadcast satellite system by means of an IP network. Service providers who wish to deliver multiple consumer services over a single network often choose IP technology because it can provide voice and high-speed data access in addition to IPTV on a single platform. In a typical system, a private, high-speed IP network is used to continuously deliver video programming to hundreds or thousands of viewers simultaneously.

The typical IPTV network shown in Figure 2.1 is separated into three physical locations: the Video Serving Office (VSO), the Local End Office (LEO) and the viewer's home. The VSO is responsible for gathering video from a variety of sources and converting the signals into IP video streams. The LEO is responsible for combining video, data and voice signals into a form that can be transmitted over a network to the home. In this example, *Digital Subscriber Loop* (DSL) technology is being used, so the LEO contains a *DSL Access Multiplexer* (DSLAM) to format the signals. Inside the home, the incoming signal is split and reformatted for a number of purposes, including telephone service, high-speed data service and video that is fed to a television by way of an IPTV *set top box* (STB).

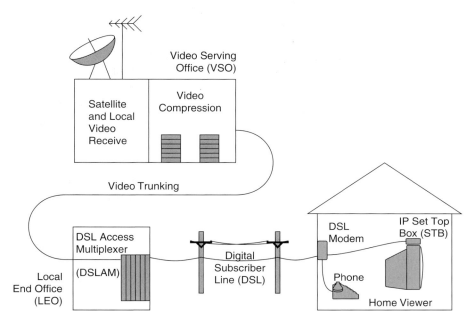

**FIGURE 2.1** *Typical IPTV Network*

Many types of technology can be used to deliver IPTV service to the home, including DSL, fiber optics, wireless, CATV and even broadband over power lines. Regardless of the delivery technology, the basic characteristics of an IPTV network are quite similar, which we will now discuss in more detail.

## Continuous Content Streams

IPTV is designed to send streams of video programming to each viewer. These streams are continuous—each viewer can select the stream they want to view, but they must join the stream in-progress. This process is functionally identical to the programming delivered by local broadcasters, CATV companies and satellite providers—the viewer is able to select the channel to be viewed, but not the content of the channels. This contrasts with Internet Video, where viewers generally select each piece of content they wish to view and play it in whatever order they want.

In most cases, the programming provided over IPTV systems is not created or owned by the IPTV provider. Instead, this programming is obtained from normal broadcast television sources, including broadcasters that may be located in the same city as the IPTV system. Broadcasters typically don't need to do anything special to their content to prepare it for broadcast on an IPTV network—the process of compressing the video and formatting it into IP packets is usually done by the IPTV network provider.

There is one significant exception to the practice of delivering continuous streams of programming to an IPTV viewer. Most IPTV systems also offer on-demand content, where viewers can select videos that are stored on a server and played out upon request. These videos can be from a wide variety of sources and may be offered for free or for additional cost to the viewer. With true on-demand content, viewers can control the playout of the video to start, stop, rewind and fast-forward through the content. As service providers expand their server capacities, more and more content will become available on-demand.

## Multiple Channels

The content that is delivered over an IPTV network is produced by a range of broadcast networks and delivered simultaneously to a large number of viewers. When viewers watch this programming, they will see regularly scheduled news and entertainment from network such as NBC, BBC and TF1; live or recorded sports from companies such as ESPN or Premier; 24-hour news reports from CNN, Al Jazeera and others; and a variety of specialized programming such as music video channels, movie channels, children's channels and home shopping channels.

IPTV networks are well-suited to deliver live programming such as sports or award shows to many viewers at the same time. Hardware inside the network is capable of making copies of the continuous content streams and delivering them to hundreds or thousands of homes simultaneously.

Viewers typically choose which channel they want to watch on their television by interacting with the IPTV STB. This can by done by simply entering the desired channel number on a remote control keypad or by making a selection from an *Electronic Program Guide* (EPG). An EPG can be as simple as a "barker" channel that passively scrolls though all of the current channel choices, or it can be interactive, enabling the viewer to navigate through a list of choices.

Once the viewer has chosen a channel, the STB must connect to the IP stream that contains the appropriate video data and use this data to create a video signal that is sent to the viewer's television. In cases where this data is already present at the input to the STB, the switch can be accomplished merely by changing to the desired data stream. Otherwise, the STB must signal the DSLAM (or other IP switching device further upstream) to deliver the new data to the STB. This is particularly common on networks with limited bandwidth connections to each home, such as DSL networks.

## Uniform Content Format

Most IPTV systems use only one (or possibly two) video encoding formats for each type of content. The choices can typically range from MPEG–2 or MPEG–4 to VC–1 (which began life as Windows Media 9), but IPTV providers will typically choose one format for all video signals. This greatly simplifies the overall management of the IPTV system, allowing for a uniform system design and easing the burden on technicians maintaining the system. This also simplifies the STB design by eliminating the need to support multiple video decompression engines.

Any content that arrives at the IPTV provider that is not in the correct format must be converted. There are two main methods to do this. The first involves taking the incoming video feed and decompressing it to a baseband digital video signal before recompressing it using the desired compression system. The second is a process called *transcoding*, where the signal remains in a compressed state but is processed and reformatted into the new format.

Most IPTV providers also convert all of the incoming content into a common bit rate, usually one value for SD and a second for HD. This greatly simplifies the process of channel changing and overall bandwidth management; one fixed-bandwidth stream replaces another stream of the same bandwidth when a viewer switches channels. The process of changing the bit rate of video stream is called *transrating*.

## Private Network Delivery

In order to deliver continuous channels of content to thousands of viewers in a repeatable manner, an IPTV network must be carefully provisioned and controlled. This task is daunting on a private network where all of the video content and other network traffic can be controlled. This task would be impossible on the Internet.

Playing a continuous video stream is a constant race against time. The video source signal must be received, compressed (usually) and converted into IP packets that must be delivered to every viewer's STB just when they are needed to create the video signal. If the packets arrive too early, they must be stored in the STB until they are needed. If the packets arrive too late, then the video signal playout can be interrupted. Some of these variations can be smoothed out using a memory buffer inside the STB, but that step adds delay in the end-to-end delivery path and can slow channel changing.

To keep the streams moving smoothly, the IPTV network must be managed to ensure that the IP connections to each STB are not overcrowded with packets. Overcrowding can be disastrous in an IPTV network, because it can affect all of the packet streams, causing delays or even packet deletions that will surely affect the quality of the delivered video. On a private network, this can be avoided with careful engineering and by ensuring that each of the packet sources and destinations is controlled to prevent more packets from entering the network than can be delivered. In a public network that contains packet sources and destinations that can't be controlled by the IPTV provider, there is no mechanism to prevent overcrowding.

## Viewed on Consumer Televisions via Set Top Boxes

Standard consumer television sets, until recently, have been very dumb devices when it comes to intelligently managing content. There is no mechanism to store video signals—any valid input is immediately displayed to the viewer. For most consumers, the television is located far away from the nearest PC, and many consumer PCs simply aren't up to the task of delivering high quality, full-screen, full-resolution video to the viewer. This is where the specialized hardware and software of an STB come into play.

The role of an STB is extremely important for an IPTV network. At a minimum, it must receive an incoming IP video stream, reassemble the data packets in the correct order, decode the video signal and produce an output that can be fed to a television (or projector) for display. It normally serves as the terminus for the IPTV network, so it must be able to receive commands from the user's remote control and send them into the network for action. It may also need some built-in intelligence to be able to generate text or other display used to communicate with the viewer, for functions like the EPG.

# Internet Video

The viewer experiences and expectations for Internet Video are very different from IPTV. Most viewers have much lower expectations for Internet Video, particularly if they have ever tried to watch video over a dial-up connection. Of course, technology marches on, and the viewer experience continues to improve. Figure 2.2 shows a very simplified view of an Internet Video network.

This diagram contains two sections: production and distribution. In production, the video content is captured from a source, digitized, edited, labeled and bundled into a file that is placed on a server where it can be accessed. In distribution, a viewer uses an Internet-connected PC to search for content, connect to the server, acquire rights to view the content, and then either download a video file or request a video stream of the content for viewing on their PC using specialized multimedia viewing software.

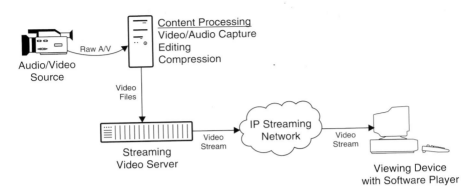

**FIGURE 2.2** *Typical Internet Video Network*

A viewer using their PC or other device initiates a typical viewing session. First, the viewer must identify where the content is located on the Internet. For example, a user might have received an e-mail from a friend with a link to a Web site containing the video. When the viewer clicks on the link, the browser on their PC connects to the appropriate Web server. Typically, the Web server then displays a screen that gives some information about the video (such as a description and the clip's duration). The viewer then may be asked to click on a link embedded in that page, which begins the video playing process. One important step that happens at this time is an exchange of information between the server and the browser software on the PC that tells the browser to run a plug-in or stand-alone application called a *media viewer*. The media viewer will properly decode the incoming video data and convert it into an image that can be displayed. If the proper media viewer software isn't installed on the PC, the user will be prompted to install it by downloading the software from a suitable source. Then, as the video file is delivered, the viewer can watch the content.

## Discrete Content Elements

Instead of continuous channels of highly produced programming, most Internet Video content is available for each viewer to select exactly what they want to watch at whatever time is convenient. Many of the video files that are available for viewing or downloading are relatively short—five minutes or less. Certainly, longer duration files are available, but they tend to be more limited in number, particularly considering the cost of server and network bandwidth needed to deliver these streams over the Internet.

Not all Internet Video is discrete content elements—there are some real-time streaming broadcasts available. For example, NASA TV offers some live video content each day from the International Space Station, as well as live coverage of major events like shuttle launches and space walks (visit www.nasa.gov/multimedia/nasatv). In between, educational, news and other programming are provided. For-profit real-time Internet Video channels are also becoming a reality, as the number of viewers with high-bandwidth Internet connections reaches a level that is attractive for subscription or advertising-based services. (See the discussion of MobiTV in the Reality Check.)

## Millions of Content Offerings

Any quick search of some of the more popular lists of video content on the Internet will show that there are well over a million different video files available for viewing, with thousands more being added each day. These can range from professionally produced music videos and movie previews to crude home videos and other amateur content. A great deal of content is available for free viewing; other files require purchase to view. Some sites allow the content to be downloaded for later playback; other sites only allow viewers to watch the content while they are connected to the site.

Locating a specific piece of content for viewing can be a challenge with Internet Video. Many viewers find content by following links on Web pages that direct them to video content sites. Others use the listings of popular titles on these Web sites. Still other viewers find the videos to watch using general-purpose search engines (such as Google) or site-specific search engines provided on some of the popular video Web sites. Unlike IPTV, there is no master EPG for the Internet— there's simply too much new content being added each day for this to be practical.

## Multiple Content Formats

There are a wide variety of formats that can be used for video files, and virtually all of them have found their way onto the Internet. There are many choices, including various camera formats (such as DV), the MPEG family (1, 2 or 4), JPEG (basic or 2000), player-specific formats (Windows Media, QuickTime, Real Networks, etc.), and a variety of computer file formats (such as AVI and Flash). Consumers who view a significant amount of Internet Video content often end up with a collection of video players loaded onto their machines to handle the various video file formats.

For content providers, this variety can present a dilemma. If the provider chooses only to support a single video format, then any consumer who wishes to watch the content must already have the appropriate viewer software installed on their PC or find a way to get the proper viewer (most of which are distributed for free). If, on the other hand, the provider chooses to support multiple formats, then they assume the burden of producing and managing content in several different formats.

In addition to the choice of video compression technology, content providers must choose the screen resolutions they will support. Low resolutions offer small file sizes that are easier to download over low-bandwidth network connections but also create small images for viewing. Higher resolutions offer increased picture quality but can require a long time to download or a high-bandwidth connection for live streaming.

## Delivered over the Internet

One big strength of Internet Video is that it can be delivered to any viewer with a connection to the Internet. Of course, high-bandwidth connections are easier to use and deliver quicker results, but even consumers with low-speed dial-up connections can download video files if they are patient enough.

Because video sites can be accessed from around the globe, the potential audience for any video can be very large, particularly if there is a good mechanism in place to inform consumers about the content that is available.

Use of the Internet also means that content providers don't need to build network facilities to all of their viewers, resulting in a significant cost savings. Unfortunately, this means that the network must be shared with a host of other applications that consume bandwidth. Also, there is no means for video content to be given higher priority than other types of traffic, which can dramatically increase the difficulty of delivering high-quality, high-bandwidth content in real-time to viewers, as is commonly done on IPTV systems.

## Viewed on Consumer PCs

A reasonably powerful PC is capable of running the viewer software required to decompress and display most compressed video formats. Performance can sometimes be improved through the use of graphics accelerator cards or additional memory that is added to the system. In some cases, viewers will watch the content on the display screen of the PC itself; in other cases, the video will be displayed on a television set that is connected to a video output port of the PC.

Other consumer video playback devices have begun to enter the market for Internet Video content. One of the most popular portable video viewers is the Apple Video iPod, which features a screen resolution of 320 x 240 pixels. Most of these portable devices have a limited range of video file types that they will support, so it is essential for the consumer to select only those content files that are compatible with their device's capabilities.

# Which Is Best?

In the preceding two sections, we discussed the principal differences between IPTV and Internet Video that we will discuss again in subsequent chapters. Table 2.1 summarizes the key points.

Now that these differences have been explained, the question may arise "How do I choose between them?" For many broadcasters, no choice may be necessary—the broadcaster may simply chose to offer content to viewers using both technologies at the same time.

- In the case of IPTV networks, there is no real difference to a broadcaster between having a signal carried on a digital CATV or a digital satellite network versus carriage on an IPTV network. In all three cases, broadcasters negotiate a contract with the network provider, and content can be supplied in almost any form that is convenient—over the air, as a digital video feed over a telephone company supplied circuit, as fiber optic connection or whatever format suits both parties. No matter what format is chosen, the IPTV network provider will most likely need to perform some sort of processing on the delivered signal to make it compatible with their network. This can include compressing the signal, changing compression format or many other changes that the broadcaster won't be able to control. Any or all of these tasks will need to be performed by the IPTV provider, just as they need to be performed by digital CATV or satellite providers.

- In the case of Internet Video networks, broadcasters will probably be heavily involved in managing which content will be offered to viewers and how it will be

| | IPTV | INTERNET VIDEO |
|---|---|---|
| Nature of Content | Continuous streams of content | Discrete content segments |
| Content Selection | Hundreds of programming "channels" | Millions of content files |
| Content Format | One or two formats selected by provider | Dozens of formats with multiple players |
| Delivery Networks | Private IP network | Public Internet |
| Viewing Device | Consumer TV via STB | Consumer PC display or portable device |

**TABLE 2.1**  *Key Differences Between IPTV and Internet Video*

offered to viewers. In many cases, this content will be delivered to viewers by means of a Web site that is owned and operated by the broadcaster themselves. However, this will only be suitable for programming where the broadcasters own the appropriate rights. (This will not be that case in many circumstances for programming that is produced by independent production companies or that comes from national network feeds.) One visible result of the ownership limitation in the U.S. are local broadcaster Web sites. These sites heavily feature video clips from local news and weather programs that are produced by the local broadcaster, but they do not include other programming that is purchased from third parties.

Many broadcasters will find that their programming is carried in both ways—as linear feeds over CATV, IPTV and satellite systems, and as discrete content elements over Internet Video services. For popular prime time programming, most local broadcasters won't have the rights to host this content on their local Web sites. Instead, these programs may be available from the Web site of a national broadcast network. The question of who pays for this content will be something that we will take up in the next chapter.

# Reality Check

For this chapter's Reality Check, we will discuss a relatively new service that combines some of the attributes of both Internet Video and IPTV delivery mechanisms. This example shows how these categories are already starting to overlap.

## MobiTV – Blurring the Lines

An innovative service has been launched to provide standard television network programming to viewers via several different user devices. The service is named MobiTV because of the substantial deployment for mobile telephone users, with more than 1 million reported users in October 2006.[1]

MobiTV has introduced service into several different markets:

- Wireless network suppliers who have chosen a group of phones that can be configured to accept the MobiTV broadcast. For this to work, selected phones can be downloaded with special software that enable the phone to locate the desired data stream so the user can select the content to be viewed.

---

1. MobiTV press release, October 11, 2006

- Certain brands of smart telephones (such as Treo and Palm) have the ability to tune to MobiTV on any wireless network. These devices still require proper configuration and a data service from the wireless carrier. In fact, many carriers recommend that their users purchase an unlimited wireless data service to avoid excessive data service charges that might be incurred by viewing video over the networks.

- PC users with broadband connections, either through wired broadband connections such as DSL or cable modems or through wireless connections such as Wi-Fi, can subscribe to yet another service. One provider of this service, AT&T, is marketing this version of MobiTV under the brand name of "AT&T Broadband TV."

The mobile/smart telephone versions require a monthly subscription fee for the programming on the order of $10 per month as of this writing in addition to a wireless data plan. The PC version has a fee on the order of $20 per month; PC users must supply their own broadband network connections to the Internet.

AT&T Broadband TV is a hybrid of both IPTV and Internet Video. Here are the ways that the service is like IPTV:

- The content is provided in a linear broadcast, with no fast-forward, rewind or pause capability.

- Some channels have commercials; others do not.

- User interactivity is limited to choosing between different television channels.

- Channel change speeds are on the order of 1 to 10 seconds, perhaps somewhat slower than some IPTV installations, but quicker than most Internet Video applications.

- No noticeable buffering time is required when a channel is selected.

Here are the ways that AT&T Broadband TV is like Internet Video:

- Viewing is done using a standard PC running Windows software and the Adobe Flash player. No television tuner card is required in the PC.

- Viewers supply their own Internet connection.

- Video resolution depends on connection speed, with some video significantly below SD resolution.

- There is a substantial delay on at least some live television channels—we measured some at more than one minute.

As of this writing, MobiTV has raised $125 million in venture capital financing.[2] Investors included companies such as Adobe Systems, who supply the Flash software used by MobiTV, and Hearst Corporation, a large media company with television stations, newspapers, Internet and other media outlets. Clearly, some large companies are interested in participating as this market evolves.

There is no single, universal definition of what is IPTV and what is Internet Video. What's important is to remember that whenever IPTV comes up in a conversation, one should be careful to qualify what the speaker is talking about before making any conclusions.

# Summary

This chapter focused on the differences between IPTV and Internet Video, terms that are often used in very similar contexts by experts. In this book, we will talk about IPTV as a video service that offers multiple channels of programming distributed on a real-time basis to viewers who typically use an STB to watch the content on a television or other display device. We'll talk about Internet Video that consists of thousands or millions of discrete content elements (files) that are viewed on a monitor for a PC.

These differences are important, because they affect the viewer's ability to control when and where specific content is viewed. As we move into the future, these differences will become somewhat less important, as IPTV providers offer more and more content on demand, and as Internet Video providers offer more linear and long-form programming.

2. From GigaOmniMedia, Inc. Web site article, gigaom.com/2006/11/01/mobitv-adobe-hearst/, November 1, 2006

# 3 Business Models

Information technology and business are becoming inextricably interwoven. I don't think anybody can talk meaningfully about one without the talking about the other.
—Bill Gates

Regardless of the technology, the key to success in delivering video services to consumers is a profitable business model. A wide variety of models are being tested in the market today for delivering video content over IP networks. Many different plans for user fees are being tried, ranging from completely free service to services that charge for each viewing of each piece of content. In the long run, it is likely that a few selected models will dominate, but for now, it is prudent to get an understanding of the many different models that are being used.

This chapter is divided into two main sections. In the first section, we will look at business models that are being used primarily for IPTV networks. In the second section, we will look at models that are often used for Internet Video businesses.

The lines can be blurry between these two groups, but here is the key point to remember: IPTV providers generally need to pay for installing and operating the network that delivers the services in addition to any costs for content, whereas most of the costs of Internet Video services relate to content acquisition and preparation. Of course, there are a number of other costs that we will discuss, but network costs can be major portion of the overall system costs.

## The Corner Office View

For the ultimate example of an incumbent telecoms firm moving into TV, you have to visit Hong Kong. When PCCW, the local phone company, launched a TV-over-broadband service in September 2003, everyone laughed; it had tried similar

CONTINUED ▶

CONTINUED ▶

ventures twice before, in 1996 and 2000, and had failed on both occasions. But its new service, Now Broadband TV, proved a success. Today it has more than 40 percent of the market and is on course to displace the local cable operator as the main provider of pay-TV in Hong Kong.

Moreover, last year PCCW became one of the first incumbent operators worldwide to arrest the decline in fixed-line subscribers. This is the kind of success that other telecoms firms dream of: a new service that not only stops line loss, but beats the cable companies at their own game and brings in new revenue. Better still, the service is expected to become profitable by the end of the year. No wonder that "just about every phone company in the world" has come to visit PCCW, says Alexander Arena, the firm's finance chief. PCCW is now advising telecoms firms in several countries about how to emulate its successful roll-out of IPTV.

—From "Tuning into the Future?",
*The Economist,* October 12, 2006

# IPTV

As we discussed in Chapter 2, for now, IPTV networks primarily deliver multiple streams of continuous content over private networks to viewers who watch the content on normal television sets. While this sounds simple, a significant amount of technology needs to be installed and managed to provide these services. Table 3.1 summarizes the key cost elements of an IPTV system.

Table 3.2 gives the monthly programming costs for several popular television networks in the U.S. Note that these costs are paid by the IPTV system provider to the content owners; part of the business plan for the IPTV network is devising a way to recoup these costs from viewers.

In addition to the costs in Tables 3.1 and 3.2, other recurring costs must be covered. These include marketing, customer support and network maintenance. These costs can be hard to quantify before an IPTV system is deployed, but they can have a significant impact on the overall profitability of a system.

The following sections describe some of the business models that can be used for IPTV systems.

| COST ELEMENT | COST BASIS | DESCRIPTION |
|---|---|---|
| Video Content | Recurring fee per month per viewer | Paid to content suppliers, such as broadcast networks |
| Delivery Network | Fixed, up front | Cost of IP network, part common equipment, part per-subscriber |
| STB | Fixed per subscriber | Often rented, sometimes purchased by consumers |
| Digital Head End | Fixed, up front | Receives video signals, converts into proper IP format |
| Content Servers | Fixed, scales with capacity | Used for on-demand and advertising |
| EPG | Recurring, scales with number of channels and subscribers | May be produced locally by IPTV provider or acquired from service bureau |

**TABLE 3.1** *IPTV System Cost Elements*

| NETWORK | FEE PER SUBSCRIBER PER MONTH (2006) |
|---|---|
| ESPN | $2.91 |
| Fox Sports | $1.67 |
| TNT | $0.89 |
| USA | $0.47 |
| CNN | $0.44 |
| Nickelodeon | $0.41 |
| TBS | $0.39 |
| FX | $0.36 |
| MTV | $0.29 |
| ESPN2 | $0.24 |

**TABLE 3.2** *Programming Cost Examples; Source: Kagan Research, LLC, a division of JupiterKagan, Inc.; used with permission*

# Subscription

Subscription services are one of the most common methods used for funding IPTV systems. In this system, viewers sign up for a package of video services (channels) and pay a flat monthly fee. Subscribers are then allowed to watch as much or as little of any of the channels that are included in their subscription package.

Often, these services come in different tiers, with basic services (such as re-broadcasts of local over-the-air (OTA) programming) being the least expensive and premium sports or movie channels being the most expensive. Service providers try to group the channels into these tiers to maximize the number of subscribers at each level while minimizing the costs of the programming. This arrangement is similar to the pricing schemes used by many CATV and satellite providers; hence it is normally well-accepted in the marketplace.

For example, a basic tier of services may have several local OTA network feeds (which may have little or no programming costs to the IPTV provider), some news and weather channels, shopping channels, and other local content. A more expensive tier of services may include a variety of national entertainment, sports and music channels, including channels such as those listed in Table 3.2. This tier could easily be priced at 100 to 200 percent premium over the basic tier. Even more expensive tiers could be provided which include more variety, such as advertising-free channels or specialized sports channels.

# Á là Carte Channels

This is similar in concept to subscription, except that each viewer is allowed to select exactly the channels they want to view, so he or she does not pay for the undesired channels. As above, the subscriber receives a monthly bill from the service provider, but only for the specific channels that have been chosen. The service provider in turn uses the revenue to pay content providers.

Within traditional CATV and satellite providers, á là carte channels have not seen widespread deployment. For IPTV providers, there are two advantages to this approach. First, since each channel that a subscriber is viewing must be individually sent from the IPTV network to the viewer's STB, it is technically less difficult to deliver only a specific group of channels to each subscriber. Second, IPTV providers may capitalize on subscribers' desires to pay only for those channels they wish to view; and á là carte channel selection option could be used as a service differentiator and market entry strategy.

## Local Advertising

Local advertising involves inserting advertisements from merchants that might only appeal to local residents into network feeds before they are distributed to viewers. The technology for dong this is well established—many national content providers include special indicators in their programming feeds that tell the local providers when to insert their local ads. These indications, called *avails*, are provided by the content owners under the terms of contracts with the local service providers. In some cases, a local service provider may earn enough revenue from the local ads to partially or completely pay for the cost of the programming.

Many CATV providers have already designed their networks to take advantage of this important source of revenue. For IPTV providers, much of the technology is already available. Specialized servers collect advertisements from a variety of sources, and these servers can monitor multiple video channels simultaneously to locate avails. When one appears, the content from the server simply replaces the content of the programming feed.

The appeal of local advertisements is not limited to local businesses. Companies with global brands may wish to tie their advertisements to items of local interest, such as soft drink companies targeting fans of local sports teams. The challenge for a local service provider is to effectively market their selection of avails to the advertisers that will value them the highest.

## Video on Demand

The idea of allowing viewers to watch any programming they desire whenever they want to watch it is not new. But, as technology advances and costs come down, *video on demand* (VOD) becomes more and more attractive to service providers.

The basic concept of VOD is based on video programming that is stored and then delivered to a viewer when it is requested. This storage can take the form of a centralized server that is equipped to send programming simultaneously to a hundreds of viewers, or it can take the form of more distributed storage throughout the network. At the limit, individual storage devices for each viewer can be located in individual STBs.

Various forms of VOD have been tried over the years, and most of them still exist in one form or another. Table 3.3 lists the most popular types of VOD services.

One of the big controversies surrounding PVR service (described in table 3.3) is the role of advertising in recorded content. Advertisers have two main concerns:

- Ad skipping, where viewers fast-forward through ads. This capability is often listed as the motivation for many consumer PVR purchases.

| TYPE | DESCRIPTION |
|---|---|
| True Video on Demand (VOD) | This is the purest form of VOD, where each viewer receives an individual video stream that they have complete control over. Viewers are allowed to start, stop, pause, rewind and fast-forward the content. Viewers typically pay a fee for each title viewed; the charges are either debited from a pre-paid account or included on a monthly bill. |
| Near Video on Demand (NVOD) | Similar to true VOD without the individual video stream control capabilities. One common form of NVOD is sometimes called staggercasting, in which multiple copies of a program are played starting at five-minute intervals, thereby limiting any individual viewer to no more than a five-minute wait before his or her program begins to play. |
| Subscription Video on Demand (SVOD) | Same delivery technology and viewer control as VOD with a different payment system. In SVOD, subscribers pay a fixed monthly fee for unlimited access to a library of titles. In many systems, the library is updated monthly. |
| Free Video on Demand (FVOD) | A variation on VOD where payment is eliminated. In most systems, this content is restricted to long-form advertisements, how-to guides and other low-cost content. |
| Everything on Demand (EOD) | For some technology visionaries, this is the ultimate form of video delivery system, where all programming is available to all viewers at all times. |
| Personal Video Recorders (PVRs) | These devices take incoming video programming, compress it, and record it to a hard disk that is typically located either in an STB or a standalone device. Viewers then control the PVR to play back content, including pause, fast-forward and rewind capabilities. Also called *timeshifting*, viewers normally program the PVRs to record specific programs at specific times. One of the pioneers of this technology is a company called *TiVo*. |
| Network Personal Video Recorders (NPVRs) | Offers similar functionality to PVRs, but recording is performed inside the service provider's network, rather than in the viewer's location. Some content owners contend that this technology is so similar in capability to true VOD that it needs to be licensed as such. |
| Pay Per View (PPV) | This precursor technology to VOD is primarily used to deliver live paid programming, such as concerts or sporting events. |

**TABLE 3.3** *Types of Video on Demand Service*

- Ad timeliness, where viewers watch programs at times far removed from their original broadcast date. This is a big concern for some advertisers who have their ad campaigns targeted for specific time windows, such as promotional ads for a movie that is being released to theaters the following day.

Service providers have a limited amount of control over content that has been recorded by a viewer on their own device for later playback. They have only a slight bit more control over PVRs that are embedded in a STB supplied by the service provider—at least they can ensure that the DRM function is working to protect any copyrighted content while it is on disk. Providers actually have the potential to influence viewers who use a networked PVR, where the video recordings are actually stored on the service providers' own video servers.

Network PVRs have exciting potential to make advertisers much happier than with other PVR technologies. Why? Well, consider what happens in a normal PVR scenario with an advertisement. The machine faithfully records the commercials along with the program content and gives the user the ability to fast-forward through any parts of the program or advertisements at their whim. For example, say the viewer recorded a program on December 20 and decides to watch the program on December 29. As you could imagine, the program contained a number of ads that pertained to special last-minute shopping opportunities for Christmas. Unfortunately, when the viewer watches the program, the sales are over and the ads are completely worthless to both the viewer and the advertiser. Now, consider the same scenario with a networked PVR and some advanced technology in the server. With this technology, the service provider is able to replace the commercials that were in the original program with ones that are timely and relevant whenever the viewer watches the content. In this example, the ads might be for something great to do on New Year's Eve, which the viewer might actually be willing to watch, and an advertiser might be willing to pay for.

All that's needed to make this a reality is some pretty serious software inside the VOD server and some kind of legal framework to govern the "bumping" of one commercial by another. The industry isn't quite there yet, but this technology is certain to be available in the not too distant future.

## Interactive TV

When viewers are given the opportunity to interact with broadcast content, the result is called *interactive TV* (iTV). This can take many forms, ranging from the simple press of a button to more elaborate menu schemes. Here are a few common applications for iTV:

- Camera angle selection, where the viewer can chose one or more different camera angles of live sporting events

- Voting/opinion polling, where the outcome of a television event is determined by a vote of the audience

- Ad response, where viewers can request more information about a product or service being advertised

The key requirement for iTV is a *return path*, where user actions are sent to the service provider. Particularly in satellite applications, this can be difficult to construct, requiring connection of modem internal to an STB to the subscriber's telephone line. In contrast, in IPTV networks, the return path is already present, allowing for simple integration of iTV.

## Triple/Quadruple Play

*Triple play* refers to multiple services being delivered by a single service provider, typically voice (telephony), data (Internet access) and television services. *Quadruple play* adds mobile telephony to the mix. Service providers typically offer discounts to customers who buy more than one service, which has proven to be a successful marketing ploy. The value proposition is that consumers benefit not only from lower prices but also the convenience of a single bill to pay (although the value of the latter is debatable).

From a service provider perspective, triple play services offer the combined cash flow from three separate services that can be used to pay for a common network that is capable of delivering all of them (such as networks based on IP technology). Of course, there are costs associated with installing the extra equipment needed to provide all three services, but these items can be paid for with moderate market penetration.

Certainly triple play has been the beautiful face that launched a thousand networking ventures. Carriers that traditionally had separate spheres of influence (for example, video versus telephony) are now rushing to deploy networks that can support all three aspects of the triple play. And these forays have been met with some success—a number of telephone companies acknowledged in 2006 (and some even earlier) that pricing and revenue for basic subscriber telephony services are in decline, partially due to the combined effects of VoIP technology and mobile telephones.

## Internet Video via IPTV – The Walled Garden

IPTV providers have a dilemma. On one hand, they want to be the sole (or at least very dominant) supplier of video content to their subscribers, which is one of the best ways of securing continuous subscription revenue flows. On the other hand, there is a huge amount of content available on the Internet, and there will certainly be pressure from subscribers to have easy access to this content. To resolve this dilemma, some IPTV providers have resorted to a concept called a *walled garden*.

A walled garden can almost be thought of as a protected copy of some portions of the Internet, or possibly a set of content offerings that have nothing to do with the Internet. It can also be thought of as a heavily censored and filtered view of the Internet. Either way, only a small fraction of all the content available on the Web is included in the garden.

Service providers see several advantages for using walled gardens. First of all, the wall can prevent viewers from accessing content that may not be technically compatible with the network equipment or content that possibly contains harmful viruses, worms or Trojan horses. Second, the wall can help increase the amount of revenue that service providers derive from their content, in the form of advertising revenue or payments for on-demand content. Third, the wall prevents viewer access to content that may compete with what the service provider offers or content that may not be suitable for some groups of viewers, such as children.

The concept of a walled garden is not new. AOL tried to provide a walled garden for all their subscribers in the early 1990s. For a while, this model worked, with a variety of custom content available only to AOL subscribers. After time, this model broke down as users started to demand access to sections of the Web that were not inside the wall. In addition, the cost of creating and preparing content to reside within the walled garden became very expensive, even for a large company like AOL with millions of subscribers. As the decade wore on, AOL eventually switched to allow subscribers to have more open access to the Internet.

# Internet Video

Internet Video delivery systems use the Internet as a means to deliver programming to viewers. As a result, the business models for this technology are significantly different from the business models that are used with IPTV systems. At the risk of completely abusing an analogy, there is no wall around this garden.

| COST ELEMENT | COST BASIS | DESCRIPTION |
|---|---|---|
| Video Servers | Fixed, scales with number of streams provided | An adequate number of servers must be available to deliver streams to all of the simultaneous viewers of the content |
| Video Content | Often paid as a percentage of the revenue earned, if not free | Paid to content owners, such as performing artists and producers |
| Internet Access Bandwidth | Fixed, scales with number of streams provided | Fees paid to ISPs to supply high-bandwidth connections |

**TABLE 3.4** *Internet Video System Cost Elements*

Table 3.4 summarizes the major cost elements for an Internet Video service provider.

Subscription-based pricing is much less common in Internet Video than in IPTV. This is most likely due to the common perception that entertainment video is better suited to viewing on a television set than on a computer display (and sofas are typically more comfortable places to sit). In addition, most Internet Video delivery services are unable to offer anywhere near the video quality of a purpose-built television delivery service when both screen resolution and freedom from service interruptions are considered.

Some common elements are shared by both technologies. Both can rely heavily on advertising; although in the case of IPTV the advertising revenues tend to go more to the content providers whereas in Internet Video most of the ad revenues are collected by the portal provider. Both architectures support a variety of VOD services. And both technologies have a wide variety of business models that have been used successfully.

The following sections describe some of the business models that can be used to operate Internet Video services.

# Pay-per-View

Pay-per-view (PPV) is often used for high-value content such as Hollywood movies. In this model, the viewer purchases the right to view a specific piece of content over a specific time period (often 24 hours). The viewer is entitled to pause, fast-forward and rewind the content, but loses all rights after the viewing window expires. Typically, the license only covers a single viewing device.

Part of the reason for these tight viewing window restrictions is simple profit maximization, but another part is security. If a viewer somehow devised a method to enable multiple devices to view content, the resulting "cracked" file would only be useful for a short period because of the display time limit. Such technologies help limit the incentive to devise these illegal techniques.

## Rights Purchase/Podcasting

Much of the content delivered over Internet Video systems is sold in the form of a permanent license, where the rights to store and view the content are delivered to the viewer for an unlimited time. Users are allowed to download the content onto their PCs or other viewing devices and play back as desired. Typically, there is a limit to the number of devices that can be used to play the content, to prevent viewers from reselling the content to other parties.

One somewhat contentious issue for providers is the concept of backup copies. Consumers want the right to make backups so they don't lose the rights to a valuable collection of content items as a result of a hard disk or other device failure. On the other hand, content owners fear that a liberal backup policy could result in widespread misuse of their valuable content.

## Subscription

Some Internet Video content is sold by subscription. Two business models are often used:

- Live Video Access, where viewers pay a monthly fee in exchange for the rights to view live streaming video (such as sporting events).

- Video Library Access, where viewers pay a monthly fee to have access to a collection of content that can be played.

Subscription models work best when there is a collection of unique content and a group of viewers who are willing to pay. Examples include Major League Baseball in the U.S., news programming from a variety of countries in different languages and a variety of adult content. Financial success depends on controlling the costs of production (perhaps by sharing production costs with other television outlets, such as local television broadcast stations) and on establishing a subscriber base large enough to cover the system costs.

# Advertising Supported

As with e-mail and Internet search portals, many Internet Video providers started out by offering free services to viewers. As the user base grows, it becomes economically feasible for the portal owners to sell advertising space, in the form of static ads displayed on the portal's Web page or as video advertisements played immediately before the viewer's selected content.

Revenues derived from advertising can be used in three interesting ways, aside from filling the pockets of entrepreneurs and venture capitalists. One way is to use the revenues to purchase more content from suppliers, either as an outright purchase or in the form of revenue sharing. Another way is to hire people and purchase equipment to create a larger-capacity and more user-friendly portal that will attract more viewers and increase ad revenues. The third way to spend the revenues is on marketing, thereby attempting to increase the number of viewers using the portal. These choices are not mutually exclusive—many providers will choose to do all three as a way of increasing the success of their Internet Video services.

# Free and User-Contributed Content

Human creativity knows no limits. The fortuitous combination of low-cost, high-quality camcorders, animation software, audio recording/mixing software, synthesizers and professional-grade editing software that can run on PCs has created an immense pool of people who have the means to produce their own digital video clips and programs. Certainly a lot of the content that is produced is only beautiful in the eye of its creator, but enough inspiring, intriguing or amusing content is being produced to populate any number of Web sites with high-quality content.

One way for service providers to create revenue from this type of Web site is to charge users a fee to host their video content, to simplify sharing between friends and family members. As demonstrated by a number of photography sites that have done this, it can be tricky to create a profitable business.

Another way to fund a "free" video Web portal is to sell advertising space on the portal itself or to push advertisements to viewers before the content is played. This can provide enough revenue for the service provider to cover their costs, particularly for bandwidth and storage.

A third common way to fund a "free" video Web portal is to offer previews of video content that needs to be purchased. For example, many professionally produced music videos are available for sale. A number of Web sites have been created that provide free previews of these clips, along with links to sites where they can be purchased and downloaded. Other types of preview content are available for movies currently in theatrical release or on DVD. Web sites that feature these previews can be funded by commissions or other "click-through" accounting methods.

# Reality Check

Clearly, the scale of investment required to install and operate an IPTV system requires some form of payment from viewers. In the following Reality Check, we will take a look at one local telecom supplier who has been able to successfully build and operate a fairly compelling IPTV delivery system.

## Canby Telcom

Canby Telcom is an incumbent local exchange carrier located in Canby, Oregon, about 20 miles south of Portland.[1] The company has provided telephone service to local residents for more than 100 years. Currently, the company provides 11,000 telephone access lines to 8,600 customers.

The geography covered by Canby Telcom consists of a good deal of agricultural land. The company provides service over an area covering 84 square miles. A large number of Hispanic people have moved into the area to work on the flower and tree nurseries that are a common feature of the area.

In October 2004, Canby Telcom received approval for their business plan to deploy a full set of triple-play services to their customers. In addition to the voice services they traditionally supplied, the company decided to offer and broadband data IPTV service using DSL technology. The company began offering service to their first customers using this new system in October 2005.

Canby's basic offering includes voice, data and video service using ADSL2+ technology. Customers have a choice of 1.5, 3.0 or 6.0 Mbps data service in the downstream direction. For subscribers within 5,000 feet of a DSLAM, Canby is able to offer up to three simultaneous video streams. Customers between 5,000 and 8,000 feet from the DSLAM can be supplied with two simultaneous video streams.

---

1. Information on Canby Telcom provided by interviews with company management (Keith Galitz, President, et al) in November 2006 and through other published sources

## System Construction

The Canby Telcom IPTV system was constructed using equipment and software from a number of different suppliers. This is the case with essentially all current IPTV deployments, because of the wide variety of different technologies involved. The following list indicates some of the key building blocks and their respective suppliers.

- Content Processors—Tut Systems Astria CP. These units are responsible for taking incoming programming from a variety of sources and converting it into the common compressed digital format that will be delivered to viewers.

- Remote Terminals (DSLAMs)—Calix C7 Multiservice Access Platform. These units sit inside Canby Telcom's facilities and generate the DSL signals that are sent to subscribers. They also receive upstream data back from the subscribers.

- DSL Modems—Best Data 542 Four Port Ethernet switch/router. These units receive the incoming DSL signals and separate the packets into up to four streams. Three streams can each be connected to one of the STBs, and one can be used to provide high-speed access for a PC.

- Middleware—Myrio. This software provides a number of functions, including supporting the channel change process and presenting information to viewers such as the EPG and the VOD selection menu.

- Encryption/DRM—Verimatrix. This software works in conjunction with the Myrio software to protect the digital content from being misappropriated by viewers or by third parties.

- STBs—Amino AmiNET 110. Small, powerful STB with Ethernet input. Supports Standard Definition MPEG–2 programming only.

## Services Offered

Canby offers quite an impressive array of triple-play service options. Basic telephone service is available throughout the company's serving area. DSL service is available to 99.6 percent of the homes and businesses in the serving area. As of November 2006, IPTV service was available to 3,000 homes in the serving area.

DSL service is offered at three speeds—1.5, 3.0 and 6.0 Mbps downstream. Upstream speeds are up to 512 kbps. While there is a slight price difference between these two options, it is important to note that either option can be used in conjunction with IPTV service.

The IPTV service offers economy television, an enhanced package and five premium programming packages. As of November 2006, the economy tier had 19 channels and sold for $17.95 per month.

The enhanced package is sold as the "Essentials" package for $48.95 per month and includes the economy channels. This package includes more than 100 channels of content, much of which is traditionally delivered to CATV head ends around the country. More than ninety percent of Canby's IPTV subscribers have chosen the "Essentials" package.

Four of the five premium packages are movie channels, each with multiple channels for different content types and time zones. Each of these packages sells for $11.95 per month.

The fifth premium package is somewhat unique, because it includes only Spanish language channels. It includes several channels produced by U.S. programmers and live feeds from several television networks based in Mexico. This $6.95 per month service is popular with many of Canby's customers who have come from Mexico to work on the local agricultural businesses.

VOD is also up and running at Canby. As of November 2006, more than 800 titles were available for viewers to watch, with 43 percent of those available for viewing at no charge. Some of this latter content includes recordings that were made at live music concerts.

## Investment

Canby Telcom was somewhat of an early mover in the IPTV market, due to the company's desire to roll out services beginning in 2005. This may have caused the cost of their system to be higher than what might be typical today for two reasons:

- MPEG–2 compression technology continues to decline in price as time passes, similar to other trends in the high technology field.

- Some of the technologies that Canby had to use were quite new and had not been fully integrated with the other technologies. As a result, the integration costs may have been higher than what would be experienced for a similar system today.

Even with these higher costs, Canby was able to install their entire IPTV digital head end for less than $2 million of invested capital. The primary cost elements that made up this total included:

- Digital head end, which includes the content processors and other signal receiving and processing functions, accounted for 70 to 75 percent of this total.

- VOD system, including the disk drives that actually store the content and the servers that create the IP packet streams that deliver the content to viewers, accounted for 20 to 25 percent of this total

- Other equipment, including the satellite receiver dishes and associated electronics, middleware servers and initial licenses, accounted for the balance of the investment.

### Results

Due to a combination of good engineering, affordable pricing and relatively weak competition from the local CATV company, Canby Telcom has been able to achieve good take rates. As of November 2006, the company had 900 IPTV subscribers, out of a total of approximately 3,000 homes passed, for a take rate of 30 percent. What's more, 77 percent of the IPTV customers take the full triple play of video, voice and data from Canby, helping to prevent erosion in the basic telephony population, which had been a concern of Canby's management.

# Summary

In this chapter, we discussed a variety of topics that relate to the business models that are being tried for both IPTV and Internet Video. Because these technologies and their applications are so new, it is difficult to determine which business models will be successful and which ones will not pan out. Only with time (and some large sums of money) will these answers start to emerge.

We began by looking at both the equipment costs and the programming costs for an IPTV system. Then, we examined some of the methods that can be used to get viewers to pay for these services, including subscriptions, local advertising and VOD. We then looked at several business models that have been used with Internet Video, including pay-per-view, podcasting, subscriptions and advertising supported. We also glanced at free video portals that have been primarily supported by investors with deep pockets who hope to devise a way to earn a return in the future. We concluded with an in-depth look at a real IPTV system that is meeting its financial goals ahead of plan.

# 4 Network Overviews

People [are not] abandoning television or going to the Internet or doing other things and taking away from television viewing activity. The pervasiveness of the medium is not being eroded.

—David Poltrack, Executive Vice President,
Research and Planning, CBS Television

IPTV and Internet Video systems can be very complex puzzles to put together. As any jigsaw enthusiast will say, it is hard to understand how each individual piece of technology fits into an integrated whole unless there is a way to look at the overall picture. In this chapter, we hope to provide this big picture view.

A wide variety of network architectures have been successfully used to deliver IPTV and Internet Video services. Describing all those variations is impractical in a single book, but it does make sense to look at typical network architectures for each delivery method. By understanding these reference models, readers will get a better understanding of all the elements that make up both types of video delivery systems.

Interestingly, in the IPTV section, we will spend most of our time describing hardware components, whereas in the Internet Video section, we will spend a lot of time discussing software. Why the difference? Because most IPTV networks have to be constructed from various hardware components to reach each of the subscribers, whereas Internet Video delivery takes place over links to the Internet that are purchased independently by each subscriber. In other words, IPTV service providers usually need to build a network to reach their viewers, whereas Internet Video service providers typically use existing networks.

## The Corner Office View

"So why now?" asked Jeff Weber, SBC's vice president of product and planning for Project Lightspeed [at NAB 2005]. "I've already been asked this question a thousand times and it's already come up today: 'The telcos have been down this path before—what is it that makes you think that SBC can pull it off this time?'"

CONTINUED ▶

CONTINUED ▶

Weber said, "At the highest level, the economics look dramatically different today than they did 10 years ago... The improvements in compression technology, the ability to do switched video instead of broadcast video, the technology development on a scale around the world makes [IPTV] real. As these standards evolve—and I think SBC can help provide that—the scale and the economics come down, driving the deployment costs [down].

—Jeff Weber, Vice President, Product & Strategy AT&T Operations, Inc. (formerly SBC Communications) speaking at NAB 2005

This chapter is divided into two sections, one focusing on IPTV networks and the other focusing on Internet Video networks. Each section includes a detailed descriptions of the major components, both hardware and software, that go into these networks. Reality Checks for both types of networks are included at the end of this chapter.

# Constructing an IPTV Network

IPTV networks can be built to serve millions of subscribers or just a few thousand. Large systems can be national in scope and can be optimized to deliver hundreds of channels of programming across thousands of miles of networks. Small systems may service a local community with just a few dozen channels. In either case, cost-effective deployment of both the central equipment and the delivery networks is crucial to successful business operations.

One thing to keep in mind is that IPTV networks are typically designed to use phased deployment. Not all services will be offered to all potential subscribers when a system is first launched. This is due to two major factors:

- The complexity of deploying an IPTV network can require many hours of engineer and technician time from both system operators and their vendors for installation and system integration. Since staffing budgets are typically limited, services must be deployed only after they have been properly tested and integrated with the other network elements. Also, the equipment needed to deploy advanced services may be too expensive to deploy without a substantial customer base to provide adequate revenue.

- Consumers will take varying amounts of time before deciding to subscribe to new IPTV service offerings, particularly if their television viewing needs are being met by other technologies. A prudent business plan will recognize that a significant amount of time will be needed to convince customers of the benefits of a new television delivery method. It is simply not realistic to assume that 20 percent of the available customer base will sign up as subscribers as soon as a new service is launched.

Because of these two factors, it is important to develop a construction and customer activation plan that grows over time. First launch may see only a very small percentage of the available customer base signing up for service. Therefore, the network must be designed to keep the cost of the central equipment low during the early phases of deployment and for the outside plant construction to target areas with high densities of customers, where the costs can be kept low relative to the number of residences that will be wired for service.

Two important statistics are used in financial plans for IPTV systems. The first is a calculation of the total number of "homes passed" by the network, which is essentially the number of residences where the network is physically present and available for connection to any residences that want to become subscribers. The second is a calculation of the total number of subscribers that have actually signed up with the IPTV service provider to receive video service. One figure of merit for a deployment plan is the ratio of the number of subscribers to the number of homes passed. Initially, this ratio will be very low (in the single digit percentages) and increase slowly over time. Note that this ratio will never reach 100 percent, due to the availability of other technologies in most service areas (such as CATV or satellite) and due to the fact that not all consumers will want to pay for television services at any price. We'll explore these concepts more in Chapter 9.

## Typical System Architecture

For very large IPTV delivery systems, there is often a hierarchy of facilities constructed to deliver video signals across a large expanse of territory. One (or two, for disaster recovery) *Super Head End* (SHE) can serve millions of customers by processing the video channels that are common to all subscribers across the serving area. A *Video Serving Office* (VSO) will be located in each region as required to handle local programming and channels specific to a single city or geographic area. A *Central Office* (CO) or *Remote Terminal* (RT) can serve as a *Local End Office* (LEO) that contains the equipment needed to actually deliver the programming to customers in a local area. This is typically a portion of an existing facility already owned and operated by a telephone company or other local utility. The roles of

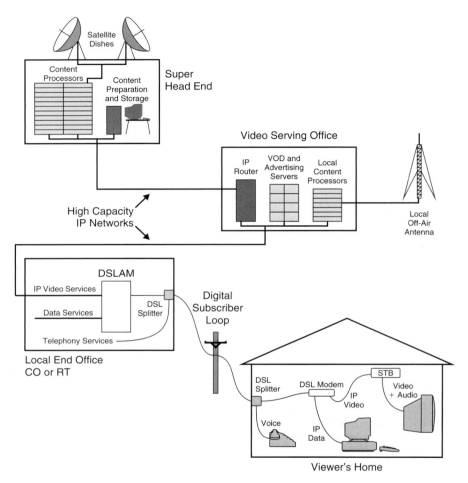

**FIGURE 4.1** *Typical IPTV System Architecture*

each of these facilities will be explained in more detail in the following sections. Figure 4.1 shows an overview of a typical IPTV system architecture.

Note that for smaller-scale IPTV systems, these three functions may be combined in a single location. The functions all need to be performed; they just might not be performed in separate facilities as described here.

## Super Head End

A Super Head End is the primary source of programming for the IPTV system. It is responsible for gathering content from programming suppliers, converting it into the appropriate form for delivery over the IPTV network and transmitting the content to the VSOs. The SHE may also be the location where content is prepared for storage on video servers that will be used to deliver VOD services. Let's look at each of these functions:

1) Content must be gathered from a number of different programming suppliers. The programming can be anything that will be delivered over the IPTV system, such as standard television network feeds; specialty programming channels such as sports, all-news, music, drama, children's or nature; premium movie; or other non-broadcast feeds. In many cases, these video signals may be gathered from a group of satellite receivers or from a terrestrial video transport network. Most often, these incoming signals will be in an encrypted digital format, so the appropriate receivers must be able to receive the necessary commands and decryption keys from the programming suppliers.

2) Incoming content must be converted into a form that will be transmitted over the IPTV system. To simplify operations, each channel will likely need to be formatted in a very standard manner—standard bit rates, standard packet format, standard compression technology and everything else that will make it possible for the viewer's equipment to understand the video signal and how to process it.

   Since the programming suppliers are free to choose the type of compression that best suits their needs, it is very common for some type of *transcoding* to be required. Transcoding is the conversion of signals from one compression format to another. The input to the transcoder may be any type of video—uncompressed video, MPEG–2, MPEG–4, VC–1—at whatever bit rate the content supplier has chosen. The output needs to be a properly formatted IP packet stream containing content compressed with the selected compression method operating at the precise bit rate that the IPTV network is designed to accept.

3) The compressed video signals must then be inserted into a transport network that provides connectivity to each of the VSOs. In some cases, this network will be owned and operated by the IPTV provider; in other cases, network capacity will be leased from a long-distance network provider. In either case, these networks will tend to be terrestrial (with some exceptions for geography) because the large bandwidths needed to supply hundreds of channels to many locations may be expensive to obtain from satellite providers.

   In many cases, the networks connecting the SHE to each VSO will be redundant. This allows operations at a VSO to continue even if a major network failure has occurred. In very large systems—those serving hundreds of thousands of viewers or more—a second SHE will be constructed to prevent a single catastrophic failure from cutting off television service to a large number of viewers. In this case, the two SHE locations will be hundreds of miles apart to enhance survivability.

4) Content intended for delivery to viewers on a VOD system can arrive in a wide variety of formats. Some content may arrive in one of a number of different professional videotape formats or on DVDs. Content may also be delivered as data files sent over an IP network. Still other content may be transmitted over real-time broadcast links (such as fiber or satellite), requiring a mechanism to receive video signals and store them for further processing.

Regardless of the source of the video server content, several key functions must be performed on each content element. The content must be transcoded and converted into a common format that can be interpreted by every STB, standardizing parameters such as bit rate and compression technology. The content will also need to be cataloged and labeled for reference, and software tags will need to be added that indicate the duration of the video, describe the content for viewers, list any restrictions on the storage or delivery of the content, etc. Formatting content into IP packets is not required at this step—that will be the function of the VOD servers that actually deliver the video signals to the users.

Advertising content may also need to be processed by the SHE. Most of the processing steps are the same for ad content as program content, with the exception that the result will be delivered to advertising servers instead of VOD servers. Ad servers may be located in the SHE for insertion into programs that will be delivered throughout the IPTV system, and they may also be located in individual VSOs for ads that will run only in specific regions. As with VOD content, proper labeling and delivery of these files is crucial to success.

Distribution of the VOD content to servers located in a VSO will typically be in the form of files sent over a standard data network. Since this content is not being viewed in real time, redundancy is typically not required. In the event of a failure of the network between the SHE and a VSO, the content can simply be transmitted again once the network is repaired. One thing that will be crucial on this network is security. Content owners will want strong assurances that their valuable titles won't fall into the hands of video pirates. Accordingly, the VOD file distribution system will use encryption and/or physically secure networks (such as private fiber optic links).

All of these different functions in a SHE will require hardware and software systems. Staffing will be required to monitor the systems operations, repair any failures in a timely manner and perform tasks that require human intervention, such as VOD file processing.

## Video Serving Office

A Video Serving Office (VSO) provides video processing and delivery services for a geographic region, such as a city. Each VSO can receive content from a SHE as well as local programming sources. It is responsible for distributing all of this content in real time to every CO/RT in the region. A VSO will also typically serve as the location of the VOD and other servers that deliver specialized content to viewers. Customer service, billing and other related operations might also be housed in the VSO.

1) One of the most important functions of the VSO is to process content specific to the local region. This might be from local OTA broadcast stations, or it might be locally originated programming from other sources, such as educational institutions, government sources or public access channels. Similar to a SHE, this content can arrive in forms that need to be converted into the standard format required by the IPTV delivery system.

2) Video content processors take many different forms of video inputs and create video outputs in the form necessary for distribution. Content processors can take video signals that have been compressed at one bit rate and convert them into a different bit rate. They can also take video signals that have been compressed using one standard (such as MPEG–2) and convert them into a different standard (such as MPEG–4). Some content processors can also take uncompressed video and compress it using any one of several compression standards.

3) The VSO will also be the location where actual IPTV streams are created. These streams will consist of packets sent out to COs/RTs. The level of sophistication of the remote equipment will determine the number of streams that need to be generated by the VSO. With simple remote equipment, the VSO will need to generate one stream for every active viewer. With sophisticated remote equipment capable of duplicating outbound video packets, only one stream for each broadcast channel will need to be generated. In this latter case, when multiple viewers are watching the same channel, the remote equipment will make as many copies as necessary (*multicast*) to feed one to each active viewer.

4) VOD servers are also typically housed at the VSO. These systems are responsible for creating the individual (*unicast*) streams sent to each subscriber when viewing VOD content. With true VOD, each viewer has the ability to pause, fast-forward and rewind the video stream. Commands from each viewer need to be processed rapidly and uniquely, so an individual stream is required for each active VOD viewer.

5) Local ads can be an important source of revenue for the IPTV operator. These ads can be inserted (with proper approval) into both nationally and locally originated

programming. Typically, the ads are for products and services sold on a local basis. National advertisers also want to use local ads to promote products in a special way to local viewers, such as tying a brand to a local athletic team or popular activity.

6) Interactivity is one of the main competitive weapons for IPTV as compared with satellite television. At the VSO, commands from individual STBs are gathered and processed. One of the main interactive functions is the selection, purchase and viewer control of VOD content. Another is actual interaction with video content, such as voting for a game show contestant or making purchases on a shopping network. To support these functions, the VSO needs to be equipped with applications servers that run the software needed to process commands from viewers.

7) STB control is important to the financial well-being of the IPTV provider. By ensuring that each STB is authorized before it can receive content, illegal viewing of video signals is eliminated. Two goals can be achieved through the use of scrambling and encryption: the IPTV operator can ensure that only paying customers are viewing content, and the content can be protected from unauthorized duplication and re-transmission.

8) The network to each CO/RT must have enough capacity to handle all of the streams destined to viewers connected to that VSO. Typically, this will be a fiber optic network consisting of multiple Gigabit Ethernet links. These can be packed onto relatively few fibers by using a different wavelength (color) of light for each GigE stream.

## Central Office/Remote Terminal

Many IPTV networks use existing telephone company physical infrastructure, including buildings. Central Offices (COs) contain telephone call switching equipment. Remote Terminals (RTs), which are often located underground, contain systems that connect subscriber lines and digital or fiber optic links to the nearest CO. In both types of buildings, equipment can be installed to deliver IPTV services over DSL circuits. The equipment located in these facilities must perform several different functions.

1) IPTV signals are generally delivered from the VSO by means of high-bandwidth (Gigabit and above) IP networks, usually by means of optical fiber. Inside a CO/RT, these networks are connected to DSLAMs.

2) The basic function of a DSLAM is to act as an Ethernet switch and connect video traffic arriving from the VSO to the DSL lines going out to each subscriber

premises. To accomplish this, the DSLAM examines the IP address of every incoming packet and forwards them over whichever DSL circuit connects to the subscriber device with that IP address.

3) Multicasting technology (also known as IGMP) is useful for IPTV video broadcasting and is supported by some of the newer brands of DSLAM. With this technology, the DSLAM is capable of taking a single stream from the VSO and replicating it to feed multiple simultaneous viewers of a single channel. Without this technology, the VSO must create an individual video stream for every viewer.

4) The DSLAM must also connect the existing telephony system in the CO/RT. A DSL splitter or hybrid bridge is used to allow both the DSL equipment and existing phone equipment to share a single pair of copper wires that leads to each subscriber's home. Inside the CO/RT, one leg of this splitter is connected to the standard voice telephone processing equipment. The other leg of the splitter is connected to the DSLAM for handling the high-speed data and video signals.

5) Several different services can all share the high-speed bandwidth offered by a DSL line to a consumer's premises. Of course, IPTV video services are one component. Another component is high-speed data service for Internet access; this traffic can be separated by the DSLAM and connected to an IP data router for processing within the CO. Services such as VoIP could also be delivered to separate outputs of the DSLAM if configured appropriately.

## Customer Premises

One of the most difficult environments for an IPTV operator is inside the viewer's home. IPTV devices require power, a physical location and a network wiring system to connect to one or more STBs located around the house. Many different technologies have been employed here, including HomePNA, coax and twisted pair, and some investigations are ongoing into wireless connections.

1) A DSL modem is installed in each home to receive the high-speed digital signals from the DSL circuit and convert the data into forms that other devices can use. This device can be stand-alone or integrated into a home gateway.

2) A DSL splitter is used in each home to separate the signals required by standard telephones from the high-speed signals processed by the DSL modem. One leg of this splitter is connected to any existing legacy telephone equipment, and the other leg is connected to the DSL modem. Note that in many cases the DSL splitter is integrated directly into the DSL modem.

3)  The home gateway is an optional piece of equipment installed by some service providers to provide control of and communication to multiple STBs. This device can also serve to manage the home network to ensure Web surfing from a PC in the home does not compromise the high-priority video traffic. It can also serve to convert between the different types of cabling used inside the house and the high-speed data lines.

4)  The STB provides much of the functionality of an IPTV system. It decodes the incoming digital video signals, produces on-screen graphics, supports user channel changing and other interactive functions, and many other tasks. Without a suitable STB for each television set, an IPTV system would be unusable.

# Typical Software Capabilities

Software performs many key functions inside an IPTV network. As is the case in a PC, an IPTV system simply wouldn't function without software. In the following sections, we will describe a number of software functions typically found in IPTV systems.

### Electronic Program Guide

The *Electronic Program Guide* (EPG) is an on-screen display that tells viewers which content is available on which channels. This can include both broadcast channels available to all viewers simultaneously and VOD content available for viewers to watch individually. Program guide information can either be produced by the IPTV network provider or, as is most often the case, can be purchased from an external supplier.

Two main types of EPGs are available. The first is a scrolling program guide, where the content on each available channel is displayed in channel number order on a grid that slowly scrolls up the television screen. This scheme does not require interactivity from the viewer and can become annoying to viewers as the number of channels exceeds 50 or more.

The second type of EPG is called an interactive program guide. In this scheme, a grid of channels and content choices are displayed on the television screen, as above. However, in this case, viewers have the ability to navigate around in the grid using their remote controls. The viewers can scroll and jump up or down in the grid to view different channels, and they can also scroll to the right to see future programs.

System operators have two choices for handling EPG functions:

•  Intelligent STBs can be used. In this case, the data for an interactive programming guide is broadcast to all the STBs on a periodic basis. Each STB is responsible for storing the latest information and for creating the displays. This is done to allow rapid response to the viewer's commands and to eliminate the burden on central equipment of having to process scroll commands from every viewer. This is also why newly connected STBs can require a significant amount of time before being able to display an accurate program guide, since it may take a while for all the information to be received and stored.

- In other cases, the interactive program guide processing is centralized in the VSO. In this architecture, the STB simply sends viewer commands upstream and receives new display information downstream. This system has the advantage of reducing the amount of processing that takes place in the STB, but has the disadvantage of requiring more communication between the STB and the VSO.

## Conditional Access System

A *conditional access system* controls which users are able to view which programming. For example, only viewers who have subscribed to a premium movie channel are allowed to have access to that content. This can be relatively simple to implement in an IPTV system, because the system simply needs to ensure that streams are never delivered to users who are not authorized to receive them.

In contrast, a different approach is needed in a satellite or traditional CATV system, where all the viewers are able to receive all the channels. In these systems, the content must be scrambled, encrypted or otherwise made unavailable to unauthorized viewers.

## Video on Demand System

A VOD system provides users with content that can be viewed at their discretion. This typically consists of a set of content files stored on a server and played out under the control of users.

Software for a VOD system needs to perform several functions, some in conjunction with other software modules. The available titles need to be listed and described by way of the EPG. Any required payment needs to be collected. A network connection (possibly via several hops) needs to be set up between the VOD server and the viewer's STB to deliver the content. The proper keys for decoding any content encryption need to be sent to the STB by the DRM system (covered in the next section). Viewer commands (such as pause, fast-forward and rewind) from the middleware system need to be retrieved and rapidly processed to control how the content is played out. All of this needs to happen fairly quickly in response to user actions, so that the system operates as "video on demand" and not "video when the system is good and ready."

## Digital Rights Management System

A *digital rights management* (DRM) system is designed to protect the property rights of a content owner. This typically involves some form of encryption or scrambling that renders the content unwatchable without the appropriate key. The key is usually some type of numeric value that controls the operation of a descrambler or decryption device.

In addition to content scrambling, the DRM system needs to be able to securely deliver the appropriate keys to authorized viewers' STBs. With these keys, the STBs will be able to make sense of the incoming stream and display it properly. Key distribution needs to be secure to prevent unauthorized viewers from obtaining the keys either by deliberate action or unintentionally.

## Subscriber Management and Billing System

The revenue stream of an IPTV provider depends on an efficient, functional system for managing subscribers and gathering the data needed to prepare accurate bills. Here is a brief list of functions that are normally required:

- Device Association, where a specific subscriber is linked with a specific set of hardware, such as an STB. Accuracy in this process is essential to ensure that the STBs have been correctly deployed and that any charges associated with an STB actually belong to the linked subscriber.

- Subscriber Services Profile, which indicates the services that the subscriber has ordered, such as a specific set of premium content channels. This system also needs to accurately track when customers call to add or remove services, so that STB control settings can be adjusted appropriately.

- Subscriber Purchase History, which records the specifics of any purchases such as premium VOD content.

- Service Call Logging and Repair Dispatch, which has a big impact on subscriber satisfaction levels. Accuracy is essential, so subscribers can be told when to expect repair technicians to arrive and when their service will be restored. It can also help technicians understand the problems that were reported by the subscriber and any steps that have already been taken to isolate the fault.

It is not uncommon for specific types of content to require direct payments to the content owner. This might be a monthly payment per subscriber for a premium sports channel or a per-viewing charge for a new-release movie offered on VOD. IPTV providers who don't have good billing systems in place can find themselves in violation of contracts requiring payment to the content owners. In extreme cases, a poor payment or faulty security system could result in the IPTV provider losing access to premium content in the future.

It's interesting to note that many companies are coming to recognize the growing importance of customer service for IPTV and other systems. Amdocs, a leading supplier of customer management solutions to service providers, commissioned a survey in 2006 of Tier 1 and 2 service providers. The results were quite interesting: "Nearly 67 percent of respondents plan to increase their spending on customer service enhancements over the next year, with the average investment increase projected at 31 percent."[1]

### Emergency Alert System

In the U.S., the federal government requires that television and radio broadcasters and cable television system operators implement an Emergency Alert System. This system can be used by the President to make an announcement to the public in a time of a national emergency. Use of the system is also permitted for state and local agencies to warn of certain hazards such as tornadoes or other dangerous weather. The system must be capable of interrupting programming on all channels provided by the television system and of inserting an appropriate warning or other instructions. The EAS must be installed in each active system and must be tested weekly and monthly. Failure to have an operational EAS can result in significant fines for the system operator.

# Constructing an Internet Video System

Building an Internet Video system is easier in some respects than building an IPTV system but more difficult in others. Construction is easier because an IP network, with all of the accompanying packet delivery hardware, does not need to be built, since the Internet will be used. On the other hand, building a delivery system that has adequate capacity to handle the peak number of users simultaneously while being affordable at the same time can be a difficult balancing act. Accordingly, many systems are designed to be scalable so capacity can be added quickly and easily as demand grows. Some hosting companies offer this as a service, where system capacity can be rented incrementally as demand grows.

---

1. "Amdocs Survey Findings Released," *Call Center Magazine*, November 22, 2006, www.callcentermagazine.com/shared/article/showArticle.jhtml?articleId=195900063

The basic elements of a content delivery system include a content preparation system, a Web portal, a video delivery server and a viewer device to watch the programming, usually a PC. Each of these elements requires software for operation, much of which can be purchased off the shelf. In the following sections, we will discuss the principal hardware elements and then the software applications hosted on them.

## Typical Hardware Architecture

The vast majority of the hardware needed for an Internet Video delivery system can be housed in a single facility, although it does not need to be. The quality of connectivity between the different systems' elements and between the systems and the Internet is a primary determinant of system performance. In very large applications that are capable of delivering thousands of simultaneous streams to viewers, hardware distributed at several different geographic locations can actually help performance by eliminating bandwidth bottlenecks that might occur. Please see Figure 4.2 for an overview of this system.

### Content Preparation System

Raw video content, such as a live image generated by a camera or video that has been recorded to a tape, is generally not well-suited for streaming applications. Normally, the content needs to be processed to make it ready for streaming. Processing can include format conversion, video compression, labeling and indexing, and publishing for streaming.

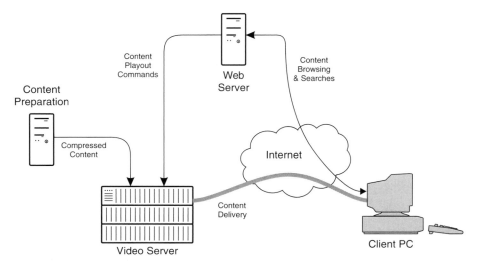

**FIGURE 4.2** *Typical Internet Video System Architecture*

Capturing and preparing content for viewing can be a simple or a highly complex process, depending on the goals of the users and their budgets for time and money. For some users, taking a home video camera and placing a compressed video image on their personal Web site is adequate. For others, professional production, with carefully edited images and graphics designed for Web viewing, is required.

Sometimes, multiple versions of a video file are required. This is the case if users are given the choice of two or more different media players or if the video is to be encoded at different bit rates. Low bit rate videos are delivered to users who have lower speed Internet connections. High bit rate videos deliver better images if viewers have access to high-speed Internet connections. A different video file must be prepared for each of these combinations, so if two viewer types are supported and three different bit rates are offered, then six different files must be prepared.

## Web Server

Web servers are used in Internet Video systems to assist viewers in selecting content to view. A typical page will contain descriptions of the videos, as well as selected stills from one or more videos. Some of these Web pages are configured to have embedded links to video content that begin video playback as soon as a user views the Web page. These Web pages can be viewed with a standard browser and searched by normal text-based search engines. Videos can be tagged with text labels by viewers to assist others in searching. Many pages also contain links to other pages of video with related subject matter.

Web servers often support a number of other functions. Here are some common capabilities:

- Some sites require payments or user logins prior to viewing. Web servers often handle the whole process of managing user profiles, collecting payments and discouraging non-members from entering the site.

- Many sites allow users to rate or vote on particular videos. Web servers can gather this information from users, store and process it, and create pages that show the summarized details to other users.

- User comments form a huge part of many sites' appeal. Web servers are used to collect, manage and display these comments. Care must be taken to ensure that the comments are associated with the proper videos and that any rules about the use of profanity or copyrighted material are followed.

- A number of video Web sites use advertising as a source of revenue. Web servers must be configured to deliver the correct, current advertisements. More sophisticated servers can deliver context-sensitive advertising, where the choice of ads to be displayed is based in part on the type of video featured on the page. For example, if a Web user is looking at a video that features a famous comedian, then the Web server could display an advertisement for a DVD of that comedian's most recent movie.

## Video Server

The video server is the workhorse of an Internet Video system. It is responsible for securely storing the video files that can be viewed. In addition, the video server must create the packet streams that are delivered to each viewer. The video server must also handle encrypting or scrambling the outbound video streams to ensure that they are protected from unauthorized use.

- Storage: The video server only needs to have enough capacity to store the video files it is providing. Accordingly, servers can have either large or small capacities. If multiple versions of the video files have been created, then the server needs to have enough capacity to store all of the different versions.

- Stream creation: The video server must be capable of delivering a stream to each requesting user. This is essentially always done on request, so each time one user wants to view a video, the server needs to create a stream of packets to send to that specific viewer. Every packet in the stream needs to be created by the server, because each one must contain the specific destination IP address corresponding to the viewer's device. While this is not an incredible burden for a few video streams, the workload on the video server increases as more users are added and more streams are requested.

- Security: Files stored on the video server are typically encrypted or scrambled for two reasons. First, by pre-encoding the files, it reduces the amount of work that needs to be done when the files are streamed to viewers. Secondly, in the event that an unauthorized user gets access to the content on the server, encoded files will be unwatchable by the unauthorized user. Content owners often specify contractually how their content is to be handled, and this may include the form in which the content is stored on the server.

## Live Streaming Server

A live streaming server is a specialized device that enables live video programming to be delivered to multiple users simultaneously. It operates by taking in a single stream of content and producing multiple copies for delivery to multiple viewers in real-time.

Typically, viewers who want to watch the live content will navigate to a central Web site that acts as a portal (covered in "Typical Software Architecture") for the content. Users who navigate to the portal are then redirected to the live streaming server as soon as they request to watch the video. Once they are connected to the streaming server, a copy of the source video is created inside the server. This new copy is then formatted into IP packets addressed to the viewer's device and sent out for delivery over the Internet.

### Client PC

Most Internet Video is delivered to PCs for viewing, although other devices are becoming available. Each PC must be equipped with software capable of receiving the incoming video packets and converting them into a video image on the user's display. In order for this software to work properly, adequate hardware must be present. Most recently produced PCs have enough processing power to decode and display standard-definition video images that have been compressed using standards such as MPEG–2 and MPEG–4. High-definition streams (which aren't yet too common in Internet Video) might require hardware accelerators in order to produce HD image output.

## Typical Software Architecture

Software is a key element of any Internet Video system. It plays a major role in enabling viewers to find and select content, delivering the content and playing the content on the viewing device. Let's take a look at some of the major components.

### Web Portals

A *Web portal* provides a common gathering point for viewers and content providers. From a viewer's standpoint, a successful portal has wide range of content that can be easily searched and navigated through to locate content that will be interesting to view. From a content provider's standpoint, a good portal will attract a large number of potential viewers.

A portal will typically have a number of different ways to search for content. One method uses a standard text-based search on the title of the video. Another method uses tags (similar to keywords) that have been added to video files by viewers that describe particular attributes of the video, such as "turtles" or "funny." Still other methods may rank videos by popularity in a number of categories or display videos that are frequently watched by viewers who have watched the currently displayed video. Many portals also allow viewers to post comments or rate videos, thereby increasing the level of viewer participation.

Portals will typically consist of a number of Web pages that serve as the user interface to video content. Different approaches are taken in the design of the user interface. Some Web sites will have a single featured video per Web page, which will begin playing as soon as the user navigates to that page. Other Web sites will have a collection of links to still video images; when the user chooses one of the thumbnails (small pictures) to view, the video will begin playing in a new pop-up window. Choosing between the two methods is really a matter of preference, and both are widely used.

Examining the HTML code for a video portal Web page reveals that the actual video content is not contained in the page itself, but is instead stored elsewhere. The portal handles interaction with the user and provides links to the locations where the content is actually stored. One benefit of using this technique is that it avoids having the user's browser attempt to load a complete video file each time the user navigates to a new page of the portal. Instead, what happens is that the portal page loads to give the user a complete page image with everything but the video, and then an automatic process takes place to stream the video file to the viewer. What the user sees is a Web page with an active video window, but in reality these two items are delivered separately and united inside the user's Web browser software. If the user navigates away from the page (or presses one of the controls to pause, rewind or fast-forward the content), then the Web page remains static, but the streaming engine reconfigures itself to deliver the user's new selection.

## Streaming Engine

The *streaming engine* is specifically designed to create a series of IP video packets for each outbound stream. Each IP packet must have source and destination IP addresses. In order for the video packets to reach the correct destination, the server must create headers for these packets with the correct IP destination address.

Since streaming is done on a real-time basis, the server must also create well-behaved streams, meaning that the pace of the packets should be regular and consistent. The rate of the packets also has to be controlled such that the player receives only as many packets as needed to render the video and audio correctly. Too fast and the player would be required to store the extra packets before playback, creating havoc with the playback if the buffer overflowed. Conversely, if the pace slows too much, the player would be starved for data and would have to freeze or interrupt the user display to compensate while waiting for new data to arrive. Although software players normally include small buffers to smooth out the inevitable variations in packet arrivals caused by IP networks, the goal of a streaming server is to deliver a 5-minute, 10-second stream in 5 minutes and 10 seconds.

## Web Browser

Web browser software resides on a viewer's PC, mobile phone or other device and enables a viewer to view and navigate through Web pages that contain text, graphics and other data. Examples include Microsoft Internet Explorer, Apple Macintosh Safari and Mozilla Firefox. Viewers use these programs to navigate through Web portals to find content to view. Web browsers work with static content such as text and graphics that can be described with HTML commands. One of the best features of HTML is the ability to embed hot links into documents—these have the effect of directing the browser software to a new Web site which is then downloaded and displayed on the viewer's device.

Browsers use multimedia plug-ins to support other functions such as video and audio playback. These plug-ins consist of pieces of software stored and run on the viewer's PC or other device that can interpret video, audio and other special types of files, such as Flash. When a Web site contains content beyond the scope of normal HTML, special commands are used to put the correct plug-in into operation when the content is selected. We'll spend more time on browsers and plug-ins in Chapter 11.

It is common for a single PC to have a number of plug-ins to support a variety of multimedia types. Different plug-ins are used for different types of media, so that one type of plug-in is used for viewing Flash animation while another is used to play a compressed audio stream. The plug-ins are also closely tied to the internal workings of specific operating systems, so a Quick-Time plug-in for a Macintosh won't be useful for playing Real Media files on a Windows PC.

## Media Player

A media player is another piece of software resident on the viewer's device. Examples include Microsoft's Windows Media Player, Apple's QuickTime and RealPlayer from Real Networks. A media player performs a very similar function to a browser multimedia plug-in, in that it takes a content stream and turns it into images and sounds that can be seen and heard by the viewer. However, there are differences between media players and plug-ins, which will be covered in the following discussion, as well as in more depth in Chapter 11.

A media player is typically a stand-alone piece of software. It can be run by itself, without having a Web browser activated. Most players contain a library function that enables them to list a variety of content that can be played by a viewer. This list can include content resident on the local device (e.g., the PC's hard drive) and content available from the Internet. Most media players can access the Internet to locate and play files from a variety of sources. In contrast, a browser plug-in is only active when a

Web page is delivering multimedia content, and there is no easy way to use the plug-in to play content that is not part of a Web page.

Most media players offer a significant amount of viewer control over content display. The video window can often be expanded or contracted. When an audio-only file is being played, some players offer visualization graphics that change shape in response to the sounds being played. A variety of skins can be chosen to change the appearance of the controls and the frame that surround the viewing window. This contrasts with the very limited control given to viewers by most Web pages—typically just pause, rewind and fast-forward (if enough of the clip has been buffered).

DRM is a key part of most media players, used to ensure that the rules and limitations defined by content owners are obeyed. Another important function is copy protection, which prevents unauthorized copies of media files from being made. Both of these technologies are typically built into a media player, because otherwise it would be difficult to get content owners to agree to allow their content to be played by that brand of player. Browser plug-ins are typically not as sophisticated; they rely on the functions of browsers to manage Web pages and media streams reliability.

It is also interesting to note that many commercial media players have different versions of their software, some of which can be downloaded at no charge and other versions which require purchase. The purchased versions typically offer greater functionality, such as support for full-screen video display or more advanced video compression techniques. Some media players offer subscriptions to special libraries of content as well as user customizable programs.

# Reality Check

In the first Reality Check of this chapter, we will take a look at two modifications to the architectures that have been successfully used for providing IPTV services. In the second Reality Check, we talk about aspects of the IPTV business that all prospective providers should consider before launching a project. In the third Reality Check, we discuss a very simple Internet Video delivery system that offers a minimum level of functionality.

# Alternative Architectures

Systems with architectures similar to the IPTV network we have described here have been implemented at numerous large telephone companies around the globe. However, one of the great benefits of IPTV is that it does not need to be tied to a specific architecture. Here are some alternatives that have been used successfully by IPTV providers.

## Shared Super Head End

There are an amazing number of small and geographically dispersed telephone service providers who could offer IPTV services if they were able to get access to programming. If each one of these companies needed to create a SHE with multiple satellite receivers, content processors, encryption units and subscriber management systems, and they had to negotiate contracts will a large bouquet of content providers, the costs would be very substantial. Instead, some services have sprung up to fill this need by offering a pre-packaged set of programming distributed from a central location. The following excerpt describing a service offered in the U.S. by the National Rural Telecommunications Cooperative (NRTC), called IP PRIME, appeared in *Telephony* magazine[2]:

"In partnership with SES Americom (a video transport provider with 44 satellites in orbit), the NRTC's program offers a basket of video content (including some 200 channels); centralized, managed middleware; end-to-end encryption; and satellite transport from SES Americom's center in New Jersey to a 3.8-meter dish at the telco's receiving site (which the telco buys through the NRTC). At the receiving site, the telco feeds the video traffic from the receiving dish to its own IP aggregation routers and sends it out to subscribers."

Once this equipment is in place, the local telco needs to negotiate a contract and install hardware to get content from any local television stations and add those signals to their IPTV channel lineup. This type of arrangement vastly simplifies and cost-reduces the process of installing an IPTV system for a smaller telephone company.

## Alternative Circuit Technology

Not all IPTV services need to be delivered over DSL circuits, although they are certainly the predominant technology. For green-field installations, namely those where a large group of housing is being built in a single tract, even DSL-oriented companies like AT&T will use *Fiber to the Home* (FTTH) technology to deliver voice, video and data services over an IP infrastructure. Similarly, it is certainly possible to deliver IPTV services over a CATV broadband system or a wireless system provided that a suitable return path is installed.

---

2. Ed Gubbins "IPTV in a Bottle," *Telephony magazine*, July 17, 2006, telephonyonline.com/mag/telecom_iptv_bottle/index.html

# Business Challenges

Several key challenges need to be overcome to create an IPTV system that will be accepted by viewers and profitable for the operator.

### Return on Investment

One of the biggest challenges is to design a system that can be installed economically in enough viewers' homes to generate a decent return on investment. A huge amount of hardware and software must be purchased to build the content collection and processing offices. These costs don't vary much whether the system needs to serve 100 or 100,000 viewers, and the costs need to be spread over a large number of subscribers to make the business models work. In addition, there is a significant cost per user, in terms of the devices that must be installed in each home, and the costs of the transmission equipment required to distribute the signals. While these latter costs vary with the number of subscribers, the total costs for the system can still be fairly high.

### Reaching Existing Homes

Another significant challenge is installing an IPTV system in an existing neighborhood. Economical ways must be found to re-use existing infrastructure (such as subscriber loops). Also, construction costs need to be watched carefully, because not all homes that have access to IPTV networks will actually purchase the services. Contrast this with the situation in newly built developments, where fiber optic connections can be made directly to each house for not much more of an investment than needed to install standard metallic subscriber loops.

### Local Permissions

One challenge that cannot be overlooked is the need to get permission (often in the form of a renewable franchise) from the local government authorities to install and operate a system. Many communities have powerful vested interests in the form of existing video delivery services, such as CATV or OTA broadcasters. While many governments favor having competitive network suppliers, the practicalities of encouraging new providers to install or upgrade their networks while at the same time maintaining fairness to incumbent providers can be a difficult balancing act.

# The Low End of Internet Video

It's important to remember that Internet Video systems come in many different sizes. In fact, it is instructive to look at a minimal system just to see how simply it can be done. Of course, with this system, performance will also be minimal, with perhaps a limit of a handful of viewers active at any one time. However, for some applications, that is all that is really needed.

Here is what a basic system could consist of:

- A stand-alone PC or server with a reasonable amount of processing power and a high-performance network interface card.

- A basic Web server package to provide the portal function.

- Content preparation software, which could be as simple as the video editing functions built into PC operating systems.

- A video streaming server package, which are available for a low cost from several different sources.

- A broadband network connection.

Of all the above expenses, probably the most expensive one—on a long-term basis—is the network connection. All of the other equipment and software can be purchased for less than $1,500.

# Summary

In this chapter, we discussed the basic architecture of both IPTV and Internet Video systems. The first section of the chapter focused on IPTV and went through the primary system hardware elements, including the SHE, VSO and CO/RT. We also discussed some of the software functions that make up an IPTV system.

In the second section of this chapter, we described the key elements of an Internet Video system. We covered the basic hardware, including content preparation, Web server, video server, streaming server and client PC. We also discussed the software elements including the Web portal, streaming engine, Web browser and media player.

In many real systems, some of the above systems will be combined with others, but the functions must still be performed. Although the tasks may be accomplished in different locations or packages, each of them is essential to the end-to-end flow of video to viewers.

# 5 IP—The Internet Protocol

> The Internet is not just one thing, it's a collection of things—of numerous communications networks that all speak the same digital language.
>
> —Jim Clark

IP is the most successful computer networking technology ever invented. A recent count shows almost 440 million host computers connected directly to the Internet.[1] Every new desktop or laptop computer produced today comes equipped with a networking connection that supports IP.

With a basic understanding of IP networking, our discussions about IP video will be much more valuable to you. It is not at all unusual for special network designs to be required in order to transport IPTV reliably. In this chapter, we will discuss the basics of IP transport, explain the key concept of a packet and show how IP fits into the overall scheme of data communications. We will then cover unicasting and multicasting, two key concepts in video networking.

## The Corner Office View

The remarkable social impact and economic success of the Internet is in many ways directly attributable to the architectural characteristics that were part of its design. The Internet was designed with no gatekeepers over new content or services. The Internet is based on a layered, end-to-end model that allows people at each level of the network to innovate free of any central control. By placing intelligence at the edges

CONTINUED ▶

---

1. From Internet Systems Consortium, Inc., www.isc.org. This number doesn't include the millions of computers that are connected within private networks and share an Internet connection

CONTINUED ▶

rather than control in the middle of the network, the Internet has created a platform for innovation. This has led to an explosion of offerings—from VoIP to 802.11x Wi-Fi to blogging—that might never have evolved had central control of the network been required by design.

—Vinton Cerf, Chief Internet Evangelist, Google Inc., and co-inventor of TCP/IP[2]

# A Simple Analogy

A very simple, limited analogy may be appropriate here. In some respects, an IP address is like a telephone number. If you know someone's telephone number, there is a pretty good chance you can pick up your phone and call him or her. It doesn't matter what country the person is in, as long as you dial correctly (adding country code when required), and it doesn't matter what kind of technology that person is using—mobile phone, cordless phone, fixed rotary or tone-dialed phone. Several different network voice technologies may be used to complete the circuit, including copper cable, fiber optics, microwave links, satellite links and other wireless technologies. However convoluted the route, the call goes through.

For data networks, an IP address provides the same function as a telephone number: it is a mechanism to uniquely identify different computers and to enable them to contact each other and exchange data over a huge variety of different network technologies.

Stretching the analogy a bit further, simply knowing someone's telephone number doesn't mean you're going to be able to communicate with him or her. A call might be placed when nobody is there to answer the phone. The phone might be engaged in another call and not available. The call might go through just fine, but if both speakers don't use a common language, communication won't occur. The same is true with IP networking—simply knowing another computer's IP address doesn't mean that two applications running on two different machines can communicate with each other.

---

2. Vinton Cerf letter to U.S. House of Representatives Committee on Energy and Commerce, November 8, 2005, googleblog.blogspot.com/2005/11/vint-cerf-speaks-out-on-net-neutrality.html

Of course, it is important to remember that IP networking and telephony are two very different technologies. Telephony is "connection-oriented," meaning that a specific circuit must be established between the sender and the receiver of information before any communication takes place (such as a voice conversation or a fax transmission). In a call, all the information flows over the same path. IP, on the other hand, is "connectionless," meaning that the information (such as data, voice or video) is broken up into specific IP subunits, called packets, prior to transmission. Each packet is free to take any available path from the sender to the receiver.

# What Is a Packet?

An IP *packet* is a unique container for data. It consists of a string of data bytes that has a defined format, including a header and a block of information bytes. Each packet can be a different length (within limits), but once it is created, each packet has a constant length.

The header of each packet contains information about the packet. Most important is the destination address, which is the IP address of the destination for the packet. The header also includes the IP address of the source of the data, so two-way communication can be easily established between two devices. This also enables packets from different sources going to different destinations to share a single physical communications link. Devices at either end of the link (called *routers*) can sort the packets out and deliver them to different destinations based on the IP addresses in each packet's header.

The biggest strength of an IP network is that many different packets, all containing data from different applications, can share a single packet transport link. This permits the tremendous flexibility of an IP network—once a device does the hard work of converting a particular data stream into packets, the rest is easy, because the IP network will take care of delivering the packets to their destination. Once they are delivered, it is again the responsibility of an application to take the data out of the packets and put the data to work. This isn't a trivial process—the receiving application must deal with any IP network delivery errors.

# How IP Fits In

IP provides a very useful mechanism to enable communications between computers. IP provides a uniform addressing scheme so computers on one network can communicate with computers on a distant network. IP also provides a set of functions that make it easy for different types of applications (such as e-mail, Web browsing or video streaming) to work in parallel on a single computer. Plus, IP enables different types of computers (mainframes, PCs, Macs, Linux machines, etc.) to communicate with each other.

IP is very flexible because it is not tied to a specific physical communication method. IP links have been successfully established over a wide variety of different physical links. One very popular technology for IP transport is Ethernet, which is often used for local area networking. Many other technologies can support IP, including dial-up modems, wireless links (such as Wi-Fi), DSL, SONET and ATM telecom links. IP will even work across connections where several network technologies are combined, such as a wireless home access link that connects to a CATV system offering cable modem services or a DSL line, which in turn sends customer data to the Internet by means of a fiber optic backbone. This adaptability is one of the things that makes IP so widespread.

IP doesn't do everything. It depends on other software and hardware, and other software in turn depends on it. IP fits between the function of data transport performed by physical networks and the software applications that use IP to communicate with applications running on other devices. Figure 5.1 shows how IP fits between applications on the top of the networking hierarchy and physical communications on the bottom.

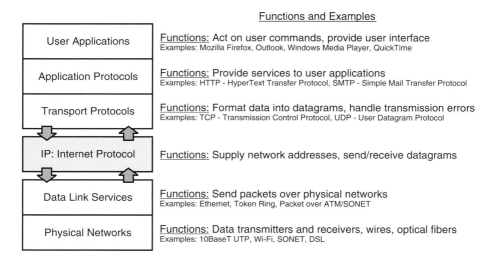

**FIGURE 5.1** *How IP Fits Between Other Layers of Networking Protocols*

IP is not a user application or an application protocol. However, many user applications employ IP to accomplish their tasks, such as sending e-mail, playing a video or browsing the Web. These applications use application protocols such as the *HyperText Transfer Protocol* (HTTP) or Simple Mail Transfer Protocol (SMTP). These protocols provide services to applications. For example, one of the services provided by HTTP is a uniform method for giving the location of resources on the Internet, which goes by the abbreviation URL.

IP by itself is not even a reliable means of communications; it does not provide a mechanism to re-send data that might be lost or corrupted in transmission. Other protocols that employ IP are responsible for that. Using the telephone analogy again, IP can connect the telephone call, but it doesn't control what happens if, for example, the person being called isn't home, or if the call gets interrupted before the parties are finished talking. Those occurrences are the responsibility of the protocols that use IP for communication.

# Types of IP Networks

Many different types of physical networks can be used to transport IP data. In this section, we'll review some of the most popular ones and describe where they are commonly used.

## Ethernet

Ethernet is almost certainly the most widespread data communications network in the world. Robert Metcalfe and David Boggs invented the technology in the mid-1970s, and the growth since then has been exponential. Ethernet is used in local area networks to connect computers, printers, servers, IP routers and many other types of devices. There are three commonly used speeds for Ethernet connections—10 Mbps, 100 Mbps and 1 Gbps. The first two technologies are often called 10baseT and 100baseT, respectively, and the fastest of the three is often called GigE. Standards have also been defined for the next logical step in speed, called 10GigE, but today this interface technology is expensive and fairly rare.

Ethernet is a *Local Area Network* (LAN) technology. This means that it is not suitable for use in *Wide Area Networks* (WANs) or Metropolitan Area Networks (MANs). The reasons for this are that Ethernet has some fairly short distance limitations (2,000 meters in many instances) and cannot be too large for timing reasons.

Basic Ethernet cabling usually consists of special twisted pairs of conductors called CAT5 or CAT6, depending on the speed rating (the higher number rating is capable of faster speed). An Ethernet network can also be implemented over optical fibers; this is reasonably common for GigE links and very common for 10GigE links.

Ethernet networks are very common in modern office settings and are often used in home networks. Many networks that were originally set up to share a printer with a small group of PCs have expanded to cover hundreds of devices throughout a building. These networks will often contain a variety of servers and network interfaces, including Internet connections. Many home networks were originally installed for the sole purpose of enabling multiple PCs to share a single high-speed network connection.

## Wireless Ethernet

Wireless Ethernet is becoming very popular for many applications, including connections to laptops and other portable devices. A couple of popular names for this technology are 802.11 (the number of the IEEE standard) and Wi-Fi.

Most Wi-Fi networks are configured with fixed central access points (AP) that provide a common node that connects to all the portable devices. Typically, the AP provides a connection to a high-speed network that supports Internet access or access to a corporate network.

Wireless transmissions can be affected by a number of different factors in the local environment, and data transmission speeds can change rapidly. As a result, systems will use automatic packet re-transmission to ensure that the data gets delivered. Unfortunately, this can cause the data transmission speed to fluctuate rapidly and without warning. This can make it extremely difficult to reliably send video information.

Wi-Fi is used inside many homes for connecting PCs to each other, printers and the Internet. The main advantages are portability and elimination of the need to string cables to every location in the home where a PC is going to be used. Wi-Fi hot spots (locations where one or more APs are located) are very common in locations visited often by frequent travelers. It is not used often for professional video networks because of the limited bandwidth and the highly variable delay.

## Cable Modems

Many CATV companies have started providing a wide variety of services to customers in the hopes of capturing a larger portion of their customers' monthly telecommunications expenses. As a result, many customers have been extremely pleased with the reliable high-speed services offerings.

Cable modems work by taking digital data signals and converting them into high frequency signals that flow over CATV cabling, in place of some of the television content. The relevant standards for these signals are called DOCSIS, for Data Over Cable Service Interface Specification, developed by a consortium lead by CableLabs. Since data services are bi-directional, transmission must take place in both directions on the CATV cable. This might require some extra equipment or maintenance on existing CATV systems to make sure that the return paths from subscribers back to the head-end are working properly.

Cable modem termination system (CMTS) shelves are located at the CATV head-end. These provide high-speed data connectivity to hundreds or thousands of CATV subscribers. The output of the CMTS system is one or more RF signal that is combined with normal video signals that are distributed to all of the viewers in an area. At each broadband user's home, a cable modem is installed that tunes to the required frequency and selects the data addressed to that user's home. The data is converted into standard Ethernet format and delivered to the user's PC or other device (such as a home router or Wi-Fi access point.) On the return trip, the cable modem accepts data from the end-user device and transmits it back to the CMTS by way of an RF channel on the CATV return path.

Cable modems are quite popular in the U.S., with roughly equal numbers of cable modem and DSL broadband households. IPTV services can be delivered over cable modems. However, since CATV systems already have a video delivery system, they are not often used for IPTV, possibly except for some VOD services. Internet Video services are frequently delivered over cable modems. Outside the U.S., cable modems are less popular but are still used for a significant number of broadband households.

## Digital Subscriber Lines

*Digital Subscriber Lines* (DSL) provide broadband data services over long twisted pair cables. They were developed to allow companies that had telephone lines installed to customer homes to offer high speed Internet connections without having to install a whole new CATV or fiber optic network.

Very special techniques are required to get high-speed digital data to move reliably over cables that were designed just to handle low-frequency voice signals. There are trade-offs between speed and distance—longer distances allow more subscribers to be served from a single office, but at lower speeds.

Special technologies have been developed to modulate the data onto the twisted pairs and to cancel any echoes that may occur during transmission. This technology requires advanced digital signal processing, with very high performance chipsets that are undergoing constant improvement. As a result, new standards are constantly being developed.

DSL is used primarily in networks that already have twisted-pair networks installed. It makes little sense to use DSL technology in new construction areas, as there is not a tremendous cost premium for installing fiber optic systems in a completely new network build. Even major proponents of DSL such as AT&T are planning to install fiber in new developments.[3]

## Fiber Optic IP Networks

Optical fibers have a number of advantages for high-speed data transport, and these benefits certainly apply to IP networks. These advantages include an extremely high data carrying capacity,[4] isolation from outside interference, long transmission distances (including undersea cables) and low cost per kilometer.

IP packets can be sent over optical fibers in a number of different ways. One popular method involves sending GigE and 10GigE signals directly over fiber. Another method involves mapping packets into SONET/SDH-compliant signals and transmitting those over an optical network. A third method involves sending IP packets over fibers in a format designed for fiber to the home transmission.

Both IPTV and Internet Video signals can be transmitted over optical fiber, and at some point, essentially all streams do pass over fiber between video sources and viewers. Fiber is often used for distributing broadcast television content on a national and international level, and it is virtually always used for long-distance Internet transport. Fiber is normally used to distribute content from VSOs to DSLAMs. Fiber can be used to deliver IP packets directly to consumers in both IPTV and Internet Video applications.

# IP Addresses

*IP addresses* are easy to recognize due to their special format. This format is called "dotted decimal" and consists of a series of four numbers separated by periods (or

---

3. From a presentation at IBC on September 9, 2006, entitled "AT&T U-verse TV" by Paul Whitehead of AT&T

4. Nippon Telegraph and Telephone Corporation reported a speed of 14 Terabits per second on a single fiber in a September 29, 2006 press release (www.ntt.co.jp). This is equivalent to 14,000 Gigabit Ethernet links on a single fiber

dots). A dotted decimal number represents a 32-bit number, which is broken up into four 8-bit numbers. For example, 129.35.76.177 is the IP address for www.elsevier.com. Most folks who have configured their own home network or laptop connection have probably seen information in this form.

Of course, being human, we have a hard time remembering and typing all of those digits correctly (even when writing a book). So, the *Domain Name System* (DNS) was invented to make life easier. DNS provides a translation service for Web browsers and other software applications that takes easy-to-remember domain names (such as "elsevier.com") and translates them into IP addresses (such as 129.35.76.177).

IP addresses are key to the operation of an IP network. They form the unique identification that each device must have to be able to send and receive packets. On any network, each device must have a unique address; otherwise the network wouldn't be able to deliver packets properly. Private networks that contain several devices and one Internet connection can use private IP addresses inside the network while sharing a single public IP address for access to the Internet.

# Key Parts of an IP Network

Many different types of equipment can be used to construct an IP network. Since purchasing, installing and operating these devices can represent a large portion of the cost of an IPTV or Internet Video system, it makes sense to describe some of the key system elements.

- Ethernet *hubs* and *switches* are used to physically move data packets from one device to another inside a physical location. Hubs have essentially no packet processing intelligence—they simply take any packets that come in on one port and transmit them out all the other ports of the hub. Switches are more intelligent—they can determine where each packet is going and send each packet out on the proper port. Switches are invaluable for connecting the hundreds of IP devices found in even a medium-sized corporation. Switches have a limited scope, however—they only pay attention to directly connected devices. Switches do not have the ability to look at a packet and figure out that in order to get to destination Z the packet needs to be sent first to devices X and Y. That is the function of an IP router.

- IP *routers* are the workhorses of an IP network. They are essential for delivering packets across a large network, because they are able to figure out a route for each packet. These routes can travel great distances through multiple devices over many different kinds of physical networks, such as wireless, fiber optic, twisted pair and DSL links. It is not uncommon for a router to manage several thousand different packet routes, even though it may only be connected to a few dozen other devices. As a result of their flexibility and intelligence, IP routers can be quite expensive, particularly for ones that can handle large bandwidth loads, as is common in video networks.

- Web and data servers provide a wide variety of data sources for a broad spectrum of purposes. These servers need to support the IP protocol to operate on the Internet and the World Wide Web. Typically, these units are set up to respond to transactions that have been initiated by client devices, such as user PCs.

- Client devices cover a wide range of different technologies, form factors and uses. They can range from desktop PCs of many different vintages and capacities to an array of portable and even handheld units. These units are typically set up to run applications that users can invoke to accomplish specific tasks.

In a typical transaction over an IP network, a user at a PC types in a command to do something, such as read an e-mail or news article. This is accomplished by means of an application running on the user device, such as an e-mail application or a Web browser application. These applications provide the user interface that appears on the user device, including displays on the device screen and a mechanism for the user to point and click or type an instruction.

When the user's command is completed, the application software will typically create a command output by sending data through a protocol such as HTTP. Referring to Figure 5.2, this process can be visualized as a downward movement through the

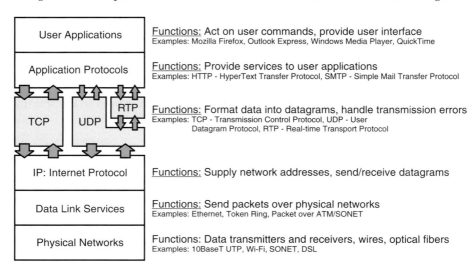

**FIGURE 5.2** *Transport Protocol Hierarchy*

different protocol layers. The command created by HTTP is then passed on to a transport protocol such as TCP, where it is given addressing information and formatted into packets for handling by IP. The IP layer takes the packets and makes them suitable for transport over the actual data network such as Ethernet. Ethernet is then responsible for actually transmitting the packet data over a physical cable to another machine, where the process is reversed, i.e., the data is passed back up through the protocol stack on the receiving device. Eventually, the data from the user is delivered to an application on the receiving machine. At this point, the user's request can be responded to either automatically (as in the case of a Web server) or manually (as in the case of an e-mail).

When the response is ready, the process is reversed. In the responding machine, data is passed down through the various protocol layers and onto the physical connection back to the user's machine. The response is then passed back to the user's application, and the transaction is completed.

The real beauty of this way of handling messages is that each protocol layer has well-defined, specific responsibilities. This also makes it possible for one layer to change without having to rework all of the other software. Consider the introduction of wireless networking over the past 5 to 10 years. While it is true that various operating systems (such as Windows or Mac-OS) had to be rewritten to accommodate these changes, most user applications (such as Microsoft Outlook or Adobe Acrobat) did not. Similarly, new versions of applications can be released without having to change the basic underlying protocols.

# Transport Protocols

Transport protocols are used to control the transmission of data packets in conjunction with IP. We will discuss three major protocols commonly used in transporting real-time video:

- *UDP* or *User Datagram Protocol*: This is one of the simplest and earliest of the IP protocols. UDP is often used for video and other very time-sensitive data. In UDP, the originating device can control how rapidly data from a stream will flow across the network. In other protocols (such as in TCP, covered next), the network can drastically affect how data transfer works. For video and other real-time streams, UDP is a logical choice for the transport protocol, since it does not add unneeded overhead to streams that already have built-in error correction functions. Because UDP does not require two-way communication, it can operate on one-way networks (such as satellite broadcasts). In addition,

UDP can be used in multicasting applications where one source feeds multiple destinations (covered in greater detail in the next section).

- *TCP or Transmission Control Protocol*: This is a well-established Internet protocol widely used for data transport. The vast majority of the devices that connect to the Internet are capable of supporting TCP over IP (or simply TCP/IP). TCP requires that a connection be set up between the data sender and the data receiver before any data transmission can take place. One of the essential features of TCP is its ability to handle transmission errors, particularly lost packets. TCP counts and keeps track of each byte of data that flows across a connection. The automatic flow control mechanism will slow down data transmission speeds when transmission errors occur. If this rate falls below the minimum rate needed by a video signal, then the video signal receiver will cease to operate properly.

- *RTP or Real-time Transport Protocol* (or Real Time Protocol, if you prefer) is intended for real-time multimedia applications, such as voice and video over the Internet. RTP was specifically designed to carry signals where time is of the essence. For example, in many real-time signals such as video, if the packet delivery rate falls below a critical threshold, it becomes impossible to form a useful output signal at the receiver. For these signals, packet loss is better tolerated than late delivery. RTP was created for these kinds of signals—to provide a set of functions that are useful for real-time video and audio transport over the Internet. Overall, RTP adds a lot of functionality on top of UDP without adding a lot of the unwanted functions of TCP. RTP also supports multicasting, which can be a much more efficient way to transport video over a network, as we will see in the next section.

In the networking hierarchy, all three protocols are considered to operate above the IP protocol, because they rely on IP's datagram transport services to actually move data to another computer. Figure 5.2 shows how UDP, TCP and RTP fit into the networking hierarchy. Note that RTP actually uses some of the functions of UDP; it operates on top of UDP.

# Multicasting

*Multicasting* is a key concept for IP networking. However, there are two very different meanings of the word that can apply to the field of IPTV:

- In over-the-air digital television broadcasting, multicasting means delivering multiple video programs simultaneously over a single digital broadcast channel.

- In IP networking, multicasting means delivering a single stream to multiple viewers simultaneously.

Broadcast multicasting became feasible with the advent of terrestrial digital television. Within a standard digital channel (19.38 Mbps in the U.S.) it is possible to have multiple video channels, each occupying a portion of the total bandwidth. For example, ION Media Networks (formerly Paxson) has more than 50 digital broadcast stations across the U.S.—each one is capable of delivering at least four different SD programs simultaneously using multicast technology.

In IP multicasting, a single video stream is sent simultaneously to multiple users. Through the use of special protocols, copies of the video stream are made inside the network for every recipient. All viewers of the multicast get the same signal at the same time.

Market penetration for both types of multicasting is limited. Broadcast station owners are just beginning to explore the types of broadcast multicast services that consumers will actually watch. Most of the IP networking equipment delivered over the past five or more years is capable of supporting IP multicasting, but it has been disabled out of fear of an excessive burden on networks. For example, IP multicasting is not currently enabled on the Internet, restricting the use of multicasting for IP video steaming to private networks. However, in newly constructed IPTV systems, multicasting is a key technology.

# IP Unicasting

To get a better understanding of IP multicasting, it is helpful to compare it to the process of IP *unicasting*. In unicasting, each video stream is sent to exactly one recipient. If multiple recipients want the same video, the source must create a separate unicast stream for each recipient. These streams then flow all the way from the source to each destination over the IP network.

Each user who wants to view a video must make a request to the video source. The source needs to know the destination IP address of each user and must create a stream of packets addressed to each user. As the number of simultaneous viewers increases, the load on the source increases, since it must continuously create individual packets for each viewer. This can require a significant amount of processing power and also a network connection big enough to carry all the outbound packets. For example, if a video source were equipped to send 20 different users a video stream of 2.5 Mbps, it would need to have a network connection of at least 50 Mbps.

An important benefit of unicasting is that each viewer can get a custom-tailored video stream. This enables the video source to offer specialized features such as pause, rewind and fast-forward video. This is normally practical only with pre-recorded content but can be a popular feature with users.

Unicasting is the norm for Internet Video for two reasons. First, the Internet is not multicast-enabled, so it is not feasible to use multicasting.[5] Second, most Internet Video viewers expect to be able to control video streams (i.e., pause, rewind, fast-forward), and this is impossible with multicast streams.

## IP Multicasting

In multicasting, a single video stream is sent simultaneously to multiple users. Through the use of special protocols, the network is directed to make copies of the video stream for every recipient. This process of copying occurs inside the network, rather than at the video source. Copies are made at each point in the network only where they are needed. Figure 5.3 shows the difference in the way data flows under unicasting and multicasting.

In multicasting, the burden of creating streams for each user shifts from the video source to the network. Inside the network, specialized protocols enable the network to recognize multicasted packets and send them to multiple destinations. This is accomplished by giving the multicast packets special addresses that are

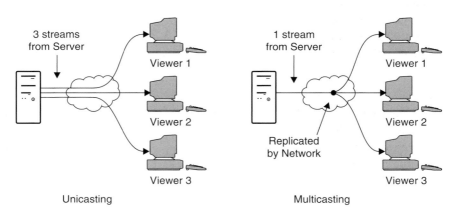

**FIGURE 5.3** *Unicasting vs. Multicasting*

---

5. Alternatively, a streaming server could be used to handle the load of creating multiple packet streams

reserved for multicasting. There is also a special protocol for users that enables them to inform the network that they wish to join the multicast.

Keep in mind that multicasts operate in one direction only, just like an over-the-air broadcast. There is no built-in mechanism to collect data from each of the endpoints and send it back to the source (other than some network performance statistics like counts of lost packets). This means that any interactivity between the endpoints and the video source must be handled by some other mechanism.

## Multicasting in IPTV

Multicasting is a key technology for IPTV because it enables a single source signal to be sent to multiple destinations. This can enable hundreds, or even thousands, of viewers to simultaneously watch a single television broadcast.

In an IPTV network (as described in Chapter 4), there are several points inside the distribution network from the SHE to the viewer where multicasting can be used to great effect.

From the SHE output, multicasting can be used to take a single live stream and distribute it to multiple VSOs. This saves the expense of constructing a high-bandwidth streaming server inside the SHE. This also greatly reduces the size of the network connection required at the output of the SHE.

When it comes to distributing broadcast television streams to viewers, multicasting is almost always used. This technology enables a viewer's STB to connect to a program feed simply by joining a multicast. However, where this happens is greatly dependent on the capabilities of the DSLAMs. Some DSLAMs are multicast-enabled, and others are not.

- When the DSLAMs are not multicast enabled, a unique video stream must be sent for each viewer all the way from the VSO to that viewer's STB. This requires a high bandwidth connection from the VSO to each DSLAM, with enough capacity to handle all of the active viewers simultaneously. This approach has the advantage of reducing the complexity (and therefore the cost) of the DSLAMs.

- When the DSLAMs are multicast enabled, the connection between the VSO and the DSLAM can be simplified, with only one copy of each broadcast channel needing to be sent. Requests to join and leave the multicast are received from STBs and processed inside the DSLAM; copies are made as necessary for each STB. While this approach increases the complexity of the DSLAM, it does significantly reduce the amount of bandwidth needed to feed signals from the VSO to each DSLAM.

## Issues with Multicasting

Multicasting is not enabled on all IP networks, because there are some noticeable drawbacks to the technology. These include network resource burdens, management complexity and unverified file transfer. Let's explore each of these in more detail.

As mentioned in previous sections, one drawback of multicasting is the additional burden that it places on the network, primarily routers. Routers are impacted in two main ways—processing the overhead packets containing multicast join and leave instructions, and processing the live streams. In most IPTV systems, broadcast channels (such as prime-time network TV) are broadcast using multicast technology. Each time a channel change takes place from one multicast stream to another, several messages must be processed, including instructions to stop delivering one stream to and to start delivering a new stream to a user's STB. In addition to this overhead processing, the IP router needs to be able to make a copy of every single multicast packet for every destination served by that router. In some cases, the copies will go to another router downstream toward the destination. In other cases, the copies will go directly to a STB. If a router has to serve hundreds or thousands of STBs, each with a multicast stream, this can require a lot of processing power.

Multicast networks can be complicated to manage. In the most popular multicasting protocol, there is a built-in mechanism to gather feedback from all of the distant endpoints. This protocol is carefully designed to minimize the amount of traffic coming back from the endpoints, with the tradeoff being that each endpoint reports less often as their number goes up. This can make it difficult to determine when several endpoints are having difficulty with a particular stream.

Bit-for-bit file copying using acknowledgments is not compatible with multicasting. Normally, when perfection is demanded (say in a million dollar financial transaction), the endpoints are designed to handshake with each other after each block of data is successfully delivered. Any mistakes require re-sending the damaged or missing packets. This is impractical for a multicast, since it is unlikely that all endpoints would always experience the same errors at the same time. Accordingly, there are other protocols (such as TCP) that can be used to transmit data when errors must be totally excluded.

# Reality Check

In this chapter's Reality Check, we take a look at the immense growth of broadband services that has taken place over the past few years. While the growth rates have slowed in some countries as penetrations increase, millions of broadband lines are

still being installed each month around the world. All of these lines service potential customers for IPTV and Internet Video.

## Broadband Network Growth

For IPTV and Internet Video to operate with any level of user satisfaction, a broadband network connection is essential. While it is technically possible for a dial-up
user to view a video signal, the long delays needed to download even a short clip at
very low resolution make dial-up impractical. So, to get a feel for the market for
IPTV and Internet Video, we must restrict our focus to broadband users.

A good working definition of a broadband connection is one that offers more
than 256 kbps of throughput. This is adequate for low resolution, low frame rate
video in real time. It may also be enough for a user to download a short video clip
from a Web site in a reasonable amount of time. This kind of speed simply cannot
be achieved with a dial-up modem operating over an analog voice line.

There are many different ways to look at broadband network statistics. One
way that makes sense is to look at the worldwide deployment of broadband links,
since this comprises the total available market for IPTV and Internet Video services.

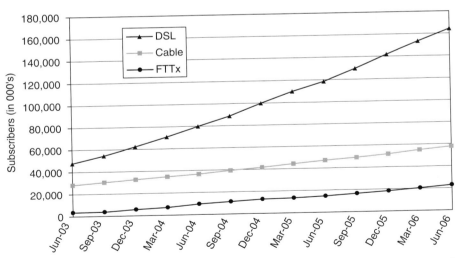

**FIGURE 5.4** *Worldwide Broadband Growth by Technology © Point-Topic, Used
with Permission*[6]

---

6. Vince Chook, "World Broadband Statistics Q2 2006" Point-Topic Ltd., www.point-topic.com/

Figure 5.4, from Point-Topic, shows the worldwide growth of broadband circuits from 2003 to 2006 in three different technologies: DSL, Cable modem, and *fiber to the node/fiber to the home* (FTTx on the diagram).

As this illustration shows, expansion has been quite rapid, growing from a total of 79.7 million lines at the end of Q2, 2003, to 247.2 million at the end of Q2, 2006. This calculates to a cumulative growth rate of just under 46 percent per year. On current trends, the worldwide penetration of broadband will reach 5 percent by the end of 2006, leaving a great deal of room for future growth. Compare this to 1.263 billion fixed line telephones in use and 2.168 billion mobile/cellular phones in use in 2005,[7] and it is easy to see the immense growth potential for broadband services.

# Summary

IP has changed the world of data communications and impacts the physical world around us more all the time. As telecommuting, videoconferencing, virtual worlds and the increasing array of online video content reduce the need for travel for communication's sake, a range of possibilities open up. As the Internet continues to grow, most people will be able to learn about whatever they want from the comforts of their own homes. More and more devices are becoming IP enabled, from cell phones to refrigerators, and they will all end up connected somehow, over networks that are becoming IP-centric. The opportunities created will be enormous due to what IP helps make happen.

In this chapter, we began with a basic discussion of the properties of IP and looked at some of the roles that IP plays in the hierarchy of data communications. We then described some popular types of devices that support IP communication and examined some of the higher-level protocols such as TCP and RTP that use IP to transmit Web pages and video. We followed this with a look at multicasting, which is one of the key enabling technologies for IPTV. The Reality Check showed how large the market has become for broadband services and how much room exists for future growth. It's amazing to consider that essentially every broadband subscriber is a potential customer for IPTV or Internet Video.

---

7. CIA Factbook https://www.cia.gov/cia/publications/factbook/geos/xx.html

# 6 Video Compression

Once you get past a few hundred kilobits-per-second, it's possible to deliver pretty good quality video and sound.

—Vinton Cerf

Video signals used in IPTV and Internet Video are almost always compressed. Compression means reducing the number of bits required to represent the video image. This is an important topic, because choosing a suitable compression method can sometimes mean the difference between the success and failure of a video networking project.

In this chapter, we will begin by examining the reasons for compression and look at some of the factors that determine what form of compression is suitable for an application. Then, we will examine MPEG video compression, since it is one of the most popular technologies used for video and audio compression. After that, we'll look at some of the other compression systems available for use with video and audio signals. We'll conclude with a look at some of the licenses needed to use some forms of compression technology.

## The Corner Office View

[itvt]: What directions do you see [compression] heading in the near future?

**Cooney**: It's not difficult to see where it's going. Yesterday's compression technology was MPEG–2; tomorrow's compression technology is one of two options: MPEG–4 or Microsoft's VC-1. Both of those technologies, by about a factor of two, outperform MPEG–2. So, half the bit rate, double the channels—however you like to look at it.

CONTINUED ▶

CONTINUED ▶

**[itvt]**: Is the cable industry eager to switch to the more advanced codecs?

**Cooney**: The biggest barrier to entry for those next-generation technologies is the installed base of MPEG–2 set-top boxes in the cable space: none of those boxes can receive and decode an MPEG–4 or VC-1 signal. So you need to replace the set-top boxes in your networks, in order to move to those next-generation technologies. If you're a telco that's getting into the IPTV space and that has no installed base of set-top boxes, and you're asking yourself, "How do we implement the next generation of compression," the answer is easy: if you're making technology decisions today, you might as well pay for the best technology available, which in the case of compression is MPEG–4 and VC-1. Actually, as it happens, if you're a telco, you're going to need to use those codecs anyway, as MPEG–2 isn't good enough to get video through your relatively small pipes. So for telcos, there's really no decision to make: they have to use next-generation compression. But for the other operators, both cable and satellite, there are definitely decisions to make, and commercial implications are the drivers of those decisions.

—Eric Cooney, President and CEO, Tandberg Television,
as interviewed by Tracy Swedlow of itvt[1]

# Why Compress?

Many communication systems that have become commonplace in the past few years depend on compression technology. For example, MP3 players use compression to take files from audio CDs and make them small enough to fit into the memory of a portable player. Compression fits a two-hour movie onto a four-inch DVD. Both CATV and satellite television systems use compression to place multiple digital video channels into the space formerly occupied by a single analog video channel, allowing hundreds of video channels to be distributed economically to viewers.

Here are some of the main reasons why compression is used for IPTV and Internet Video systems:

• Compressed streams can be transmitted over lower bit rate networks than uncompressed streams. For Internet Video applications in particular, this can mean the difference between getting the stream to a user or not. For example,

---

1. Interactive TV Today blog, August 31, 2005, blog.itvt.com/my_weblog/2005/08/eric_
cooney_pre.html

many home users have Internet connections over standard ADSL lines that operate in the range of 1.5 Mbps. Unless a digital video stream is substantially compressed, it will not fit into this bandwidth.

- More compressed streams can fit into a given bandwidth. This is particularly important for IPTV systems that have a fixed upper limit on bandwidth for a given distance. For example, ADLS2+ has a limit of just over 10 Mbps at a distance of 9,000 ft (2,750 m). With normal compression techniques, 10 Mbps has enough bandwidth for two or three video signals. As compression technology has advanced, more and more signals can be squeezed into the same amount of bandwidth.

- Raw, uncompressed HD video signals occupy 1.5 Gbps of bandwidth, which is roughly 1,000 times the capacity of a standard ADSL link. Without compression, there would be no way to deliver HD video to a viewer over any of the normal IPTV networks.

- A compressed video or audio file will occupy less space on a disk drive or other storage medium than an original uncompressed file. This enables users either to put more content in a given space or to use less space for a given file.

- In many real-world video signals, there is a large amount of redundancy and underused bandwidth. Often a good portion of a single video frame is identical to the frame immediately before or after it. A good compression technique can use this redundancy to greatly reduce the amount of bandwidth.

Of course, there are compromises that must be made in order to achieve these benefits, such as:

- Compression can introduce delay into a video or audio signal, at both the compression and decompression stages. This occurs because most video compression systems operate by looking at the differences between adjacent portions of the input signal, such as the changes from one frame to the next in a video signal.

- Compression can be difficult on signals that have a lot of noise in them, such as static or other interference. When there is a lot of noise in a video signal, the compression system has difficulty in identifying redundant information between adjacent video frames.

Overall, the benefits certainly outweigh the drawbacks, particularly when you consider that IPTV and Internet Video providers really don't have a choice about using compression.

# Groups of Pictures and Why They Matter

Users of any MPEG system will quickly encounter a variety of frame types, including *I frames, P frames* and *B frames*, as well as the term *Group of Pictures* (GOP). These terms all describe the way picture data is structured in an MPEG stream or file.

A frame is a single image from a video sequence. In NTSC, one frame occurs every 33 milliseconds; in PAL, one frame occurs every 40 milliseconds.

- An I frame is a frame that is compressed solely based on the information contained in the frame; no reference is made to any of the other video frames before or after it.

- A P frame is a frame that has been compressed using the data contained in the frame itself and data from the closest preceding I or P frame.

- A B frame is a frame that has been compressed using data from the closest preceding I or P frame and the closest following I or P frame.

- A GOP is a series of frames consisting of a single I frame and zero or more P and B frames. A GOP always begins with an I frame and ends with the last frame before the next I frame. The GOP is usually a fixed, repetitive pattern that is configured on the compression device. Different content suppliers may use different GOPs for different channels, but they are normally fixed within each channel.

To understand why MPEG uses these different frames, let's look at the amount of data required to represent each frame type. With a video image of normal complexity, a P frame will take two to three times less data than an I frame of the same image. A B frame will take even less data than a P frame—a further reduction by a factor of two to five. Figure 6.1 shows the relative amounts of data for each frame type in a typical MPEG GOP.

## The Impacts of GOP Length

One parameter that system providers have a lot of control over is GOP length. Choosing the right length can be quite controversial.

Remember that a GOP always begins with an I frame. To determine the length of a GOP, you simply count the number of B and P frames between each consecutive I frame and add one for the I frame. For example, in the frame sequence shown in Figure 6.1, the GOP length is 12: one I frame, three P frames and eight B frames.

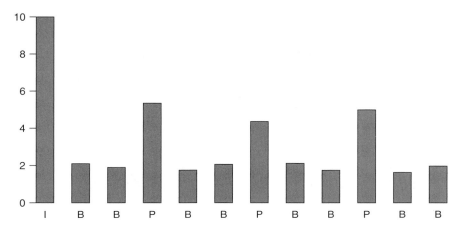

**FIGURE 6.1** *Relative Amounts of Data in Each MPEG Frame Type*

A GOP is considered short when the GOP length is low, say three or five. Some systems use GOPs that are quite long; values of 15, 30 or even 60 have been used in some applications.

Selecting a suitable GOP length can have a big impact on a video network. Many system performance factors are affected by GOP size, including the bit rate of encoded streams, channel change time and the ability of the stream to tolerate errors. Let's examine each of these factors in more depth.

### Bit Rate

As Figure 6.1 clearly shows, I frames contain more data than P frames or B frames. With a short GOP length, the total number of I frames in the stream is increased, thereby increasing the average amount of data that needs to be transmitted for each frame. This translates into heavier demand for bandwidth, which can affect the performance of both IPTV and Internet Video services. With longer GOPs, there are fewer I frames per second, so the aggregate data rate drops.

### Channel Change Timing

Whenever channel changing occurs in a video stream, the decoder has to have enough data to accurately produce a new image sequence. The decoder's ability to do so depends on which type of frame it receives. If the decoder receives an I frame, then no problem, because each I frame contains all of the data to completely reproduce one frame of video. If the decoder receives a P frame or a B frame, then it has a problem, because these frames only contain enough data to tell the decoder about any changes that have happened since an earlier frame. So, what typically happens after each channel change is that the decoder waits for the first I frame of the new video channel to arrive before it begins to produce an image.

With a short GOP, of, say, five frames, channel changing isn't much of a problem. In a 30-frame-per-second system (such as those used in the U.S.), this means that the decoder needs to wait, at most, 166 milliseconds for the first I frame, and that amount of delay is insignificant to viewers. If, on the other hand, the GOP is 30 or 60 frames long, it could mean that the decoder may need to wait one or two seconds before the first I frame arrives. This can be quite annoying to viewers.

Two different approaches have been demonstrated to address this issue. One method uses a server that stores decoded copies of all the videos present on an IPTV network. When a user changes channels, the STB momentarily connects to the server to get a sequence of I frames for the new channel and then rejoins the regular long GOP stream once a new I frame is delivered. This approach can deliver very fast change times, but there are some questions about how well this technology will scale to thousands of users all changing channels simultaneously during a major live sporting event.

Another system actually makes available two versions of each stream for use by STBs—one with low resolution and a short GOP, and another with normal resolution and a long GOP. Normal viewing is with the long GOP, normal resolution stream. When a channel change occurs, the STB connects to the low-resolution stream and *upconverts* it to a normal size picture. Once the normal stream is ready (i.e., when an I frame arrives), the STB switches back to the normal stream.

This method has the advantage of not requiring any special servers or targeted streams to be delivered to each STB, but it does require two versions of each stream to be available. The low-resolution streams can also be used for picture-in-picture applications when they aren't being used for channel changing.

## Error Tolerance

One major benefit of an I frame is that it permits the STB to wipe out any memory that it has about previous frames. This contrasts with P and B frames, which require the STB to store a copy of the preceding frames so it can properly create the new frame. Consider what happens if one of the incoming frames in the middle of a GOP has an error. This error can persist in the STB for a while, until the next I frame arrives. Once this happens, the error can be cleaned out.

# MPEG

The *Moving Pictures Experts Group* has developed some of the most common compression systems for video around the world and given these standards the common name of MPEG. Not only did this group develop video compression standards including MPEG–1, MPEG–2 and MPEG–4, but it also developed audio compression standards, which we will discuss later in this chapter. This group continues to meet and to set new standards (which we won't discuss here), including work on MPEG–7 (a standardized means for describing audio and visual content) and MPEG–21 (standards for describing content ownership and rights management).

MPEG standards have enabled a number of advanced video services. For example, MPEG–based DVDs have replaced the videotape as the preferred medium for viewing Hollywood movies in the home. Digital television, including digital satellite television and digital cable television, is based on the MPEG video compression standards. High definition (HD) television also uses MPEG technology. Also, much of the content for streaming media on the Internet is compressed using MPEG or closely related technologies.

## What happened to MPEG–3?

Some readers may be curious about the lack of an MPEG–3 standard. In fact, there was originally a working group called MPEG–3 set up to develop a standard to focus on multi-resolution encoding. This group's work was completed before the work on MPEG–2 was completed, so the work was simply incorporated into the MPEG–2 standard.

Readers should be careful not to confuse the MPEG audio coding standard called Layer III, often abbreviated as MP3, with the non-existent MPEG–3 video compression standard. MP3 files are popular in many music file-swapping and portable player systems.

## MPEG–1

MPEG–1 was the first standard developed for video compression by the Moving Pictures Experts Group. It was intended for use in creating video CDs, which had some popularity in computer multimedia, but never completely caught on as consumer movie rental or purchase format. MPEG–1 is still in use today for a number of applications, including low-cost surveillance cameras and some Web video applications. It is also interesting to note that MPEG–1 is allowed as a video compression method for DVDs, and many DVD players will play video CDs. Stand-alone and software-based MPEG–1 encoders are available for very reasonable prices from several sources. MPEG–1 does not support interlacing, so standard full-resolution PAL and NTSC signals are not usable with MPEG–1.

# MPEG–2

MPEG–2 is the predominant standard for MPEG video today. It is used in a wide variety of applications, including digital TV production and broadcasting, HDTV, satellite television and cable television. Each day, thousands of hours of MPEG–2 video are recorded, processed and played back by television broadcasters around the world. Millions of hours of MPEG–2 recordings are sold to the general public each day in the form of DVDs. Thousands of PCs with MPEG–2 playback capability are sold each week, and the installed base of MPEG–2 devices continues to grow.

MPEG–2 supports standard NTSC and PAL signals at full resolution, as well as 720p and 1080i HD signals. MPEG–2 also enables multiplexing of a number of video and audio streams, so applications like multi-channel satellite television become possible. MPEG–2 also supports five channel audio (surround sound) and the Advanced Audio Coding (AAC) standard.

Many MPEG–2 devices, including highly sophisticated MPEG–2 encoder and decoder devices are available as custom semiconductors; these are in their third or fourth generations. There are literally hundreds of millions of STBs, digital satellite receivers and DVD players installed in consumers' homes that can decode MPEG–2 signals. A wide variety of MPEG–2 equipment is available for functions such as statistical multiplexing, bit rate converters, telecom and IP network adapters, and more.

Various software tools are available for producing MPEG–2 streams using general-purpose PCs. With sufficient processing power and memory, a PC can be used to create an MPEG–2 stream in real time. However, for many applications, such as program editing and production, real-time performance is not necessary, and even moderate-performance PCs can create MPEG–2 compressed video files for later playback.

Software-only decoders for MPEG–2 exist, but they can be difficult to run without the addition of a hardware accelerator to a desktop PC. Adding an accelerator can drive up the cost and complicate the deployment of networks intended to deliver video streams to a large number of desktops or homes.

Overall, MPEG–2 is a well-defined, stable compression system with a wide variety of applications. Hundreds of millions of devices installed around the world are capable of receiving and decoding MPEG–2 video in a wide variety of flavors. MPEG–2 is commonly used in contribution, distribution and delivery networks. However, MPEG–2's video and audio quality are not competitive at stream rates below 2.5 Mbps.

# MPEG-4

MPEG-4 is a much more recent product of the standards process, the first version having become formally approved in 2000. As would be expected, MPEG-4 incorporates a whole range of new technologies for video compression that have been developed in the past decade. All of the necessary support technology for MPEG-4 systems, such as custom semiconductors, is being developed to widely deploy MPEG-4. MPEG-4 AVC may also make it possible for high definition signals to be encoded at bit rates below 10 Mbps, opening up a much bigger range of technologies for transporting HD video signals.

Prior to the introduction of the MPEG-4 *Advanced Video Coding* (AVC) standard, MPEG-4 did not offer truly dramatic performance improvements over MPEG-2 for compressing live natural video sequences, including most types of news, entertainment and sports broadcasts. Basic MPEG-4 has a number of advantages for synthetic (computer-generated) video and has already deeply penetrated IP video streaming applications (e.g. Apple's QuickTime has fully migrated to MPEG-4). Most desktop PCs can already decode MPEG-4 video using media player software that is freely available on the Internet.

MPEG-4 AVC is a more recent offering (circa 2004) and has the potential to replace MPEG-2 in the long run. The reason is that MPEG-4 AVC can achieve quality levels that compare favorably to MPEG-2 at half the bit rate. Of course, there is a cost to this, in terms of the greater processing power needed to encode and decode AVC signals. In addition, because AVC is newer, the technology has not had a chance to pass through as many learning and optimization cycles as MPEG-2 has undergone since 1996.

One potential drawback of MPEG-4 is that decoders are more complex for MPEG-4 than for MPEG-2. According to the MPEG-4 Industry Forum (www.m4if.org), an MPEG-4 decoder will be 2.5 to 4 times as complex as an MPEG-2 decoder for similar applications. This means more complicated (and therefore more expensive) hardware devices and greater demand on processor resources for software decoders. Before the decision is made to use MPEG-4 in a video delivery system, it is important to test any user devices (STBs, desktop PCs, laptops, etc.) that will be used to decode the video signal. Service providers may need to avoid using some of the advanced features of MPEG-4 and stick to the simpler profiles. Also, service providers may need to work closely with STB vendors to ensure that adequate supplies of decoder chips are available to meet deployment schedules.

Overall, MPEG-4 is an exciting new collection of technologies that promises to greatly increase the amount of video information that can be squeezed into a given amount of network bandwidth. Through MPEG–4 AVC, much more efficient video coding is possible, and the variety of object types available makes integration with computer-generated graphics simple and extremely bandwidth efficient. Because of MPEG–4's complexity and its relative newness, much development work needs to be done to reach the level of sophistication and maturity enjoyed by MPEG–2 technologies.

# Audio Compression

Just like video compression, MPEG has a variety of audio compression options. There are three layers of MPEG audio (conveniently called Layers I, II and III) and a newer audio compression standard called *Advanced Audio Coding* (AAC). In this section, we'll take a short look at each one of these. Note that any of these audio compression methods will work with any type of MPEG video compression, except that MPEG–1 streams do not handle AAC audio.

MPEG audio Layer I is the simplest compression system. It uses 384 input samples for each compression run, which corresponds to 8 milliseconds of audio material using 48 kHz sampling. Each band is processed separately, and then the results are combined to form a single, constant bit rate output. Layer I can achieve a compression ratio of 4:1, which means that a 1.4 Mbps CD-quality audio signal can be compressed to fit into a 384 kbps stream with no noticeable loss of quality. Compression beyond this—to 192 or 128 kbps—results in lower quality.

MPEG audio Layer II uses more samples for each compression run, 1,152 to be exact. This corresponds to 24 milliseconds of audio at 48 kHz sampling. This enables frequencies to be resolved more accurately. Layer II also eliminates some of the redundancy in Layer I coding, thereby achieving better compression, up to 8:1. This means that CD-quality audio can be achieved with a stream rate of 192 kbps.

MPEG audio Layer III uses the same number of samples as Layer II, but it uses them more efficiently. Layer III has an audio mode called joint stereo, which capitalizes on the strong similarities between the signals that make up the left and right channels of a stereo program. It also uses variable-length coding to more efficiently pack the compressed audio coefficients into the output stream. As a result, Layer III encoders can pack CD-quality audio into streams as small as 128 kbps, achieving compression ratios as high as 12:1.

MPEG AAC is available only with MPEG–2 or MPEG–4 video streams. It supports up to 48 audio channels including 5.1 audio. Very good quality results for surround-sound applications can be achieved with AAC at 192 kbps.

### Dolby AC-3 Audio

Dolby AC-3 audio coding is also commonly known as Dolby Digital. It offers a high-quality audio experience with good compression characteristics and has been approved for use in both DVDs and in digital television broadcasts in the U.S. Dolby AC-3 audio is included in some versions of MPEG–4 and is used on a number of satellite television systems.

Overall, MPEG audio is flexible and does not require near the magnitude of processor involvement of MPEG video. As the layer number goes up, the complexity of both the encoder and the decoder go up, but so does the compression ratio. Software-only Layer III decoders can run smoothly in a wide variety of personal computers. AAC decoders are not as common, possibly due to the complexity involved. When choosing an audio-encoding method, remember that the overall transport bandwidth must be high enough to carry the video signal, the audio signal and some overhead to make the streams operate correctly.

# Microsoft Windows Media and VC-1

Windows Media Player has a long development history from Microsoft. With a recent version, Microsoft took two unusual steps. First, Microsoft pledged to freeze the video decoder design for a number of years, to provide an incentive for semiconductor and other hardware device manufacturers to spend the time and resources necessary to incorporate Windows Media into a variety of low-cost products. Second, Microsoft won approval of the video decoder design as a public standard named SMPTE 421M (informally known as *VC-1*) from the *Society of Motion Picture and Television Engineers*. Now, any company that wishes to design a VC-1 decoder will be able to do so, provided that it obtains a license to use any of the patented intellectual property in the specification that belongs to Microsoft or other parties.

Microsoft intends to address a broad cross-section of the video compression market with VC-1 technology. The company has already released a number of implementations of its technology that range from low bit rate streaming for handheld devices all the way up to digital projection of first-run theatrical motion pictures. In addition to the VC-1 video-encoding technology, Windows Media covers other aspects of the complete package, including audio coding, stream formats and DRM. In addition, the company is very aggressively pricing licenses to make VC-1 attractively priced relative to other technologies, such as MPEG–4.

Some readers may wonder about the differences between VC-1 and MPEG–4 AVC. Both codecs offer significant advances in coding efficiency (i.e., fewer bits for a given picture quality) as compared to MPEG–2. To date, there hasn't been any compelling evidence to say that one is clearly better than the other for any large group of applications. Interestingly, many vendors of encoders and decoders are designing their hardware to support both technologies, through the use of general-purpose digital signal processing (DSP) hardware and downloadable firmware.

# Other Compression Technologies

MPEG and Microsoft are not the only games in town. Here are a few other compression technologies that bear consideration for service providers, primarily those in the Internet Video market.

## JPEG

Standards developed for compressing still images by the *Joint Photographic Experts Group* are named JPEG files. These standards have been adapted for video use by treating each frame of video as a separate picture and compressing it. The approach brings some benefits, most importantly is the ease in which motion sequences can be edited. Since each frame of video is compressed individually, there are no structures like the GOPs of MPEG and therefore no restrictions on when one frame sequence can be stopped and another started. JPEG files are used in some video editing systems precisely for this reason.

## JPEG2000

JPEG2000 is an advanced form of still image compression that was finalized in 2000 (hence the name). It uses a completely different technology for image compression than JPEG, but performs the same tasks. JPEG2000 also compresses each frame of video individually, so the technology is not able to take advantage of the similarities between adjacent frames. As a result, streams tend to be higher bandwidth than those commonly used in IPTV and Internet Video applications.

## Proprietary Codecs

A number of proprietary video and audio *codec* systems are on the market, and many of them are suitable for use in Internet Video networks. Because they are proprietary, the exact details of their operation are normally not provided for general publication. In addition, the different codec manufacturers are currently engaged in heated competition, so product cycles are short and performance and other specifications can change rapidly. Let's look at two of the largest codec suppliers for the video streaming market: Real Networks and Apple.

Real Networks is a major supplier of proprietary codec technology. Most of Real's products are targeted at the video streaming market, but more developments are sure to come. As with Microsoft's products, a number of third-party tools (from suppliers such as Adobe) can be used to create compressed video streams in both real-time and off-line production environments. A good deal of content is available for streaming on the Web in Real's SureStream format, which is designed to automatically adapt to suit the wide range of different network connection speeds used around the globe.

Apple Computer supplies QuickTime technology, which has migrated to using standards-compliant technology such as MPEG–4. Apple was one of the pioneers of video streaming and still has a significant amount of development activity underway for new technology.

One distinguishing feature of both of these codec suppliers is their willingness to provide a free software client (player) for receiving their compressed video streams. Literally hundreds of millions of personal computer users have downloaded and installed these players onto their desktop and laptop computers. In addition, most of these companies also supply a free encoder with limited functionality. More sophisticated encoders are generally available for a fee; these versions often contain advanced features that can make the job of creating content files easier, as well as using more efficient compression algorithms.

There are no easy answers when deciding whether or not to use proprietary codecs. All of the main software-based codec suppliers mentioned in this section have a long and distinguished track record of innovation and customer service. The same can be said for many hardware-based codec suppliers. Nevertheless, any users of a proprietary codec run the risk that their supplier will, for one reason or another, stop providing products. Prudent users will assess this risk and have a contingency plan in place. Here are some advantages and disadvantages of proprietary codecs:

## Advantages

- Innovation: As compression technology advances, innovations can be incorporated into proprietary codecs very rapidly. Industry standards tend to have a slower rate of change because of the need to achieve agreement between many different parties.

- Pricing: Many proprietary software codec suppliers offer basic versions of their players (decoders) free and have very low cost encoder options.

- Backward Compatibility: Proprietary codec suppliers have a strong incentive to ensure that new versions of their codecs work with previous versions and have typically done a good job in this area. This may not be as true with designs based on standards, unless backward compatibility is explicitly defined in the specification.

### Disadvantages

- Portability: Because a single vendor controls when and how proprietary codecs are implemented, versions for alternative platforms may be late to arrive or never produced. This can limit users' choices, particularly in the selection of operating systems.

- Change Control: Major codec suppliers determine when new features are released to the market and frequently encourage end users to upgrade to the latest version. This can make it difficult for large organizations to ensure that all users have the same version and to ensure that the codec software doesn't interfere with other applications.

- Platform Requirements: As codecs become more powerful, the minimum requirements for other system components (operating systems, processor speeds, etc.) can also increase. This can force users to deploy system upgrades in order to use the latest versions of some software codecs.

- Archival Storage: As with any rapidly evolving technology, long-term storage of encoded video files is useful only as long as suitable decoder software is available. In the case of proprietary codecs, the supplier controls software availability over the long term.

# Digital Turnaround

*Digital turnaround* is the process of taking video and audio signals that are encoded in one format and converting them into another format. This normally occurs under the control of a service provider to help standardize the operation of a multi-channel system. If each stream has the same compression technology, GOP length and bit rate, then the process of channel changing is greatly simplified. One fixed-bandwidth stream simply replaces another stream of the same bandwidth whenever a viewer decides to switch. Digital turnaround usually consists of two tasks: transcoding and transrating.

*Transcoding* is the process of converting a video signal that is encoded in one technology (say MPEG–2) into another technology (say MPEG–4). The best quality results can usually be obtained if the signal is never fully decompressed or recompressed, enabling the output signal to retain some of the information embedded in the original video feed.

*Transrating* is the process of changing the bit rate of video streams. Most IPTV providers convert all of the incoming content into a common bit rate, using one rate for all SD content and a second rate for HD content. Transrating needs to happen frequently, because most content suppliers use a higher bit rate for distributing their content than the rates that most IPTV and Internet Video service providers choose to use.

# Reality Check

In this chapter's Reality Check, we discuss the licenses necessary to use some of the compression technologies we have described here. Many readers may not be aware of this, but every DVD player and every DVD disc sold includes the cost of a mandatory license fee collected for each unit produced. Service providers need to consider license terms when analyzing the costs of installing a video delivery system.

> ### Disclaimer
>
> Neither the authors of this book nor the publisher claim any expertise in licensing law or in the terms of the MPEG LA license agreement. Readers should consult with MPEG LA and any other licensing bodies to confirm all details of the required licenses prior to installing a video network that relies on this technology.

## Technology Licensing

As we have seen in this chapter, a huge number of clever technologies have been applied to the art and science of video compression. Even though much of this technology is governed by international standards, not all of this technology is in the public domain. In fact, many of the key technologies used in MPEG and other compression systems were developed by individuals and corporations who still retain ownership of their technology in the form of patents and other legally protected rights. For example, the patent portfolio for MPEG–2 technologies includes 630 patents from around the world.

Fortunately, the owners of these technologies banded together to set up an organization known as the *MPEG LA* (the LA originally stood for Licensing

Administrator, but now LA is the official name). MPEG LA is responsible for establishing and collecting the license fees on the technology and for distributing the collected funds to the patent owners. This central clearinghouse provides big benefits to the users of this technology, because one simple payment to MPEG LA satisfies the patent obligations for the covered technology. Contrast this with the headaches and complexities that would be involved in negotiating separate license agreements with the 20+ companies that have patents included in the MPEG–2 technology pool.

The license fees are assessed on a per-item basis and are officially described on www.mpegla.com. For example, the fee listed on the Web site for an MPEG–2 decoding device (such as a DVD player, STB or computer with a DVD player, whether hardware or software) produced after 2002 is U.S. $2.50. Other fees are assessed for MPEG–2 encoders, MPEG multiplexers and other devices. Fees are also assessed for recorded media, such as DVDs, but the fees are relatively low (e.g., $0.03 for a single-layer DVD disc—although there are a number of different ways of calculating the fee).

There are similar fee arrangements for MPEG–4 devices. In addition, there are fees based on the number of streams created and on the number of subscribers served in cable and satellite television systems. In addition, there are fees for individual titles sold to viewers on a DVD or via pay-per-view, such as a VOD system. These fees have created some controversy in the industry, because they include charges for the device itself (like MPEG–2) and also charges for viewing content using the device.

Where does this leave the owner of a video networking system? First, it is important to understand that fees for devices are normally collected from the device manufacturers, so end users of equipment generally don't need to worry about technology fees. Second, publishers of media, such as DVDs, are also responsible for paying the fees required for those items. Third, most of the MPEG–4 license fees that are payable on a per-stream or a per-subscriber basis are targeted at companies that are charging users to view the videos. However, this arrangement will be subject to revision in 2008, so users of MPEG–4 would be well served by investigating the necessary license arrangements in detail before launching a large-scale system.

# Summary

Video compression is a requirement for essentially all IPTV and Internet Video systems. We began this chapter with a discussion of why compression is so important. GOP length, a very important topic for service providers to consider, was discussed in depth. We then took a look at the varieties of MPEG for both video and audio applications, as well as other compression systems, including Microsoft's VC-1, JPEG, and offerings from Real Networks and Apple. We concluded with a brief look at digital turnaround and a discussion of licensing issues.

Any service provider needs to make a careful evaluation before choosing a compression technology. Each technology has benefits and drawbacks in terms of performance, cost, availability and scalability that can have major impacts on business plans, deployment schedules and viewer experiences. This choice cannot be taken lightly, because providers will need to live with their choices for years to come.

# 7 Maintaining Video Quality and Security

> Television is like the invention of indoor plumbing. It didn't change people's habits. It just kept them inside the house.
>
> —Alfred Hitchcock

Quality and security are important for any video delivery system. Quality is a prerequisite to keeping viewers happy (and therefore paying their monthly subscription bills) and to providing advertisers and content owners with image quality complimentary to their desired public images. Security is needed to keep viewers from watching content they aren't authorized to view and to prevent them from making unauthorized copies of content that only they are authorized to view.

In this chapter, we will begin with a discussion of the main factors that affect quality and how they can be controlled. Then we'll take a look at the function of conditional access, which manages which viewers have the ability to watch which content. We'll conclude with a discussion of rights management and how it relates to the types of digital video signals that are often used with IP-based delivery systems.

## The Corner Office View

Film piracy has been seen by some as a "soft" crime, yet it brings harm and other serious criminal activity to local communities. Criminals made over £270 million ($358.7 million) from film piracy in 2005, making this the worst affected single sector for

CONTINUED ▶

CONTINUED ▶

intellectual property crime out of all [intellectual property] industries. This is revenue that has been lost to the local and national economy and is affecting British jobs.

—Kieron Sharp, Director General,

Federation Against Copyright Theft (U.K.)[1]

# Factors that Affect Video Quality

A wide range of factors can affect the quality of a delivered video signal and have important impacts on the viewer experience. Managing the video delivery system to minimize these factors will result in more satisfied viewers.

## Audio/Video Synchronization

In real life, when people move their lips during talking, the sounds change accordingly. Similarly with physical objects—when a person's shoe hits a hard pavement, a sharp sound can be heard. Viewers find it objectionable when these sounds don't match the image being displayed in a video presentation. This is called a loss of "lip sync" or a loss of audio/video synchronization.

One potential source of lip sync problems is clock differences between the transmitting and the receiving ends of a video link. Careful management to ensure that both the encoder and the decoder in a link are referenced to a common clock signal—and that these clock signals are properly transmitted along with the compressed video stream—will help ensure that synchronization doesn't become an issue.

Assuring lip sync can be difficult on IP networks, which are inherently asynchronous. The solution lies in careful network provisioning (to ensure that adequate bandwidth is available for all the traffic) and in making sure that there are no processing bottlenecks (such as overloaded routers) that can delay or scramble the order of packets. Some IP receivers (including STBs and PCs) can be configured to use large incoming packet buffers to smooth out any delay variations or to realign packets that arrive in the wrong order. This has the side effect of delaying the signals flowing through the device, which should be avoided if possible.

---

1. Stuart Kemp, The Hollywood Reporter, Dec. 7, 2006, www.hollywoodreporter.com/hr/content_display/international/news/e3i4383520b62392ae146f52d45c4842913?imw=Y

# Source Image Quality

As with many complex processing systems, the adage "garbage in, garbage out," applies to IP video transport. For example, source signals that have a lot of noise (i.e., random changes in the video image that are not present in the source scene) can greatly affect the performance of MPEG encoders. When this happens, the encoders see the noise as changes in the image that need to be captured in the compressed data stream, thereby creating more work for both the encoder and decoder. This can divert processing power away from other portions of the image that could otherwise benefit.

Several things can be done to improve source image quality. First, service providers can work with content providers who have high quality source images and get the content directly from them, rather than through intermediate sources. Second, high quality, light compression or uncompressed video links can be used to bring the programming from the sources to the network. Third, noise reduction equipment can be used to clean up video signals making them easier to compress.

# Macroblocking

When images are compressed using MPEG or other block-based compression technologies, the image is broken up into groups of pixels before the compression operation begins. For MPEG–2, the pixels are grouped into macroblocks that measure 16 pixels on a side. Borders between adjacent macroblocks on a video screen can be quite noticeable to the eye if there is an abrupt change in color or intensity between adjacent blocks. This can occur if the image has been compressed excessively; i.e., there is not enough data in the MPEG stream to accurately reproduce the source image in each block. When these borders appear, the perceived image quality for human viewers drops significantly, and steps are often taken to prevent this.

Macroblocking is more likely to be noticed in scenes with a lot of motion, with subtle gradations of color or in scenes where the overall light level in the scene is moving higher or lower (i.e., a fade to black) when essentially every pixel on the screen is simultaneously changing intensity. When macroblocking reaches an extreme state, each $8 \times 8$ block of the image may be represented as a single color, which can be very objectionable to viewers.

To prevent macroblocking, video providers need to make sure that the video stream bit rate is high enough to handle the motion and detail levels in the original pictures. In addition, many MPEG streams use error correction to prevent minor bit errors from causing macroblocking.

If longer-duration errors occur in the path between the encoder and the decoder, then some of the data needed to reconstruct the picture is lost or corrupted. When this happens, the decoder is not able to correctly recreate the source image, and the output for that block of data may be corrupted. To the viewer, this loss of data often appears as one or more macroblocks with very poor resolution. This problem can be corrected by eliminating the errors in the data path.

# Resolution

The resolution of a video image refers to the number of pixels present. Images with higher pixel counts have higher resolution (unless the image has been degraded in some other manner). In IPTV systems, image resolution is normally matched to the display resolution, so an SD signal for an NTSC system would have 720 pixels on 480 lines. In Internet Video, many different video resolutions are used, ranging from QCIF at 176 × 144 to full HD at 1920 × 1080 pixels and everywhere in between.

Delivered resolution needs to be managed carefully. Viewers typically prefer higher resolution signals to lower ones, but high resolution can carry a high price in terms of system design. If the number of pixels in each dimension (vertical and horizontal) doubles, the total number of pixels in the image goes up by a factor of four. This not only adds to the amount of bandwidth required for a signal, it also adds to the amount of processing power needed to encode and decode the signal. Higher resolutions generally increase the burden on the entire system, from start to finish.

Many Internet Video systems deliver signals at less than full SD resolution, both to save bandwidth and to make images easier for PCs to display. Virtually all IPTV systems offer SD resolution video (comparable to broadcast, CATV and satellite systems) and many offer HD video.

# IP Artifacts

Artifacts are image impairments that are visible to a viewer. They can be caused by noise, encoding errors, transmission errors, decoding errors, poor cabling, display errors and other sources too numerous to name. Let's focus on some of the common causes of artifacts in an IP video delivery system and how they can be avoided.

### Packet Loss

Packet loss is one of the most common errors that can happen on an IP video delivery system. It can be caused by many sources, including bit errors that corrupt IP packet headers (forcing them to be discarded), overloaded links that force routers to discard packets, inadequate or malfunctioning networking equipment, and other sources. Packet loss is a routine occurrence on the Internet, and Internet Video delivery systems must be designed to handle it. In IPTV systems, packet loss can be minimized through the use of careful system design practices (including over-provisioning) and by careful control of the amount of traffic that is allowed to enter the system. However, occasional packet losses that cannot be completely avoided must be handled in a graceful manner by the equipment.

## Packet Jitter

Packet jitter is created when the packets that make up a data stream do not arrive in a smooth, continuous flow. For example, if an application was trying to send 100 packets per second in a smooth stream, it would try to send one packet precisely every 10 milliseconds. If these packets were sent across a jitter-free network, they would arrive with the same timing: one packet every 10 milliseconds. When this pattern is disturbed—packets start arriving too soon or too late—jitter occurs. This causes the gaps between the packets to be either too short or too long—say 9 milliseconds or 11 milliseconds.

For normal data, such as e-mail or a Web page, jitter is not an issue, because this information is not time-based. It really makes no difference if the Web page is displayed a few milliseconds early or late, because such differences are imperceptible to people. However, for data streams containing audio or video information, such variations can be very harmful.

To understand how jitter affects a video stream, recall what makes up a video stream. It is, in effect, a series of pictures taken 30 times per second (25 times per second in most countries outside the U.S. and Japan) that, when played back one after the other, gives the illusion of motion to the human eye and brain. This technique works fine when the series of pictures is displayed in a smooth, continues flow. But, when the picture display times vary excessively, the illusion of motion can be broken, and the video becomes uncomfortable to watch.

In actual applications, jitter will affect both uncompressed and compressed video data. This is due to the clock information carried with a compressed signal. These clocks are fundamental to the operation of MPEG and other types of decoders. When these clocks get disturbed, there can be many different impacts on the video signal. For example, excessive jitter can cause the receiver buffers to overflow or run out of data. In either case, the video image can be disturbed, by suddenly freezing when the data runs out or by losing picture information when the buffer overflows. In addition to these effects, jitter can also interfere with lip synch.

There are two main ways to fight jitter in an IP network—prevent it or use a buffer to fix the timing at the receiver. Many successful systems employ both techniques to keep jitter under control.

Preventing jitter is simply a matter of ensuring that any packets containing video data are not delayed at any point during their transit through the network. This means there needs to be an adequate available bandwidth on each link, minimizing the random chance that video packets will be blocked or delayed by other traffic. In addition, the data routers that form of the core of many networks need to be able to send certain types of packets (such as those containing video files) as a priority over other packets, eliminating the chance that they will be delayed.

Buffering incoming packet data is also commonly used to reduce jitter. The buffer is set up on a FIFO basis (first in, first out), with the size of the buffer limited by the amount of delay that can be tolerated. Incoming packets are put into the buffer as soon as they arrive, at a variable rate due to any accumulated jitter. Packets are removed from the buffer according to an evenly spaced clock signal, so the jitter is removed. This clock rate needs to be carefully tuned to make sure that the buffer doesn't overflow with too many packets or underflow with too few packets. The clock may also have to adapt to changes in the underlying packet rate.

One disadvantage of buffering is that it adds delay to the overall delivery system, which increases the amount of time it takes the system to recover from a failure or to switch to a different packet stream due to a channel change or other event. As a result, there is a lot of pressure to minimize the amount of buffer used while still providing enough to handle the amount of jitter expected at the input.

## Bit Errors

Bit errors occur when the digital information delivered to the user device is different from the data originally sent. Bit errors are caused by a wide range of physical phenomena on any network, including over-the-air broadcast, fiber-optic and satellite systems. When errors occur, they can affect any of the data used to create the picture. Some errors are harmless, affecting only a single pixel, while others can be quite serious and affect multiple frames of video. Unfortunately, since bit errors tend to be randomly distributed, there is no good way to predict whether a given bit error is going to be harmful or not.

There are a number of schemes for correcting bit errors. One method involves re-transmitting errored packets; this is the method used by the TCP protocol. As we discussed in Chapter 5, this isn't usually the best solution for streaming video, due to the potential delays in re-transmission.

Another method to handle bit errors is called *Forward Error Correction* (FEC). With FEC, additional data is added to each packet of data that enables the receiver to correct a limited number of bit errors in each packet. One popular method for calculating FEC data is called Reed-Solomon, based on a seminal 1960 paper by I.S. Reed and G. Solomon. Some schemes even allow a limited number of missing packets to be recreated using FEC data from the surrounding packets that made it through. Even a modest amount of FEC can have a significant impact on system bit error rate. However, this protection comes at a price—the extra FEC data consumes bandwidth on top of that needed for video and audio data. As a result, not all service providers use FEC, depending on their overall system error rate performance targets and network quality expectations, among other factors.

## Signal Availability

Availability is a measure of the amount of time that a signal is active and meeting minimum performance levels. Availability is calculated by measuring the duration of any interruptions in the signal and dividing by the total length of the program being delivered. For example, if a program lasts 100 minutes, and it was unwatchable for one-tenth of a minute (six seconds), then the availability of that signal would be 99.9 percent.

Generally, for IPTV networks, availability statistics need to be quite high to provide acceptable levels of consumer satisfaction. A system that offers 99.9 percent availability for a year can be expected to be unavailable to every viewer for an average of 8.7 hours. This probably won't be acceptable to most subscribers if all of unavailability occurs in one day. As a result, many systems are built to offer 99.99 percent availability to each viewer and 99.999 percent availability in the common core (routers, feeder networks, etc.) of the network.

# Conditional Access

*Conditional Access* (CA) is a group of techniques used to ensure that only viewers meeting the correct conditions are given access to certain content. The basic technology for doing this involves encrypting or scrambling the content, so an unauthorized viewer who receives the signal is unable to view it. Authorized users are given numeric keys which permit the operation of special hardware or software within an STB or PC that is able to decrypt or descramble the signals. CA systems are available from a number of vendors; typically these are integrated systems that provide both the content scrambling/encryption devices and control the distribution of the keys required to view the content.

Encryption can take many forms, but most major systems have a few core traits in common. First, the encryption and decryption must be computationally easy to perform when the key is known. Second, decryption must be difficult when the key is not known. Third, the keys must be manageable so they can be distributed to the appropriate viewers.

Many different encryption systems have been designed that embody these core traits. Some of the more common ones are described below.

## Smart Cards

One common form of key distribution for STBs is the smart card. These cards are called "smart" because they incorporate a processor and memory that can be used by a variety of applications. Billions of smart cards are sold around the world each year for a variety of uses, including identification cards, pre-paid telephone cards (outside the U.S.), debit/credit cards and a host of other applications. Typically, a smart card contains a processor capable of performing basic calculations and executing simple programs, as well as memory that can hold both variable and permanent data.

Smart cards must be connected to a reading device in order to operate. In some cases, this connection is made physically, using gold-plated contacts. Some cards can also connect wirelessly to special readers using short-distance radio signals, eliminating the need to physically insert the card into the device.

A key feature of many smart cards is their ability to securely store data. The cards can be programmed to store secret information, such as the private part of a public/private key pair. Any unauthorized attempts to read that data would result in the card becoming permanently damaged and the data destroyed. The smart card's internal processor can be used to decrypt data using this stored private key, and the results can be sent back out of the card without ever exposing the key to any external device.

For video applications, smart cards are one way to deliver video content descrambling/decryption keys to a user device. Each content stream (or television channel, if you prefer) has a unique descrambling key that is created when the content is prepared for broadcast. This key must be delivered to the viewer's device for it to be able to properly descramble the content. One way of doing this would be to simply send the key to the viewer's device; however, any other device that was connected to this communication path (think of a satellite link) would also receive this key and be able to decrypt the content. Instead, the descrambling keys are encrypted before they are sent to a viewing device.

When smart cards are used for delivering descrambling keys, each viewer device must be equipped with a smart card reader, either built in (as in many STBs) or connected through an external port (such as a USB port on a PC). When an authorized viewer wants to watch scrambled content, the viewer's device sends a request to a central server. This server checks to see if the viewer is authorized to view the content. If so, the server locates the correct descrambling key for the desired content and encrypts it using the appropriate public key that corresponds to the user's smart card. The server then sends the encrypted descrambling key out over the communication path to the viewer's device. When it arrives, the encrypted key is fed into the smart card, and the smart card performs the decryption operation. The viewer device can then use the decrypted descrambling key to process the incoming signal and play the content for the viewer.

Smart cards offer a lot of benefits for service providers. The cards are portable and can be associated with a single viewer. For example, this could be used to control access to adult content in a viewer's home, with one card issued to the family and another to the adults. Smart cards can also be delivered separately from the STB, making it more difficult for thieves to get access to both components.

One of the big downsides to smart card management is that they need to be kept physically secure (under lock and key). If stolen, they can be deactivated, but this can be a difficult process. Also, smart cards can lock a service provider into a single encryption vendor for long periods of time, because it is difficult and expensive to swap out cards that are in the hands of thousands of viewers. This is particularly true in the unlikely event that the encryption system is cracked by malicious users. If this were to happen, it would be very expensive for the system operator to re-program all the STBs and to issue a whole new set of smart-cards.

# Watermarking

Watermarking is the process of inserting data into video or audio streams to track usage or prove ownership of the streams. It is similar in concept to some of the techniques used to protect currency and checks against forgery or counterfeiting. The basic idea is to insert identification without impairing the user's enjoyment of the content. Digital photographs can be watermarked to show copyright ownership and terms; these watermarks can be read by most of the major image-editing software packages. Video and audio content can also be watermarked with copyright data that can be read by some video recording and playback equipment to prevent unauthorized copying or distribution.

With digital content files, inserting a pattern into some of the less important bits in the file can be quite effective for watermarking purposes. For example, in a file with 16-bit audio samples, the least significant bit of any sample represents 1/65536th of the total output signal. When these bits are subtly manipulated, a watermark pattern can be inserted in the file with essentially no impact on the sound of the resulting piece.

Watermarking is implemented in different ways depending on the objectives of the creator of the watermark. A watermark can be specifically designed to be fragile so any change to the file destroys the watermark, thereby proving the file was tampered with. Alternatively, a watermark can be designed to be so robust that even if the file was significantly altered, the watermark could still be discerned. The latter is useful for tracking content that has been duplicated without permission; there are even Web crawlers that spend their time looking at millions of Web pages to see whether they have unauthorized content that contains certain watermarks.

Watermarking helps in rights enforcement when a unique watermark is created for each individual user. Individual watermarks can serve as a deterrent to unauthorized use of the content, since any misappropriations can be traced back to the specific source of the leak. If users know that any misappropriated files can be traced back to them, it can be a powerful incentive to *not* share files illegally.

## Personal Computers

Providing security for valuable content in PCs is a very difficult task. A major factor is that a determined user can read essentially all of the data contained on a hard disk drive, so it is very hard to keep information secret. The solution is to have a very robust encryption scheme for the content and to ensure that the keys used to unlock access to the content are very secure. Two main forms of key protection are used on PCs: hardware-based and software-based.

In hardware-based key protection systems, a physical device must be connected to the PC for it to be authorized to decrypt or descramble the content. This device can take the form of a smart card attached to a reader connected to the PC. Another approach is to encapsulate a small processor (like those found in smart cards) into a device that can be attached to a serial port or a USB port. With either device type, the hardware must be physically attached to the viewer's device for the content to be unlocked. Descrambling keys are obtained from the device through a process of handshaking that prevents the secret data stored within the device from ever being revealed.

In a software-based key protection system, special modules of software loaded onto the user's device control access to the key. These modules of software are not stand-alone—they must be in communication with a central server that ensures that the modules on the user devices have not been corrupted or had their security compromised. Software-based key control offers a big advantage over hardware-based systems, because it enables complete system updates on a regular basis without the difficulty and expense of changing out a large number of deployed hardware devices.

# Digital Rights Management

*Digital rights management* (DRM) is a set of software and hardware technologies designed to protect ownership rights of a content provider. The goal of DRM is to directly control the ways in which a viewer can use specific pieces of content. DRM systems will typically control uses such as repeated viewings, time windows when content can be viewed, copying or recording the content to other devices, or recording the content to removable media such as a CD or a DVD.

The concept of digital rights management is very close to that of CA. In fact, the two systems often work in close harmony in many digital video delivery systems. The key difference is that a CA system controls whether or not a viewer is allowed to view content, whereas a DRM system controls what the viewer can do with the content during and after viewing. In other words, CA governs which viewers can get access to content, whereas DRM governs what viewers can do with the content.

# Reality Check

In this chapter's first Reality Check, we look at the one of the most widely deployed (and widely discussed) systems for protecting audio and video content from unauthorized use. Development of a reliable DRM system was essential to Apple's successful negotiation of contracts with the major record labels to supply content through iTunes. In the second Reality Check, we take a look at why it makes sense, in some circumstances, to provide DRM for free content.

## Apple's Fair Play DRM System for iTunes

Apple Computer's iTunes music store has been very successful in selling compressed digital music files to millions of iPod owners. Fair Play, which is Apple's name for its DRM system, is an integral part of the iTunes software client and the iPod operating software.

A large part of the negotiations that surrounded the launch and commercial success of iTunes was to convince content owners (mainly record companies) that users would not be able to make unlimited copies or redistribute content that was protected by Fair Play. This was very important to the recording industry because of the perceived revenue impact of file sharing systems such as Napster during 1999 to 2001.

The Fair Play system is quite comprehensive and is able to control a variety of different content uses. As of November 2006, users who purchased audio content on iTunes were permitted the following uses of their content:

- Authorize up to five computers that can share content purchased through the use of one computer

- Burn an unlimited number of custom CDs with a playlist and cover art of the user's choosing

- Copy content from a computer to one or more iPod devices

- Make a complete backup of an entire iTunes library through the use of recordable DVDs.

One aspect of DRM of concern to some consumers is the prospect for future revision of the rules for using content they have purchased. Although the rules for using content tend to relax as time passes, there is no guarantee that the rights might not become more restricted in the future. Also, some consumers are troubled by the fact that tracks purchased under Apple's DRM system can only be played on portable devices manufactured by Apple. These concerns, however, has not seemed to have a major impact on iTunes sales volumes, as Apple has sold well over two billion digital music tracks to date.

## DRM for Free Content

At first it may seem paradoxical for content available for free on a Web site to be protected by DRM technology. After all, once the content owner has decided to deliver the content for free to any viewer who wants to see it, why should they care if someone makes an unauthorized copy? Well, there are a couple thoughts to keep in mind:

- If any portions of the content belong to a third party (such as some of the songs on a movie soundtrack), the content owner may not have the right to allow others to make copies of that content. Similarly, the content owner might wish to establish a certain time window for the content to be available, say for a cinematic movie preview. Without downloads, a time window is relatively easy to enforce; a window is essentially impossible to enforce if there are unprotected downloads of the content circulating within the viewer base.

- If the goal of the service provider is to get viewers to look at advertising on their Web portal, then clearly allowing viewers to simply pass the content from one viewer to another will work against that goal. By protecting the content on the Web site, and by allowing users to freely share links to content pages, the service provider can drive more viewers to their portal. This in turn will create more page views and more exposure for the advertisements.

# Summary

This chapter focused on protecting video quality and security. We began by discussing a number of potential video impairments and how they can be avoided or corrected. We discussed network impairments as well as those caused by the video signal processing itself. We took a look at the various types of errors that can occur in IP network processing and what system designers have done to minimize or compensate for those errors. In the second part of the chapter, we took at look at the several different techniques used to provide CA functions for service providers, including the benefits and drawbacks of each. We also looked at DRM and how it is closely linked to but slightly different from CA. We concluded with a look at two interesting applications of DRM.

# 8   Sizing Up Servers

While you are destroying your mind watching the worthless, brain-rotting drivel on TV, we on the Internet are exchanging, freely and openly, the most uninhibited, intimate and, yes, shocking details about our "CONFIG.SYS" settings.

—Dave Barry

One of the most commonly used devices in digital video production and delivery is the video server. Almost all content ends up on a server during part of its lifecycle, whether for production, delivery, archiving or playout. Each of these applications has its own set of requirements and group of manufacturers offering specialized products. Because servers can be some of the more expensive items to purchase in an IP video delivery service, it is important to understand the demands of each type of application.

In this chapter, we will begin with a brief description of the major types of servers used in video applications. Then, we will examine a few of the categories in detail as they pertain to IPTV and Internet Video. We will conclude with a table that compares the key performance parameters for several types of servers.

## The Corner Office View

SEAGATE BREAKS WORLD MAGNETIC RECORDING DENSITY RECORD—421 GBITS PER SQUARE INCH EQUIVALENT TO STORING 4,000 HOURS OF DIGITAL VIDEO ON YOUR PC

Achievement underscores strong advancement and future for hard disc drive storage

CONTINUED ▶

CONTINUED ▶

SCOTTS VALLEY, Calif.—15 September 2006—Seagate Technology (NYSE: STX) today announced the results of a magnetic recording demonstration, setting a world record of 421 Gbits per square inch (421 Gbit/in$^2$). The demonstration used perpendicular recording heads and media created with currently available production equipment that validates Seagate's ability to scale the technology for the foreseeable future without major technology changes or capital additions. Dr. Mark Kryder of Seagate unveiled the findings during his keynote presentation at the IDEMA DISKCON show in celebration of the 50th anniversary of the hard drive.

The demonstration is evidence of the continued momentum in disc drive innovation and reaffirms the disc drive as the undisputed king of storage when capacity and cost-effectiveness are both required. At the demonstrated density level, Seagate expects the capacity ranges to result in solutions ranging in 40 GB to 275 GB for 1- and 1.8-inch consumer electronics drives, 500 GB for 2.5-inch notebook drives, and nearly 2.5TB for 3.5-inch desktop and enterprise class drives. At 2.5TB capacity, a hard drive would be capable of storing 41,650 hours of music, 800,000 digital photographs, 4,000 hours of digital video or 1,250 video games. Seagate anticipates that solutions at these density levels could begin to emerge in 2009.

"Today's demonstration, combined with recent technology announcements from fellow hard drive companies, clearly shows that the future of hard drives is stronger than ever," said Bill Watkins, CEO of Seagate. "Breakthroughs in areal density are enabling the digital revolution and clearly indicate that hard drives can sustain their advantage to meet the world's insatiable demand for storage across a wide range of market segments."[1]

# Video Servers

Video servers perform two main functions: storage and delivery. Storage is the physical act of keeping files of digital video content (usually on hard disk) for processing or playout. Delivery is the act of transmitting video content over a network to viewers or other devices that need the content. Depending on the application, servers may be optimized for one task or the other or may need to strike a balance between them.

Video servers are often made up of a number of physically separate hard disk drives and processors. This is done both for greater reliability and for better

---

1. Seagate press release http://www.seagate.com/www/en-us/about/news_room/press_releases/

performance. Reliability is increased through the use of RAID (Redundant Array of Inexpensive Disks) technologies, which store extra data for each file. This extra data can be used with a simple algorithm to replace any data lost due to a failure or replacement of one of the disk drives. Multiple disk drives are used to increase the storage capacity of the total system beyond what is available on a single disk and also to increase the speed at which files can be written or read from the disk array. Similarly, multiple processors are used to enable the system to continue operating even if one processor fails and to provide greater computing power than would be available from a single processor.

Here are quick descriptions of some of the different applications where video servers are commonly used.

- **Ingest servers** are used to collect content from a variety of sources and make it available for use in a variety of applications. Video content can come directly from a studio camera or satellite feed, from a videotape that has just been removed from a camera or from archival storage, from another storage device such as a hard disk inside a camera or a remote server or from essentially any other source that can produce a video signal. Once the video has been ingested, it can then be handed off to a variety of other devices for further processing and storage.

  One of the most important roles of the ingest server is the proper tagging and description of each of the ingested video files. This information, called *metadata*, which can be produced automatically but usually requires human intervention, is crucial to the later processing and manipulation of the video content. If, for example, a mistake is made in the date of video file, then an editor looking for the latest version of a shot may not be able to find it. High quality in this data can be aided by the software that operates inside the ingest server to support rules for capturing this data and processes that require proofreading of the data by a second person once it has been entered.

- **File servers** are used in the video production process to handle content that is being manipulated into its final form. For example, a file server may be used to temporarily store a video clip from a color correction workstation before it is moved to another workstation that will be used to overlay graphics. The file server may also be used to store content or other data that is used repeatedly in the production process, such as theme music for a recurring program or common graphic elements.

- **Production or playout servers** are used to take finished video content that is ready to air and play it out in a continuous, highly reliable stream. With these servers, reliability is key, because any failures can cause a broadcaster to go off the air. Various technologies can be used to provide redundancy and fail-safe operation; these features are commonly found on this type of server.

- **Archive servers** are designed to store massive amounts of content. This can be from all types of sources, such as live feeds, news clips, purchased programming, etc. Archive servers typically emphasize large amounts of storage at a low cost, with speed of access being a secondary consideration. Archive servers can also be used to keep video records of programming as it has actually been broadcast in order to comply with local government regulations and to answer queries from advertisers.

- **Video on Demand servers** are designed to store content that viewers can order for viewing. These servers are typically designed to generate as many simultaneous streams as possible, often multiple copies of the same content. High bandwidth network connections are almost always used, whether the connection is to a private IPTV network or to the Internet.

- **Advertising servers** take advertising spots and play them back live inside video feeds. Although they typically don't need a massive amount of storage, they do need to interface to multiple simultaneous video channels and carefully synchronize the content playout to fit into the allotted advertising window. These servers need to be able to accept video content in a variety of different formats from multiple sources. In addition, these servers need to provide flexible scheduling tools that can be easily reconfigured to comply with rapidly changing advertising campaigns and keep good records of the ads that have actually run to support advertiser billing.

- **Live streaming servers** take live video streams and create multiple copies for transmission on the network. Although they need practically no storage, they need to have a large amount of processing capacity to create IP packets that are individually addressed to each recipient of the stream. Live streaming servers also need high bandwidth network connections to transmit all of the streams that they generate out into the IP network.

The last three types of servers listed above are often used in IPTV and Internet Video applications, so we will go into a bit more detail regarding these devices in the following sections.

# Video on Demand Servers

Video on Demand (VOD) is a common form of delivery for both IPTV and Internet Video networks. By allowing users to select content from a library at any time, this technology can be a powerful draw for attracting viewers to a service provider. It can also be a competitive weapon against services that rely on broadcast distribution, such as satellite and digital terrestrial networks. Most IPTV and Internet Video services providers, as well as many CATV systems, offer VOD.

VOD servers must perform four main functions:

- Video content storage, which is essentially the same function as any other video server. However, the server must be capable of transmitting multiple, asynchronous copies of a single piece of content (more on this later).

- Network interface, which again is similar to other video servers, with the exception that a very large number of simultaneous streams may need to be supported.

- User interaction support, which enables a viewer to pause, rewind and fast-forward video content. This can require some sophisticated software to manage all of the viewers and to interface to the systems that process user commands.

- Catalog and ordering support, which provides support for the systems that are used to display the list of available content, as well as the transactions necessary to capture payment from the viewers.

Content on a VOD server is essentially always stored in a compressed format that is ready to deliver to the viewer. This simplifies the delivery process by eliminating the need to process the video before it is delivered. Since many IPTV systems have a narrow range of allowed video signal rates and normally support only one (or at most two) compression formats, all of the content stored on the VOD server must be stored in the same format.

Accordingly, all incoming content must pass through a video compression device before it is placed on the server. In some cases, the content owner does the compression, and compressed files are simply copied directly into the server. In other cases, content may arrive in an uncompressed format and must be compressed before it can be placed on the server. This compression can be done in real-time as the content is streamed or it can be done off-line on a file basis.

In still other cases, content may arrive compressed using a different bit rate or type of compression. If an incompatible format is delivered, transcoding is used to convert it to a compatible format. If the bit rate of the content needs to be changed, transrating is used to convert the content. Note that transrating is normally only done to reduce the bit rate of video content.

When purchasing a VOD server, it is important to match the capabilities of the server to the task that needs to be performed. The amount of storage can be large or

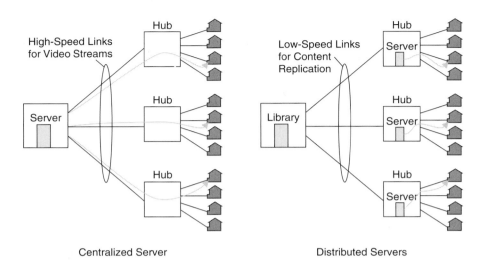

**FIGURE 8.1** *Centralized versus Distributed Servers*

small, and the number of streams supported can be large or small. These are not correlated; it is perfectly sensible to have a server with lots of storage yet little streaming capacity, if it is being used to hold video content that is rarely viewed. Conversely, it is also sensible to have a server with relatively little storage (say, 50 to 100 hours of video content) but very high stream capacity, if it is being used to serve first-run Hollywood movies to many viewers simultaneously.

IPTV service providers have two main philosophies of network server distribution, as shown in Figure 8.1. The first is centralized, where large, high-capacity servers are installed in central locations and the streams for each viewer are delivered over high-speed communications links to each local service provider facility. The second is decentralized, where smaller servers are located at each facility and provide streams only to local viewers. A central library server provides content to the distributed servers whenever necessary. On one hand, the decentralized concept makes sense because it helps reduce the amount of bandwidth needed between locations. On the other hand, the centralized concept is appealing because it reduces the number of servers that must be installed. It also reduces the costs of transporting, storing and managing redundant sets of content in multiple locations. In reality, both centralized and decentralized systems are deployed depending on system architecture, capabilities and user viewing habits that affect VOD traffic patterns.

Service providers need video servers capable of delivering video streams to hundreds or thousands of simultaneous viewers. For this application class, specially designed servers are required. These units typically have a large number of disk drives and use multiple processors in parallel to format streams and deliver the content. The capacity of these systems is staggering; in order to supply 1,000 simultaneous users each with a 2.5 Mbps stream, the server needs to be able to pump out 2.5 Gbps of data. Since no single disk drive or processor in a typical server is capable of this amount of data, servers use load-sharing among the devices. This means that each piece of content is spread out across multiple disk drives and that a high-speed backplane interconnects the different drives to the different processors.

## Calculating Server Storage Capacity

In order to properly calculate the amount of storage needed for a VOD server, two things must be known: 1) the number of hours of content to be stored and 2) the nominal bit rate of the video signal. With this information, calculating storage capacity is fairly straightforward.

Let's look at an example. Consider a one-hour video signal (with accompanying audio, of course) that runs at a bit rate of 2.5 Mbps. Recognizing that there are 8 bits in a byte and 3,600 seconds in an hour, you easily calculate that the total file will be 1.125 billion bytes, or about 1.05 GB. Note that this value is approximate, since the exact format of the file on a hard disk will be different. In addition, a small amount of metadata will be added to the file to provide description of the video and make it easier to transmit in multiple copies.

Here are a few more examples of required video server sizes for various amounts of content:

- 200 hours of SD content at 2.5 Mbps = 210 GB

- 500 hours of SD content at 4 Mbps = 900 GB

- 10,000 hours of SD content at 2 Mbps = 9 TB

- 300 hours of MPEG–2 HD content at 14 Mbps = almost 2 TB

- 500 hours of H.264 HD content at 6 Mbps = 1.35 TB

It is also interesting to note that some content owners place limits on how much compression can be applied to their video streams. Sometimes there are even contractual terms regarding the type of compression algorithm to be used. These limits are put in place to help ensure that the end viewer receives a high quality image. This can be very important to large production companies who have a public image to maintain and who stand to lose credibility or viewers if their products are over-compressed.

One example of such a company might be a broadcaster who holds the rights to a large number of sporting events. If local IPTV providers use excessive amounts of compression, then not only will that group of local viewers get an inferior video feed, but there could also be a negative impact on the broadcaster's brand image in other aspects of their business.

# Advertising Servers

An advertising server can be a key revenue producer for IPTV systems and may also have a role to play in live streaming Internet Video applications. The server's job is to insert advertisements into video streams at specially indicated times called *avails*. The result is a video stream delivered to a viewer with specialized advertising inserted.

Let's look at an example of how this technology works. A national broadcaster such as CNN designs their programming to accommodate advertisement inserts throughout the day. Many of these times will be sold to national advertisers and broadcast by CNN to every viewer in a country. Other times will be made available for local providers to sell to local advertisers. During these times, CNN will include audio tones or special digital codes that indicate that these times are available for local ads to be inserted. The ad server will recognize the indicator and replace the feed from the network with a video file stored on the local server. Any viewers watching CNN through the local provider will see the local ad in place of the ad broadcast by CNN. Because the timing of each avail is under CNN's control, the network can make sure that local ads are not inserted in place of high revenue national ads, but rather in place of ads that may not bring direct revenue to the network, such as advertisements for upcoming programs.

In the case of Internet Video, ads are commonly delivered in two ways. One way is as a graphic or video clip on the Web portal, where viewers navigate to select the clip they want to view or download. The second way is as a video spot advertisement delivered to the viewer immediately before or sometime during the requested content.

From a business standpoint, local advertising can be a big source of revenue to any video delivery system operator. Over-the-air, CATV and satellite broadcasters all utilize this technology, and IPTV and Internet Video operators can earn revenue as well. This revenue can be used to help offset the costs of programming and delivery systems, such as IPTV networks or Internet Video servers. Both local and national advertisers will use local advertising for certain purposes. For example, it makes no sense for a local automobile dealer to advertise on a national basis. National advertisers may also want to deliver advertisements selectively to local audiences, such a beverage company that may have an advertising tie-in with a local sports team.

# Live Streaming Servers

Live streaming servers are used to support broadcasts over the Internet. They are necessary because each video stream delivered must be made up of packets specifically addressed to each individual viewer's device—there is no mechanism on the Internet to make copies of a video stream and deliver it to multiple users (i.e., multicasting). Another way to describe a live streaming server would be as a unicast replication server, because their principal job is to take in one unicast stream, make multiple copies and then send them on towards multiple viewers.

Unicasting is the standard mode for sending packets over the Internet. In this mode, each packet has a single source address and a single destination address. If a source wants to send packets to multiple destinations, it must create a unique packet for each destination. This requires processing power, because each packet needs to have a correctly formatted header, with a destination IP address, a correct set of flags and a properly calculated header checksum. Once the packet is created, it flows essentially intact directly from the source to the destination over the Internet.

Live streaming servers need very little storage, because the content is moving through in real time. Instead, these servers need a lot of processing power, because they need to receive incoming streams, make copies for each viewer and create properly formatted IP packets in a continuous stream for each viewer with little or no delay. In addition, the servers must be capable of processing transactions to add and drop viewers as people tune in to watch the video or tune out when they have seen enough or want to switch to other content. These servers may also need to capture data as needed to produce invoices for paid content, although that task is normally the responsibility of the Web portal that authorized the user to view the video.

In contrast to most other types of servers, live streaming servers don't have to be purchased by each company that wants to use them. Instead, service bureaus will (for a fee) provide processing power and Internet bandwidth when a company wants to host a live event. These bureaus, often called *Content Delivery Networks (CDNs)*, will also host normal Web site content for delivery to Web surfers located around the Internet.

# Encryption and Rights Management

Purchasing and installing a major server system can be a challenge. But, getting the rights to enough content to fill the server can be a much more daunting task. Owners of the content will often refuse to permit their programming to be placed on a server until they are satisfied with the security arrangements. Securing these rights often involves direct negotiations with the content owners and may depend on the certification of the DRM system.

There are a number of vendors of DRM systems who have taken the necessary step of proving the security of their systems to the satisfaction of major content owners, such as Hollywood movie studios. At a minimum, a DRM system must ensure that the content is unusable (for viewing or copying) unless the viewer has been provided with the proper key. There are a number of mechanisms for controlling and distributing these keys, which were discussed in Chapter 7.

DRM is not only important in a VOD delivery network, but also for the content storage itself, directly within the VOD server. This is to prevent unauthorized uses of the content, which could occur from an outside intruder gaining access to the server or from an inside user misappropriating the content. Content owners will typically insist on protection of their property both in storage and during delivery.

VOD vendors have taken a number of steps to protect stored content within their systems. In addition to standard encryption techniques used in DRM, some vendors have developed a proprietary file system that is separated from the normal server operating system. This can help prevent hackers and viruses from reaching the stored content. A second security technique involves breaking the content up into small files and distributing those files to physically separate hard drives. In the event that one of the drives is stolen or compromised, the content is useless, because it is only a small portion of the overall file. This system also provides extra reliability, because files can be stored along with error correction data so all files can be properly reconstituted even after a drive fails.

# Reality Check

In this chapter's Reality Check, we will discuss three novel server implementations. In the first two examples, we will discuss ways to use servers to increase revenue and in the third, a way to change the physical location of the stored video content.

# Selling Space on a VOD Server to Advertisers

On most VOD servers, there is a significant amount of space allowed for expansion. While this space may eventually be used up, for a good part of many system life-cycles, the space is simply empty. Some clever system operators have figured out a way to leverage this asset: selling space to advertisers.

In this situation, the advertisements are not the normal 30- or 60-second spot ads. Instead, they are long-form ads designed to appeal to the relatively small proportion of viewers who might want to get more information about a specific product or service. For example, a manufacturer of an innovative flooring product might want to sponsor an instructional video that shows consumers how easy it is to install and maintain their product. Or, a luxury automobile manufacturer might want to host a program that shows a classic car rally featuring their products. Or, a golf equipment manufacturer might want to sponsor a golf training video. Or, the visitors' bureau for a tropical island might want to host a tour of their natural features. There are many possibilities.

To make this successful for both system operators and advertisers, a few conditions must be met. First, there must be a way for viewers to find out about the content and navigate to it. This will certainly involve the use of listings in the interactive program guide, but may also involve splash screens or inserts in more popular pages to inform viewers that the content exists. Second, the system operator may want to exercise a minimal amount of editorial control, to help ensure that the sponsored content doesn't end up being larded with hard-sell infomercials that have little value for viewers. The system operator may also want to gather some viewing statistics to see which types of content are popular and to provide feedback to the advertisers on the effectiveness of their offerings.

# Ads Attached to VOD Content

As discussed above, not all VOD content needs to be paid for by viewers on a per-transaction basis. As we discussed in Chapter 3, many different models can be used to pay for on-demand content. Deciding how to implement an advertising-supported VOD system can be quite interesting.

One of the most basic decisions that must be made is to decide when the advertisements will appear. Many viewers have become accustomed to pre-roll advertisements, where a few short spot ads are played before the desired content begins to play. This is, of course, common practice in movie theaters (previews of coming events, reminders to not smoke and advertisements of the snack bar in the lobby are common themes). Pre-roll advertising is also common on Web sites and is part of many purchased content items such as DVDs and VHS tapes. The secret to not upsetting viewers is to ensure that the ads are brief and few in number.

A more controversial form of advertising consists of advertisements actually inserted into the content itself. This technique certainly does not appeal to some viewers. However, if the service provider makes it clear that advertising is required in order to pay for the content, then viewers are more likely to understand.

One very controversial aspect of advertising and VOD content is whether commercial *zapping* should be allowed. Commercial zapping occurs when a viewer decides to fast-forward past a commercial. Most live video recording devices (such as personal video recorders) allow users to fast-forward through advertisements.

## Legal Blues for SonicBlue

Some PVR devices have been produced with a button on their remote control that allows the viewer to skip ahead exactly 30 seconds, allowing ads of that length to be easily skipped. This technology, which was included in Replay TV units sold by SonicBlue, ended up being the subject of a lawsuit against the company by a number of major media companies. SonicBlue ended up in bankruptcy in 2003 before the case was decided, so there wasn't a clear ruling in the U.S. about the legality of this technology.

The two sides of the controversy regarding VOD services can be summarized as follows:

- If zapping is not allowed, then users who are not willing to see advertisements will become less likely to watch the content. This in turn could translate into fewer overall viewers, meaning that revenues that depend on viewers (such as subscription fees) will drop.

- If zapping is allowed, then advertisers will be less likely to pay for advertising, since there is a lower probability of their ads being viewed. Service providers may then find it necessary to charge more for VOD content.

Of course, it is not necessary that this decision be made on an all or nothing basis— service providers are free to have different amount of advertising for different types of content. They can also experiment both with advertisements that allow zapping and ads that don't, at the risk of truly confusing viewers.

# Push VOD as an Alternative to Centralized Servers

*Push VOD* uses hard disk storage located inside the viewer's STB to store content locally that can be viewed on demand. Push VOD is a relatively new concept being used to provide VOD over networks that don't have interactive capabilities. This is certainly the case with satellite networks, which simply don't have the bandwidth to create a separate video signal stream for each user.

In an IPTV system, push VOD might be useful for a few reasons. First, by storing video files locally in each user's STB, the burden on the network could be reduced when a viewer is watching a VOD program, and the load on centralized VOD servers is lightened. Second, locally stored content could be used to provide entertainment or troubleshooting information to users in the event that their network connection failed. Third, local storage could be used to provide highly interactive programming or entertainment (such as games) that would be difficult or impossible to provide from a centralized server.

Of course, there are some factors that must be considered before using push VOD. First, a very strong DRM technology will be required, since push VOD content is literally sitting in a hard drive in the viewer's home. Second, a fairly sophisticated control system will be needed to manage which content gets delivered to each STB and to collect the payments from viewers that chose to watch the content. Vendors are appearing that offer to manage both of these issues for service providers, and as hard drive capacities increase, more content can be stored.

One interesting concept that can benefit both viewers and service providers is installing a partitioned hard drive in an STB. In one partition, the service provider can push a dozen or two popular movie titles being featured for VOD. The other partition can be used to give the viewer a PVR capability for their favorite broadcast shows. This combination gives system operators two ways to pay for the extra expense of purchasing and maintaining hard drives in STBs—by selling push VOD content and by increasing the rental fees to viewers for STBs that include PVR capability. STB manufacturers are starting to respond to this market by placing large hard disk drives into STBs and supporting partitioning in the STB operating software.

# Summary

In this chapter we have discussed a variety of different server types and examined in detail three types often used for IPTV and Internet Video systems. VOD servers can be large or small, centralized or distributed, but they are always rated on the

| SERVER TYPE | CAPACITY | SPEED | COST | KEY ATTRIBUTE |
|---|---|---|---|---|
| VOD | Varies | High stream capacity | Low to moderate | Bandwidth–number of simultaneous streams |
| Archive | As large as possible | Not important | Lowest cost per terabyte | Large capacity at low cost |
| Playout | Low | Low | High | Reliability/redundancy essential |
| Advertising | Low | Able to handle multiple channels simultaneously | Medium | Easy to operate software, excellent record keeping |
| Live Streaming | Very Low | High stream capacity | Medium | Bandwidth—number of simultaneous streams |
| Ingest | Low | Low | Medium | Flexibility for video inputs, good software for metadata workflow |

**TABLE 8.1** *Key Attributes of Different Types of Servers*

number of simultaneous streams they can support. Advertising servers are typically not large or hugely powerful, but they need to be able to monitor multiple live network feeds, reliably insert ads and keep good records. Live streaming servers need almost no storage but are rated like VOD servers on their total throughput in terms of number of simultaneous streams. Table 8.1 summarizes some of the similarities and differences between the various types of servers.

# 9 The Importance of Bandwidth

Here we go again! First music, then TV shows, and now movies.

—Steve Jobs

Both IPTV and Internet Video services are critically dependent on adequate network bandwidth. Without it, Internet Video files can be excessively slow to download, and streaming video won't work. IPTV simply cannot operate without sufficient bandwidth to carry the signal. So, ensuring adequate network capacity is extremely important for operations and quality of service.

Until recently, skeptics have maintained that delivering bandwidth-hungry television channels over broadband would vex providers seeking to build a new business with an incomplete technology foundation. The complaint was that operators would be "challenged to ensure that they have enough bandwidth over their DSL infrastructures to compete with cable."[1]

## The Corner Office View

**Greenfield**: Forrester's Josh Bernoff says there will be a huge bandwidth crunch for telco, cable, satellite providers. What do you think?

**Mark Cuban**: He is right. There isn't enough bandwidth for all the existing TV networks; some will die, some will stay standard definition, some will go HD.

---

1. Ovum, http://store.ovum.com/Product.asp?tnpid=&tnid=&pid=38267&cid=0

Regardless, any solution depends on the crucial need for dependable throughput from head-end to home viewer. Just as building a fire requires a balance of fuel, heat and oxygen, the elements for the IPTV consumer experience are equipment, network services and content. However, bandwidth is what sparks and sustains the combustion. Without understanding how to provide adequate throughput for data packets that comprise smooth playout, quality of service will degrade, and subscribers will not pay. The standard has already been set by conventional TV service. An audience will accept an occasional dropped pixel or an audio blip, but realistically, the threshold for this and other jitters, blurs or frozen frames is low.

Provisioning bandwidth to deliver on the exciting promise of personalized, interactive IPTV content opens up a new market. But the challenge of solving quality of service issues that accompany scalable, bandwidth-intensive HDTV and triple-play service offerings will increasingly go with the territory. To date, these challenges and costs for infrastructure investment have been significant, but most industry analysts see these as a minor speed bump along the way. Among the initial solutions for addressing improved bandwidth, which we'll discuss later in this chapter, are emerging DSL technologies with higher bit rates or greater range, media compression advances, and deployment strategies such as constructing remote terminals closer to the home.

Bandwidth needed for broadband transport services ranges from relatively low for Web pages and voice, higher for standard definition broadcast quality television, and very high for demanding HDTV, which must display one to two million pixels and needs at least three or four times SD bandwidth, around 12 to 15 Mbps. Though new compression standards such as MPEG-4 and H.264 lower that number to 6 to 9 Mbps there is still a gap between what is today's state of the art and the technology that will be robust enough to effectively carry all content to all destinations. The industry winners of tomorrow will be those able to calculate the best price/performance curves and provide services expediently ahead of the competition.

Bandwidth requirements vary greatly depending not only on the type of content being transmitted, but also on the quality of service expected. In the 1980s, a modem speed of 2,400 bps allowed for basic text communications. Networks soon reached ISDN speeds at 128 Kbps but were still too limited to carry significant multimedia content. Today's average global DSL speeds are reaching 1.5 Mbps and rising with many at much higher speeds, such as cable modems at 6 Mbps and higher. We are fast approaching a widespread, mass commercial IPTV capability.

Advances in compression are steadily making headway in delivering video services over broadband. MPEG-2 video broadcast, once standard for digital television and DVD, requires 4 to 6 Mbps. However, new and more efficient *codecs*, such as MPEG-4 H.264 and VC-1, only need 1.5 to 2.5 Mbps and can render DVD-quality video within 2 Mbps. Additionally, more recent classes of DSL can carry far higher bandwidth than before, such as ADSL2+ and VDSL2 at roughly 25 Mbps and 50 Mbps respectively.

Nonetheless, the bandwidth bar is continually being raised as more and more network services are bundled together into triple-play and quadruple play offerings. We will examine various forms of DSL and their capabilities in the next section.

# DSL Technologies

Twisted-pair-based DSL facilities are widespread, with more than a billion telephone lines globally, and 140 million DSL lines installed as of the end of 2005.[2] As an incumbent technology, DSL is a popular, cost-effective way for telcos and other service providers to enter the new market for delivering broadband and video services without having to lay new cable and reconstruct a system.

Also, because of the popularity and prevalence of high-speed data DSL telephone lines, many consumers are aware that they can purchase DSL service for Internet access. Some service providers now even routinely offer video content using DSL service.

To understand the mechanics of DSL, it is useful to consider the main components in data and video traffic over DSL transport. All DSL systems make a trade-off between speed and distance: the longer distances must operate at lower bit rates because losses in the cable increase as the length of the cable increases. As technology improves, these limitations are easing, but network designers still need to plan accordingly and usually make compromises due to these constraints.

Following are the key DSL network components that must be configured strategically for performance and cost-effectiveness (Figure 9.1):

1.  The main hub, or central office (CO), the source of the signal

2.  Remote Terminals (RTs) positioned between the provider's main offices and customers

---

2. http://www.budde.com.au/Reports/Contents/Global-Broadband-Infrastructure-DSL-Market-Statistics-3333.html

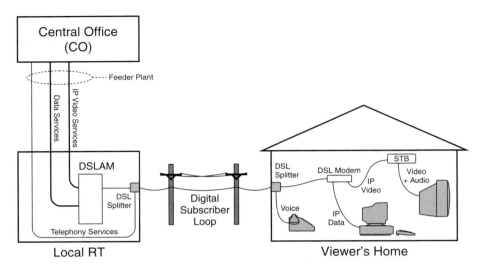

**FIGURE 9.1** *DSL System Diagram*

3.  The Feeder Plant where fiber-based voice, video and data signals often travel over different transmission equipment

4.  The DSLAM, which generates the DSL signals and places them onto the pair of copper wires (or local loop) leading to each home

Among the more crucial factors in this equation is the *DSLAM*, which we'll learn more about later in this chapter. Every DSL customer must install a DSL modem to receive DSL signals from the DSLAM and convert them into the proper form for the customer's other devices, such as a PC, a data router or a television set. The modem also takes data signals from the customer and transmits them back to the service provider.

Of the more common types of DSL services available, each has its advantages and disadvantages. These can be summarized at a high level as shown in Table 9.1.

To put this all into perspective, dial-up modems, once the norm for e-mail and Web access, operate at a maximum speed of 56 kbps today. Also, note actual bit rates that can be achieved on a DSL circuit are highly variable. They depend on many factors, including the length of the subscriber's loop and the amount of noise or interference present on the line.

In addition to using existing wires already run to many homes and businesses for telephone service, another advantage of DSL circuits is that they are normally designed to fail gracefully. This means that if a customer loses power or the DSL equipment fails, normal telephone calls can still be made. A disadvantage of DSL services for video is that very few broadcast quality signals can be sent down a DSL line. Also,

| | BANDWIDTH | PROS | CONS |
|---|---|---|---|
| G.lite | Up to 1.5 Mbps downstream; up to 512 kbps upstream. | Provides greater reach; does not need the splitter required on ADSL circuits to separate voice and data signals | Not fast enough for video |
| ADSL | Up to 8 Mbps downstream, up to 1 Mbps upstream | Mature technology | Will handle one or two SD channels, at best, but not HD; splitter required to separate voice and data signals |
| VDSL | Up to 50 Mbps downstream and up to 12 Mbps upstream | Better bandwidth at short distances | Maximum distance is quite short (~2,000 feet) |
| ADSL2+ | Up to 24 Mbps downstream and 1 Mbps upstream | Smoother roll off; as you go further out, there is a gradual decrease in performance | May not work on all existing copper cable |

**TABLE 9.1**   *DSL Service Type Options for Broadband and IPTV*

a separate stream must be dedicated to each television or other video-receiving device (VCR, digital recorder, etc.) and each must be equipped with an STB.

We've learned the basics of how DSL technology works. It's equally important to see how IPTV systems are implemented over advanced ADSL and VDSL circuits, as understand the dynamics of home delivery and regional penetration.

## More About VDSL and ADSL

It is said that there is broadband and then there is broadband, varying widely depending on geography, standards and adoption rates. Most companies deploying IPTV currently use VDSL and ADSL2+.

In the UK, there have been announcements to roll out ADSL from 5,300 telephone exchanges at up to 8 Mbps that will reach most households. France Telecom and Telefonica are basing their service on ADSL2+, and Deutsche Telekom will deliver IPTV television enabled VDSL on T-Com's 50 Mbps fiber/copper network to 40 cities by 2008, reaching 11 million German homes.[3]

---

3. http://www.iptv-forum.com/

Compared to what's ahead, prior generation DSL technologies, such as *Asymmetric Digital Subscriber Line* (ADSL), provide relatively limited amounts of bandwidth from the service provider to the consumer and even more restricted links from the consumer back to the provider (hence the "asymmetrical" element of ADSL). With current MPEG-2 processing technology, it is difficult to produce good-quality standard definition video and audio streams with a combined bit rate of less than 2.5 Mbps.

To keep overall speeds reasonable and to allow for other services (such as Internet access) on the ADSL link, it is normal to find only one, or at most two, video signals on a single ADSL circuit. High definition video, which requires at least 10 to 12 Mbps with MPEG-2 technology, is out of the question for ADSL deployment.

VDSL technology (*Very high-speed Digital Subscriber Line*) supports significantly more bandwidth on each subscriber line. Accordingly, more video channels can be transmitted to each VDSL subscriber, with three or four simultaneous videos possible. HD video signals could also be transmitted (possibly multiple ones), VDSL speed permitting. One drawback to VDSL is that the range of operational distances is less than that of ADSL, so subscribers need to be closer to the service

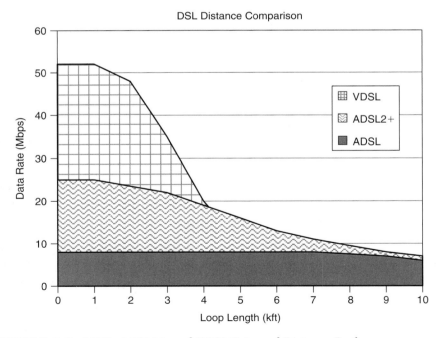

**FIGURE 9.2** *ADSL, ADSL2+ and VDSL Rate and Distance Performance*

provider facilities. Also note that the speed of DSL services varies with distance, so good planning for varying data rates is essential.

Each television set that receives IPTV signals over DSL requires an STB to decode the incoming video. (However, television sets with an RJ-45 Ethernet connector and built-in MPEG decoder have already appeared on the market.) Some STBs can act as the residential gateway in the home and provide connections for other voice and data communications equipment.

Because of DSL speed limitations, each time a viewer changes channels on the DSL IPTV system, a command must be sent back to the service provider to indicate that a new video stream needs to be delivered. We'll look more closely at both home gateways and channel changing latency issues later in this chapter.

## DSL Deployment: Homes Served, Homes Passed

Calculating ROI on IPTV and DSL business cases can become a complex calculation. There are many costs to take into account, including network infrastructure, operations and maintenance; content rights and royalties; and customer marketing. One way to keep an eye on the bottom line is using a deployment measure, homes passed, which refers to the number of potential subscribers who are ready to be served, though they may not actually choose to subscribe to the service. In other words, creating a network with a significant quantity of homes passed is an up-front investment for provisioning full service to communities.

In traditional OTA and satellite broadcast settings, the ratio of homes passed to homes served is not a significant issue because the ability to multicast to a region is mostly about skillful broadcast tower and satellite transponder deployment: essentially, a single transmission reaches all. In IPTV implementations, however, covering a region requires more planning and deployment steps to connect a line to every home and arrive at an optimum, profitable ratio of homes served (HS) to homes passed (HP). The penetration ratio of HS to HP is what counts. One benchmark of success for achieving ROI is that penetration must reach 20 percent at an early stage of deployment.

Because IPTV services are still at an early stage, there have neither been enough launches nor enough churn experience to determine what's working and what strategies should be adjusted. With no magic formula as yet, creating a system of measurement is still a work in progress closely watched by industry planners. Until you have subscribers, there's no additional cost. However, with IPTV, providers must continue to build out the network and be prepared to provide full-coverage service on a risk/reward basis.

# DSLAM

Subscribers gladly or grudgingly pay for "delivery services" that networks are so elegantly engineered to provide. What they really want is the goods: *content* in the form of entertainment and communications. One of the main delivery service elements in IP video transport that makes it all happen is the Digital Subscriber Line Access Multiplexer (DSLAM), supporting express connections between IP telephone or PC devices and the Internet. The DSLAM provides a high-speed data conduit between multiple DSLs and the network backbone's vast bandwidth.

DSLAM technology performs a mission-critical function in digital media data routing and transport. If we start with a look at the legacy of the communications world, plain old telephone service (POTS) provided telephony and served telecoms customers. The POTS acronym dates back to its "post office" roots when the postal system in certain countries also maintained the phone operations. POTS was never designed to operate as data lines, and typically it does not offer guaranteed transfer rate levels.

POTS' modern digital counterpart is IP Switching, which provides reliable data flow benchmarks and supports the switching of video and audio signals. In the IP Switching model, each digital video or audio signal is converted into a stream of IP packets and sent onto a local area network where the actual switching is done by standard IP networking equipment. The great advantage of this digital approach is that many different types of signals can be carried over IP, such as video, audio, voice and other signal types. Likewise, in connecting to wide area networks and supporting IP traffic, IP Switching enables more universal development and communications.

Location, location ... well, you've heard it before. To facilitate faster traffic flow and allow for the efficient transport of data—be it for phone, video or Web content—DSLAMs must be physically located at the right points and distances along the network. But, regardless of the strategic deployment of DSLAMs and their seamless inter-operation with server and network, another challenging demand placed on the new IPTV architecture is channel changing performance, which we'll examine later in this chapter.

# Home Gateway

A DSL home gateway facilitates integration and ease-of-use of broadband connectivity and various devices in the home to improve customer experience. It connects the networked devices in the house with any server storage and the Internet through a high speed DSL modem and communications ports. Benefits to consumers include connectivity with IPTV content, PC downloads and media, as well as VPN (virtual private network) and security features.

## The On-Demand, Network Smashing Future

In television's new "fast-forward, on-demand, network-smashing future" (*Wired* magazine, October 2003), the promised land is a single, seamless infinite world of content. This means the aggregation of the previously separate communication domains of video, music, Web pages, movies, Internet search, telephony and games. It also means that whether by Web, TV or mobile phone, whether through prime-time TV channels or amateur me-channels, your home is the intersection where this is about to take place.

The home gateway supports DSL and accommodates the expanding functionality and a converging set of devices. In what some refer to as the "living room war," an increasing market share of broadband content combined with broadcast over IP offers a new commercial prize for service providers: delivery billing for a new array of entertainment programming and information services.

## Cable: Coax and CAT6

The central nervous system, as it were, for connecting this in-home media entertainment complex, is the various internal wire line and wireless technologies such as coax and CAT6.

It is common for the residential gateway to be permanently installed in a central location in each home. IP traffic from this gateway is then routed to each STB located inside the subscriber's home. In many systems, connections on this gateway are also provided for the customer's telephone and PC.

In addition to being used in homes by the cable television industry, coaxial cabling is common for supporting computer networks, including Ethernet. Because it carries more data and a clearer signal, it has often been considered worth the added expense over regular telephone wire and is a legacy in many homes today.

CAT6 (Category6), comprised of copper wire pairs, is a higher performance — and higher priced—cable that supports GigE at bit rates of up to 1,000 Mbps at a maximum length of 90 meters. Considered a little bit of overkill for current data flow in the home, many experts maintain CAT6 is the right future-proofing choice for the long haul.

## Home Phoneline Networking Alliance

The *Home Phoneline Networking Alliance* (HPNA), with technology members such AT&T, HP, IBM and Intel, is an industry organization that explores ways to establish home networking standards that drive innovation and interoperability between telecom and IT data, device and service providers. HPNA's stated goal is to "develop triple-play home networking solutions using existing coax and phone lines." Their 3.0 technical specification has the mission of enabling devices to "simultaneously communicate at their native speed" in networks without degrading *quality of service* (QoS). Its aim is also to optimize for "broadband entertainment, voice, data file, peripheral and Internet sharing applications throughout the home without affecting standard telephone service."[4]

## Home Networking Growth

Home networking is anticipated to grow significantly, with the number of enabled households increasing to 111 million by 2008[5] (52 percent of online households),[6] and industry consortiums pushing for a goal of 500 million subscribers by 2010.[7] Momentum will likely build from home networking advantages such as shared Internet and printer access and home entertainment distribution, as well as home device control, security and telecommuting benefits. Furthermore, this is just the beginning, as we start to connect not just living room, home office and bedroom, but also the utility room, kitchen and beyond.

# Multiple Televisions

"It's what I call the dirty little secret of IPTV," says Entone Technologies CEO Steve McCay. "The huge issue today is that it's one thing to get the signal to one TV, but what if you have four or five TVs in the home?"[8] In conventional TV broadcast scenarios such as terrestrial, cable and satellite, there is no overhead or impact when

---

4. From Home Networking MR-002, ABCs_home_networking_final.pdf, www.dslforum.org

5. "Worldwide Home Networking 2004-2008 Forecast and Analysis," IDC

6. DLNA (Digital Living Network Alliance)

7. DSL Forum has the goal of 500 million subscribers by 2010

8. From Light Reading www.lightreading.com/document.asp?doc_id=73558&site=lightreading

adding additional televisions to the household, except possibly the addition of an STB for certain services. Not so with IPTV. Each IPTV node requires its own bandwidth allocation, taking an additive toll on IP packet delivery. Thus, stringing new TVs into bedrooms, dens and kitchens requires greater bandwidth, which is a challenge for IPTV to scale as gracefully as its multicast broadcast counterpart.

# How to Calculate Bandwidth

Long before the growth and influence of broadband, network communications professionals have understood first-hand the challenge of estimating and planning for required bandwidth. It's a practice that's as old as the science of networking itself. From the earliest days of telephony, designers were faced with the task of predicting user-base growth and demand and making tough, pragmatic economic choices to invest wisely in robust networks.

Another booming IP sector, VoIP provides an insight into the factors that go into creating a successful bandwidth strategy. For one thing, different codecs for various VoIP systems (with their respective protocols and bandwidth characteristics) must be taken into account in planning for telephony traffic. Also, other services, such as video teleconferencing, may need to share the bandwidth, and crunch peak activity during business hours—particularly spiking at start and close of the business day—can affect sound quality, which users expect to remain at a practical level for business and personal conversations.[9]

Turning back to IP video, calculating the amount of actual bandwidth consumed by an MPEG stream, for example, is very important. It is also somewhat tricky. We can get a sense of this by looking at how one manufacturer, HaiVision Systems of Montreal, Quebec, does this for one MPEG-2 product, the hai500 series multi-stream encoder/decoder/multiplexer.

As in most MPEG devices, the hai500 user is given control over the rate of the raw MPEG stream. For this device (which is pretty typical), the video bit rate can be set anywhere from 800 kbps to 15 Mbps, in steps of 100 kbps. For a more elaborate technical view of how this is handled, please refer to *Video Over IP: A Practical Guide to Technology and Applications* (Wes Simpson, Focal Press, 2005).

Today, some approaches to bandwidth calculation must cover current implications to planning for IPTV deployment such as MPEG-4, H.264. There are two

---

9. "Bandwidth: Calculating current and future requirements," Teejay Riedl, August 8, 2006, searchnetworking.techtarget.com/tip/0,289483,sid7_gci1209041,00.html

different incentives, or forces, acting on IPTV service providers when they determine the bandwidths that will be used for new DSL networks.

- One force is to offer as many different services as possible, thereby giving subscribers the widest variety of offerings to choose from. However, as each additional service requires room on the DSL circuit, this approach tends to increase the amount of bandwidth used.

- Another force is to maximize the number of subscribers that can be served from each DSLAM location. Since there is a tradeoff between distance and speed, higher data rates means shorter distances are covered, and therefore fewer homes are reached. This force tends to reduce the amount of bandwidth used.

Since video signals are typically the largest users of bandwidth on an IPTV system, calculating the amount of bandwidth required for video and audio streams on an IPTV system is extremely important. Here is how one supplier of video compression equipment does the calculations for a standard television feed with two audio channels and some associated data.

Begin with the raw video and audio bandwidths. The video elementary stream is a constant bit rate MPEG-2 stream operating at 2.60 Mbps. The two audio signals are MPEG AAC audio, each operating at 192 kbps. The data signal in this example is some low speed data, such as closed captioning data or possibly a description of the content.

The first processing step after the compression is completed is to convert the raw streams into MPEG *Transport Streams* (TS). This important step makes it possible for the decoder in the STB to determine which audio and data signals belong with which video signals. The TS also contains the Program Clock Reference, which enables the decoder to play back the video with proper timing and to synchronize the audio and the video. When this is done, the video stream is now 2.79 Mbps and each audio stream becomes 199.75 kbps. The data stream will be added later.

The next processing step is to convert the MPEG TS into IP packets. This process adds UDP, IP and Ethernet headers to the TS data, in the ratio of 46 bytes[10] of header to every 1,316 bytes of TS data. This brings the audio and video stream total up to 3,301 kbps plus 12 kbps of data, making the total stream run at kbps.

The next step is to convert the total stream into ATM for transmission over a DSL line. (This is common on many DSLAMs; other, newer devices can transmit

---

10. Note that standard Ethernet headers include a preamble and a Start Frame Delimiter that would add another 8 bytes to this total. However, since these frames are to be transmitted over ATM, those bytes are not used

their content directly in IP format). To do this, we need to add 5 bytes of ATM headers on every 48 bytes of the video/audio/data stream. This works out to 3,739 kbps of total bandwidth occupied on the DSL, or a total overhead of 25.3 percent on the original stream. It is also important to note that though most current generation DSLAMs use ATM, IP-based DSLAM units are steadily arriving on the market and moving into the operations architecture.

This example clearly shows the importance of viewing an IPTV system as an integrated whole. Video bandwidth decisions can affect network bandwidth decisions, which in turn can affect network geography and DSLAM deployment decisions. All of these factors can affect the IPTV system business model and need to be considered when technology decisions are made.

# Channel Changing

Channel changing is a very important issue for IPTV networks. It's important to grasp why many consider this part of the technical holy grail for attaining viable, scalable IPTV deployment. As one industry Web site reports it, "Simultaneous delivery of channels is necessary to keep IPTV competitive with cable. Obviously, multiple streams are needed to support picture-in-picture, but they're also needed by DVRs, which can record one show while a user is watching another. For IPTV to become a viable whole-house solution, it will also need to support enough simultaneous channels to allow televisions in different rooms to display different content, and juggling resulting bandwidth issues is one of the trickiest parts of implementing an IPTV network that will be attractive to consumers."[11]

On conventional television, changing channels is relatively straightforward. The television simply sends a signal to connect to another already existing radio frequency (RF) and then displays it through hardware and monitor to the viewer. There is usually little latency, and no significant technical issues standing between viewer and clicker—not even for the fervent channel surfer. In an IPTV system, that is not the case.

Instead of merely switching between an existing flow of content being delivered over satellite or cable, IPTV system programming control must first traverse a series of data flows, or digital transport points and processes, to complete the cutover from one channel to another. Some of those points along the way from viewer

11. From "An introduction to IPTV", By Nate Anderson, March 12, 2006
http://arstechnica.com/guides/other/iptv.ars

to IPTV channel change include the STB, DSLAM, routers, servers and source broadcast feed itself.

Here is a break down of the basic steps entailed in the IPTV channel changing process:

1. The customer presses a button on the remote control.

2. The STB recognizes that the user has requested a different stream than the one it is currently sending.

3. The STB sends request and an IP Multicast Join command upstream to the service provider.

4. When the DSLAM receives this command, it determines whether the stream requested is available.

5. If the stream is available, DSLAM initiates making copies of packets that are, in turn, sent to the user.

Another challenge in IPTV channel change is that the system must determine if the requested stream is currently in the middle of a long, inaccessible play-back segment. If so, the system will have to compensate for that.

Among the factors affecting channel cut-over and streaming performance, the television itself and EPG are usually not the culprits. The real bottlenecks are more likely to occur in server, encryption and middleware processes,[12] so encoding, encryption, STBs and network design must all be coordinated. Other technical certainty includes ensuring consistent sound quality, solving networking issues (such as the *jitter buffer*) and accommodating other data traffic, such as triple-play content, that strains network performance.

In IPTV channel changing, there are many latency issues. The purpose of this book as an executive briefing would not be well served by dwelling there in too much detail. Nonetheless, the parsing of MPEG streams is important to understand in a little more depth. Content in an MPEG stream or file is structured into Groups of Pictures (GOPs). Long GOPs can present a challenge in channel changing. As described in Chapter 6, the configuration of GOPs can cause serious delays for IPTV MPEG decoding when a channel is changed.

Upon attempting a channel change to a new stream, the system must determine "where in the stream" the video is currently playing. It's possible the decoder could

---

12. "Managing Delay in IP Video Networks," Cisco Systems

have no idea at that point in time what's going on in the image, and require 10 to 40 frames before the right information (from what's called an I frame) puts the system back on track, instructing it correctly for display.

The über-issue, of course, is scalability: if thousands of viewers are simultaneously watching a major sporting event or popular television drama, will there be a crunch? Namely, how well can the systems retain low-latency, high-user satisfaction when there are thousands of deployments per community in district after district?

IPTV is new. It's a digital packet-based service model that's still being refined. Nonetheless, its performance must match or exceed the prime-time standard, because the whole world is watching—for results. Until IPTV moves beyond the early release phase, troubleshooting will be part of the landscape. New tests for monitoring that performance will keep the pressure on providers to meet or beat broadcast TV quality. Technologies from QoS testing vendors, such as IneoQuest's Cricket[13] and others, will report on quality until the day the customer experiences no QoS issues when they switch channels or interact with their IPTV programming.[14]

# Bandwidth for a Triple-Play, HD Future

Bandwidth is key to the future of IP environments. Some industry observers project that IPTV will flourish to full potential only after video bandwidth becomes a commodity—low-cost and ubiquitous. And as we have discussed, as if raising the bar for broadcast-quality video over DSL weren't daunting enough, other serious developments pose an even higher standard, creating what some analysts refer to as a *bandwidth crunch*.

One of those developments is an increasingly common triple-play service offering that demands ever more voluminous data over existing pipes. The other is the increasing expectation, and prevalence, of an HDTV future: "Consumers lust for the new big, flat TV sets ... as HDTV penetration grows past 50 million homes in the next five years," according to Forrester Research, adding that, "telcos should make the breadth of HDTV choices a selling point as they roll out TV over IP."[15]

---

13. http://www.ineoquest.com/page361.html

14. http://www.exfo.com/en/support/WaveReview/2006-June/WRArticle1.asp

15. "HDTV And The Coming Bandwidth Crunch," Forrester Research, February 17, 2005, http://www.forrester.com/Research/Document/Excerpt/0,7211,35146,00.html

Without adequate bandwidth, drop-out, flicker and frozen frames mean a lost market window through the failure to meet prime-time quality that audiences have come to count on. Your network either has the right capacity video flows or it doesn't—there's no in-between.

Despite the long, winding technical path to TV programming over IP, from broadcast head-end to the residential viewer, high-speed networks are arriving. Channel changing response times are improving, and advanced technologies will continue to drive increased price performance. In conjunction with slick, efficient EPG interface design and increasing prime-time and niche content, users are responding favorably.

# Reality Check

This chapter's reality checks focus on two issues at the front line of bandwidth provisioning and change. The first, describing Passive Optical Networks (PONs), is the emergence of high-powered fiber network technologies that tackle the bandwidth question head on. The second is the problematic side of PONs that entail power requirements that sometimes must sit with the customer. Traditional telephone services don't have batteries that require customer intervention when they need replacement. Will this be tolerated as part of the for a new residential responsibility fiber optic deployment sites?

## Fiber-Based Future

Technology does not stand still, and competing fiber technologies are fast on the heels of DSL's popularity. Fiber communication technology is fast and has high bandwidth with low power and maintenance requirements. Recent work on Passive Optical Networks (PONs) has created a new method for delivering video services to the subscriber. PON subscribers will increase from 3.4 million to 31 million in 2009, and revenues worldwide are expected to rise to $2 billion for optical line termination (OTL) and optical network termination passive optical network (ONT PON), driven by video and IPTV applications.[16]

In essence, a PON is an all-optical network with no active components between the service provider and the customer. The network is optical because the path

16. "Report Says Video and IPTV Driving PON, FTTH" Lightwave, April 5, 2006

from the service provider to the customer is entirely made up of fiber-optic and optical components. The network is passive because there are no active elements (such as electronics, lasers, optical detectors or optical amplifiers) between the service provider and the customer.

One key feature of a PON network is the use of an optical splitter near the customer premises, which greatly improves the economics of the system. In the case of one popular standard, up to 32 customers can be served by one fiber from the service provider. A second key feature of a PON network is that the optical fibers and the optical splitter are configured to handle a wide range of laser wavelengths.

The promise of PONs are in providing both GigE capacity for business applications as well as "supporting the multiple simultaneous streams of High Definition time-shifted IPTV—crucial for future residential deployments," says Shane Eleniak, vice president of marketing and business development for Alloptic, a PON provider.[17]

## Installation and Power Issues

PONs offer numerous features and advantages that exceed previous-generation copper cable, but they do not come without their price. One major drawback of PON technology is that it requires the service provider to install a fiber-optic connection to each PON customer. Replacing a large installed base of copper cabling with optical fiber and supplying each user with an ONT can be a very large investment for existing customers. And because each customer must have an ONT, which typically operates using power supplied by the customer using normal commercial power, the ONT must have a method to power itself (i.e., a battery) in the event of a power outage if it is required to support emergency communication.

# Summary

In this chapter, we learned about the amount of bandwidth needed for various services, including Internet access, VoIP and SD video, and the implications of HD video as well as competitive triple-play service. We talked about current and emerging varieties of DSL and improvements in capacity and throughput steadily brining the pieces together for quality end-to-end video delivery. We also discussed

---

17. http://www.lightreading.com/document.asp?doc_id=105053, October 2, 2006

the important role of DSLAM and IP switching in the twisted-pair architecture that once ran over POTS.

With that in mind, we saw how some of the contention and latency issues can be caused by adding multiple televisions and by the channel change process itself. We took a look at how home gateways and networks facilitate DSL data flow and the internal home wiring technologies of coax and CAT6, and how the HPNA is driving adoption. Finally, some examples showed how to calculate bandwidth before discussing an increasing demand for throughput that will lay the groundwork for greater digital IP video offerings.

# 10  Set Top Boxes

Navigation is almost the crux of the future of television; not everyone has figured it out yet, but they will.

—Tim Hanlon, vice president, Starcom MediaVest

Probably the most visible component of an IPTV network to most consumers is the *set top box* (STB) that usually resides in close vicinity (or even on top of) their television sets. This box provides a number of significant functions and can have a huge impact on the customers' viewing experiences. The STB also produces essentially all of the information shown on a user's display that is not video and audio programming.

STBs can represent a significant portion of a service provider's total investment per subscriber, so selecting the correct set of functions is critical. In fact, the portion of overall IPTV system capital cost absorbed by STBs can approach 60 percent. In addition, maintenance practices and procedures need to be developed to resolve STB issues. Because they are located inside viewer homes, STBs may be more failure-prone than other devices that make up an IPTV network.

In this chapter, we will review the key functions of the STB, including internal features and external connections. User controls will be discussed briefly. We will also

## The Corner Office View

So it's not just software for the PC or software for the phone or software for the videogame, it's software for the user . . . As I move between devices, the people I've

CONTINUED ▶

CONTINUED ▶

chosen to share my presence with becomes available to them. A friend can see, if I want, what game I'm playing and say they might want to play with me . . . Even watching TV, the ability to chat with your friends while you're watching the same show or different shows should be something that's very straightforward. . . .

There's a lot of themes there, themes of personalization, themes of empowerment, themes of everything moving to the Internet. What is telephony moving to the Internet? That's voice. What is TV moving to the Internet? That's Internet TV or IPTV. People have to have confidence in these things, automatically backed up, security built-in, very reliable systems that use the cloud storage for those kinds of guarantees, and easy connections, connecting to people, connecting up to devices, a very strong way of driving through all these different scenarios and making them very simple.

— Keynote Remarks by Bill Gates,
chairman and chief software architect, Microsoft Corporation 2006
International Consumer Electronics Show Las Vegas, Nevada January 4, 2006

discuss the middleware that supports a variety of software applications on the STB, which can be a crucial part of the viewing experience. We'll conclude with a look at some of the business and economic issues that can influence the STB selection process.

# Basic Functions

The main job of the STB is to receive the incoming IPTV signal and convert it to a video signal that can be displayed on the viewer's television. In addition, the STB provides the user interface that allows viewers to select the video programming to be viewed. To accomplish these tasks, the STB must contain the following functional elements:

- Network interface, to receive the IPTV signals and transmit user commands

- Video and audio outputs, which are connected to the viewer's video display and speaker system

- User interface, both on the front panel of the STB and by way of an on-screen display and remote control

The following features are often also provided in STBs

- *Conditional access* hardware/software, to support secure viewing of valuable content

- Hard disk drive, for recording video programs

In the following sections, we will discuss each of these elements in more detail.

## Network Interface

The network interface on the STB is normally a bi-directional Ethernet interface that allows IP traffic to flow into and out of the STB. IP packets flow through this interface, containing data such as encoded video information, user commands, device status information and other useful information. Typically, these flows are highly asymmetrical, with lots of data flowing into the STB and very few packets in the return direction.

Typically, the STB interface is not connected directly to a DSL or other type of line circuit, but rather to the home gateway that takes the DSL data and converts it into Ethernet. While this might seem somewhat wasteful, it provides several benefits. First, this removes the need to make different versions of the STB for different types of DSL or other data circuits—with a standard Ethernet interface, all STB connections can be the same. Also, from a safety and reliability standpoint, it is better to have the home gateway connected directly to the DSL or other circuit in a permanent, out-of-the-way location, rather that being part of a customer's furniture that may be moved from time to time.

Several new types of network interface are being considered for use in STBs. Wireless connections have a certain attraction, because they can eliminate the headache of connecting network cables; however, issues of speed, interference and dropped packets typically reduce the attractiveness of this solution, particularly with early generation technologies such as Wi-Fi. At least one large carrier in the U.S. is using *Home Phoneline Network Alliance* (HPNA) connections that utilize existing home telephone wiring, only at much high data speeds (100 megabits and up). This scheme has the advantage of eliminating the need for rewiring a home, but relatively few devices have been equipped to handle HPNA interfaces directly. Another alterative is power line networking; as this technology matures it may become interesting for use in video delivery around a house.

## Video and Audio Outputs

As consumer home theater systems continue to grow in popularity and complexity, the demands placed on the STB will grow apace. In addition to supplying clean, noise-free signals in a variety of formats and connectors, these connections can be the weak link in the content security chain unless they are constructed appropriately. A number of popular choices for these interfaces are illustrated in Figure 10.1.

## Analog RCA Jacks

A composite video signal contains all of the information required to form a full-motion, full-color image on a television screen. A composite signal is normally sent on a single coaxial cable between devices such as a videotape player and a television set. Standard RCA jacks, which are slide-on coaxial connectors, are often used in threes—a yellow connector for video, a red connector for right audio and a white connector for left audio.

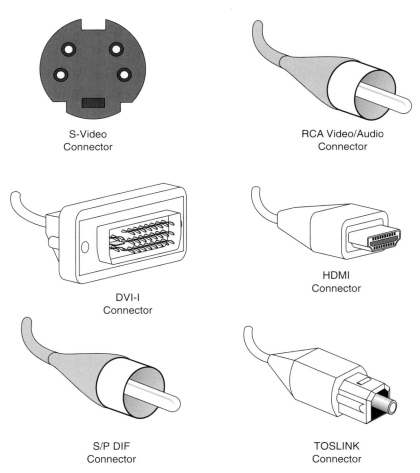

S-Video
Connector

RCA Video/Audio
Connector

DVI-I
Connector

HDMI
Connector

S/P DIF
Connector

TOSLINK
Connector

**FIGURE 10.1** *Popular connector styles for STB Video and Audio Outputs*

## S-Video

S-video signals are similar to composite video signals, with one crucial difference. In S-video, picture luminance and color information are carried on different wires. This is why an S-video cable has four pins: one pair for the chroma signal and another pair for the luma (plus an outer shield). Particularly for the digital STBs used in IPTV applications, S-video can deliver a higher quality image to the display by avoiding the step of combining the luminance and color information in the STB output and the step of separating those two signals again when they enter the display.

## Component Video

Component analog video offers benefits over composite and S-video. Because different color signals are carried on different sets of conductors, processing of the signals is kept to a minimum. YUV or YPbPr (also know as Y R-Y B-Y) component video signals use three signal paths: one for a luminance signal (Y) and one for each of two color difference signals (U and V or Pb and Pr).

## Component Colors

The Y signal contains information from all three color channels (red, green and blue) and is formed by combining different amounts of each color. The two color difference signals have the advantage of requiring less bandwidth than the Y signal, which is useful for reducing the signal bandwidths needed in digital video signals. RGB is another component video standard that uses one conductor for each of the three main video component signals: red, green and blue. Each signal carries a full resolution image, with data for every pixel. Most consumer video devices such as DVD players, projectors, and LCD and plasma displays use YPbPr.

## Digital Visual Interface

The *Digital Visual Interface* (DVI) connector can be used to carry digital or analog video signals and audio signals. DVI connectors are found on many computer monitors and video graphics cards, and for a while were used on some brands of STBs. Recently, this connector has been largely replaced with the HDMI connector (which appears to be significantly less expensive to manufacture), so DVI tends to be more often on found in computer, not home video applications.

## High-Definition Multimedia Interface

The *High-Definition Multimedia Interface* (HDMI) connector format can be used to carry digital video and audio signals. It builds on the DVI spec by adding digital audio capability to the same cable, but retains electrical compatibility to the DVI-Digital spec, so the possibility of changeover cables exists. HDMI appears to be the HD connection of choice for newer consumer televisions.

## High-Bandwidth Digital Content Protection Security

*High-Bandwidth Digital Content Protection* (HDCP) can be used on both DVI and HDMI interfaces to prevent unauthorized copying of HD digital video signals by encrypting the data for each pixel. This encryption happens on-the-fly in many types of devices that can generate HD content, including STBs, HD-DVD players and other sources. At the display device, the pixel data is decrypted and used to generate an image on a digital display, such as plasma, LCD and DLP projectors.

HDCP is normally implemented inside specialized chips in both the source and the display (Intel was one of the early developers of this technology). This makes it very difficult to remove or bypass this technology for making perfect copies of digital HD content. When an HDCP source is connected to an HDCP display, a handshake process takes place, resulting in an encryption key that can be used to encrypt the content in the source and decrypt it in the destination.

Broadcasters, DVD suppliers and other content owners have the ability to require that HDCP be in place in an operation before any true HD signals are delivered. If HDCP is not in place, then the source hardware may be restricted to only providing a degraded HD or even an SD output in place of the desired HD signal.

## Sony/Philips Digital Interface Format Audio

*Sony/Philips Digital Interface Format* (S/PDIF) is a widely used interface for carrying digital audio signals between different system components, such as from an STB to a home theater sound system. Because this interface has been standardized internationally (IEC 60958-3), it can be found on a huge number of different devices, including many STBs. This interface is used to carry uncompressed audio signals and can be physically implemented with either an RCA jack or a BNC.

## Fiber Optic Audio

A variation of the S/PDIF interface is an optical version that carries the same data, also known as a TOSLINK, which is a registered trademark of Toshiba. This connection, while not as common as the electrical S/PDIF interfaces, can be found on a significant number of high performance audio devices.

# User Interface

Beyond the physical presence of the STB exists the combination of software and hardware that provides the user interface, literally where the human is able to communicate with the machine. When this is poorly done, it can be a great annoyance to viewers; when created with skill and style, it can becomes so much a part of a viewer's experience that it becomes invisible.

Physically, the STB user interface consists of three main elements. First, the front of the STB may have a display and/or status lights that give basic information to the user, such as channel selection, time of day, power on/off status, etc. These indicators may be the only means of communicating with a user if the video display is not available; as such, they can be very important during the installation and setup process.

Second, some form of infrared remote control is used to allow the user to sit a comfortable distance away from the STB and issue commands to interact with the information being displayed on the display.

Third is the software that resides inside the STB and creates the menus and displays that support viewer interactions. The bulk of the user experience is focused on the latter two elements, so we will focus our discussion on them.

Many different functions need to be supported by the user remote and on-screen display. Here is a list of some of the basic functions that need to be provided:

- Device control, such as power, sound volume, input selection, etc.
- Channel selection and changing
- *Electronic Program Guide* display and navigation
- Access control, including parental control and secret PINs used to secure payment for some types of programming
- Basic interactivity, such as pause, rewind and fast-forward for on-demand content viewing
- Advanced interactivity, such as on-screen shopping or audience participation

In some cases, users can program the STB infrared remote device to control other devices in the audio/video setup, such as audio systems, DVD players and video displays. Care needs to be taken to balance the benefits of consolidating many functions into a single device against the need to add more buttons (and thereby complexity) to the remote control device.

## Conditional Access Hardware/Software

As discussed in Chapter 7, *conditional access* and *digital rights management* (CA/DRM) are very important to IPTV system operators. Without an effective CA/DRM system in place, it would be hard for operators to ensure that viewers are paying for the content they are viewing. It might even be impossible to obtain some types of content (Hollywood movies, for example), unless the owners of the content had confidence that their properties would be protected from unauthorized copying and distribution. The STB is one of the most important links in the CA/DRM system for IPTV operators.

Any security system depends on the capability to uniquely identify a user. In a system to verify the identity of a human, secret passwords, PINs and responses to security questions are often used. In the case of an IPTV system, the STB needs to play a similar role—the STB must be able to uniquely identify itself to the content delivery system and must also be in a position to safeguard the security of any content streamed through or stored within the device. Both hardware-based and software-based technologies have been successfully used for this purpose.

One of the most familiar hardware-based technologies is the smart card. These cards are called "smart" because they incorporate a processor and memory that can be used by a variety of applications. Each device that uses smart cards must be equipped with a smart card reader, usually in the form of a slot in one side of the STB into which the smart card is inserted. Of course, some system needs to be set up to distribute the cards to consumers, deactivate them when services are cancelled, and so forth.

Software-based technologies have also started to emerge that suppliers claim can provide the same (or higher) level of security as hardware-based systems. This consists of a specialized module of software code located in each STB that offers many of the same security capabilities as smart cards without requiring management of physical smart cards and associated reader hardware.

Software-based techniques seem to be winning some converts in the realm of IPTV service providers. This is due to the major logistics problems associated with hardware-based systems. Every smart card needs to be kept physically secure to prevent unauthorized parties from using stolen cards to obtain unauthorized services. In addition, if a smart card technology became compromised due to hackers, the service provider would be faced with the task of distributing thousands or even millions of new smart cards in order to re-secure their networks. In contrast, with a software-based system, new code could be downloaded from the central servers to each STB in the event of a security breach. Of course, no CA/DRM system is useful unless content owners are satisfied with the level of security provided, so any discussions of hardware versus software technology security need to include these parties.

# Hard Disk Drive

As in desktop and laptop computers, hard disk drives can be installed inside STBs to provide large amounts of digital storage. Of course, in an STB, this storage is going to be used for digital video content. With current compression technology, it is possible to store more than 100 hours of standard definition or more than 20 hours of high definition video content on a single disk drive. And, as disk technology continues to progress, even larger storage capacities will soon be available.

When it comes to deciding how the content gets recorded into this vast pool of storage, there are two schools of thought. The first school leaves it entirely up to the user to select programming to record, thereby making the disk a *PVR*. The second school uses the disk drive as a storage location for content that has been downloaded by the service provider to make it available to viewers, a service that has been called *push VOD*. Both of these concepts deserve a little more discussion.

PVRs (also known as DVRs) have become a very popular new device for consumers. Popularized in the U.S. under the brand name "TiVo," these devices record television programs in compressed digital form on hard disk drives for later viewing. Users program the units to record certain programs; an important function of the PVR is to provide a user-friendly way to select the programs to be recorded. Basic services simply show a list of upcoming programs and enable the user to choose the ones to record on a one-time or repetitive basis. More advanced services help viewers select programs by displaying recommendations similar to other programs that have been previously recorded by the viewer.

PVRs give viewers the ability to select when they want to watch each of their recorded items. Viewers are given VCR-like controls, so they can pause, rewind, fast-forward and skip commercials when they are playing the video back. This latter feature has caused a great deal of concern for advertisers, who not only fear commercial zapping but also worry about viewers not being exposed to their advertisements at the correct time (say, ads for a movie the night before a big release). How these issues impact broadcasters in the long run is a subject of much current concern and analysis.

Push VOD uses idle network bandwidth to deliver content to STBs that can be played back in the future by a viewer. This content can be free to viewers, distributed as a part of a paid service funded by viewer subscriptions or used to deliver content that viewers can purchase on a title-by-title basis. Since the service provider selects the programming to be pushed to the STBs, push VOD content is often restricted to a few popular titles, although these may be distributed without inserted commercials.

Push VOD is typically used by service providers with very restricted two-way capability in their networks, such as in the case of satellite and terrestrial over-the-air broadcasters. In IPTV applications, these types of network restrictions tend to be less prevalent, but push VOD can be used to help ease the burden on network bandwidth and centralized video servers for extremely popular VOD offerings or highly interactive content such as games.

# Middleware

Trying to define the term "middleware" is like try to define the term "beauty"—it is truly in the eye of the beholder. However, for our purposes, we will define middleware as software functions or services that link specific components (such as application servers, VOD servers and STBs) and application software (such as conditional access control, billing systems and interactive services).

Middleware also links client and server systems used for CA and DRM purposes. Because part of the function for these technologies is implemented on the STB while another part is implemented on a centralized server, a secure means of communication is needed between endpoints. This is an excellent role for middleware, because it is often designed to operate in the middle ground between STBs and central servers.

Middleware can be thought of as a form of operating system for both an STB and an IPTV system. In particular, there are a couple of standards that have been designed specifically to enable third-party developers to write applications for a generic STB, without having to adapt the code for each different type and manufacturer of STB in the marketplace. Two significant examples of a standard are *MhP* and *OCAP*, both of which will be the subject of a Reality Check at the end of this chapter.

## Understanding Middleware

Middleware is the glue that holds IPTV systems together. It provides mechanisms to accomplish many of the key tasks that must be performed to give users the ability to select and view programming and to support payment systems that drive revenue to the IPTV system operator. Here are some of the key functions often proved by middleware.

### User Identification

Keeping track of exactly which users are connected to which portions of the network is crucial for a number of reasons. First and foremost, the middleware system must be able to deliver video and audio content to the user who requested it. To accomplish this, the middleware system must be able to track which IP network connections are associated with each user.

## Screen Navigation Functions

Moving a cursor around in real time on the screen involves close coordination between the user's remote control, the STB's operating system and the application software driving the displayed image.

## Text and Menu Generation

Middleware will typically support mechanisms for managing a variety of different fonts and type styles that can, in turn, be used by other applications that interface with the middleware.

## Electronic Program Guide Primitives and Utilities

Creating a program guide can be quite complex for an IPTV system. Gathering all of the required data from broadcast sources, formatting it into a readable grid that the viewer can scroll through, and taking action once the desired content has been selected all require a significant amount of work. Middleware can provide support for some or all of these tasks and remove the need for the system operator to develop a different version of the program guide software for each different STB deployed in their network.

## Channel Changing

With IPTV, each time a new television channel is selected by a viewer, new and different data needs to be sent to the viewer's STB. This can require a whole sequence of events, such as leaving one multicast group and joining another at the DSLAM, or passing instructions through the DSLAM to the video serving office upstream of the DSLAM. Managing this process in a speedy and efficient manner is a sign of well-designed middleware.

## Back Office Integration

Middleware can also provide the link between different applications and the back office systems used by a service provider. Back office systems can include subscriber billing and management systems, installation and repair crew scheduling and tracking, VOD systems and more. Without a good middleware system to act as translator between these devices, it would be uneconomical to offer many advanced services that IPTV providers are using as market entry strategies.

## Interactivity

Middleware can be heavily involved with interactivity at all levels. Virtually any time a viewer presses a button on the remote control for an IPTV STB, middleware can take over. Even basic interactivity, such as channel changing, involves middleware. More sophisticated forms of interactivity also involve middleware, such as playback control (rewind, pause and fast-forward). Even content interactivity, such as voting on a talent contest, requires middleware to accept user votes from remote controls and change that data into a form that can be forwarded to the program provider to tally the votes.

## VOD Middleware Example

In the following example, we consider the process that must take place when a viewer decides to order a pay-per-view movie.

- First, the user must decide which content to view. This is normally achieved through the use of an EPG. The guide application needs to obtain data from the VOD server that indicates the titles available on the server, along with related data. This data might include the price, the length (in minutes) of the title, a synopsis, a list of the cast and possibly reviews or recommendations from either professional reviewers or from other subscribers. All this data needs to come from somewhere, and there is a significant chance that the data coming from different sources is in different formats. Middleware can help by providing conversion filters from different data formats into a common format that can be displayed on the screen. In addition, middleware can provide the proper protocols and handshakes to the other data sources to get the required information.

- Next, the user needs to navigate through the EPG and choose a program to watch. These tasks are supported by middleware in several ways. First, the middleware can take care of distributing the program guide data to all of the STBs in the service provider's network. Secondly, the middleware provides a clean interface for the software to create display elements needed to show the guide information. (Any former software designer knows the agonies of counting pixels on a display in order to create on-screen graphics.)

- Once the viewer starts to interact with the EPG, the middleware really gets a workout. Any information that flows between the central systems and the STBs will pass through the middleware, which will help to ensure that the information is delivered securely and reliably.

- When the user makes a selection of VOD content, the middleware plays an important role in the financial transaction. A query is made to the subscriber information database to determine if the viewer is permitted to order VOD content of the type selected. Once the reply is affirmative, the middleware system will send the appropriate information to the VOD server so playback to the proper IP address can begin. Also, a message must be sent to the billing system to record the transaction details to enable the proper fees to be collected from the viewer.

# STB Selection Issues

There are many different STBs on the market today offering a wide variety of features and functions. Here is a checklist of some of the items that service providers need to consider when selecting STB technology:

- Supported video output types: analog or digital? SD or HD? component or composite?

- Audio types: analog or digital? stereo or surround sound?

- Video compression standards: MPEG–2, MPEG–4, AVC or VC–1?

- DRM system: hardware-based (smart card) or software-based?

- Network interface: Ethernet, HPNA, Coax or Wi-Fi?

- Hard disk drive: present or not? PVR or push VOD?

- Middleware platform: MhP, OCAP or proprietary?

# Reality Check

The reality check for this chapter focuses on two very important standards for middleware. Both have been developed for applications other than IPTV, but because of their popularity and widespread adoption in the STB market, it is prudent to study these examples as they are likely to affect set top middleware development.

## MhP and OCAP

Both the MhP and OCAP standards have been developed by industry groups for STB middleware. The benefit of these standards is that they enable applications developers to write programs that will run on any STBs that support the MhP standard, thereby greatly increasing their target market. Similarly, system operators who deploy STBs that support MhP or OCAP gain access to a large selection of compatible applications.

Both MhP and OCAP require a fair amount of processing capacity in each STB. In particular, MhP requires a JAVA Virtual Machine on each STB, which requires a reasonable amount of processing power and memory. As a result, some of the older STBs with limited functionality may not be capable of supporting this technology.

Keep in mind that neither of these specifications is targeted directly at IPTV, but STBs with both technologies have been used in IPTV deployments. MhP was developed for the *Digital Video Broadcasting (DVB)* Project, focused primarily on terrestrial broadcasting and to some extent satellite broadcasting. MhP was developed with the European broadcast market in mind. OCAP was based on MhP, but it was developed to meet the needs of digital CATV providers in the U.S. Fortunately, many of the functions of the STB are the same regardless of the type of digital data link used to receive programming.

The work to develop MhP formally began in Europe in 1993 and was provided under the auspices of the DVB. Membership consists of companies involved in manufacturing, broadcasting, regulating and serving the television broadcast market. The aim of the group is to produce a series of standards that enable different devices to interoperate smoothly across national boundaries. In December 1997, the DVB formally approved the functional requirements for MhP, upon which subsequent standards were based. In May 2000, the MhP standards were approved and formally launched to the world that same year.

The path toward developing the OCAP standard was significantly quicker. In October 2001, CableLabs, a group based in the U.S. that develops standards and practices for the CATV industry, adopted MhP as the basis for OCAP.

# Summary

This chapter focused on a crucial component of any IPTV network—the STB. The STB is responsible for accepting IP packets that contain the video, audio and related digital content and producing signals that can be displayed on television sets and played through audio loudspeakers. The STB is also responsible for receiving and processing user commands and sending messages back to the central systems when action is required (say, for a channel change command).

Middleware also plays a key role in IPTV deployments. By enabling many of the key functions of an IPTV network, middleware can greatly simplify the deployment of a variety of advanced, integrated services. With the right platform combined with one or more compatible STB choices, service providers can readily offer the innovative, consumer-friendly services that consumers will be willing to pay for.

# 11 Internet Video Technologies

I see streaming media as the building blocks ... whether it's to deliver content to a cell phone wirelessly or to a set top box via IPTV.
—Dan Rayburn, *The Business of Streaming Media*

Throughout this book we have discussed the deployment of IPTV and explored various technical and business implications of broadband video in general. In this chapter, we'll review the ways that people are streaming video over the Web, including basic concepts and technology building blocks. We'll look at various forms of streaming, download and play as they relate to video portals, Webcasting, podcasting and video-blogging. We'll also take a look at the production workflow process running from capture to playout.

As the state of the art continues advancing quickly, delivering primetime broadcast-quality video over broadband is increasingly attractive to more and more organizations. "We're excited about IPTV," says Jeff Karnes, Director for Multimedia Search of Yahoo! "It opens up a new channel for us ... to expose online content onto the TV set and break the barrier between PC, TV, and other media devices."[1]

## The Corner Office View

"Video on PCs and iPods actually is expanding the audience for broadcast and cable programs," the study said, citing data that total TV usage was at an all-time high in U.S. households at 8 hours, 14 minutes a day during the 2005-2006 TV season.

CONTINUED ▶

---

1. *Interview, "The Changing Face of Video on the Internet", by Howard Greenfield, Euromedia Magazine, August, 2005*

---

CONTINUED ▶

The report by Nielsen Analytics, a unit of market research firm Nielsen, found that Internet broadband "expands the market for programming by offering the potential for watching shows at the office, and in non-traditional locations, such as coffee shops equipped with WiFi connections."

Moreover, the audience watching shows over broadband is highly attractive for advertisers, who spend about $70 billion a year on TV commercials.

"The broadband consumer is really the sweet spot for TV — younger, more affluent, better educated and tech savvy," Larry Gerbrandt, general manager and senior vice president of Nielsen Analytics, said in an interview.

— "Young, affluent viewers drawn to network TV shows on the Net"

USA Today, January 24, 2007

---

In this chapter we will discuss the different formats and building blocks of streaming Internet video, highlighting some of the differences between streaming video on the Internet and a true, managed IPTV broadcast quality offering. To characterize this, we'll look at further at the industry context for correlating these two worlds.

We've gotten an exposure to the various underpinnings of IPTV and Internet video, particularly in Chapter 2 ("IPTV versus Internet Video") and Chapter 4 ("Network Overviews"). There is a blur, sometimes a debate, between strict definitions of and distinctions between IPTV and streaming video. A couple of years ago, this was explored in a magazine article about the differences between streaming and IPTV:

IPTV is coming. Better place your orders now.

Wait, you might ask, doesn't it already exist? After all, "IP" (Internet Protocol) media has been streaming on the Web for more than a decade. Isn't any video stream on the Web arguably IPTV:

TV (video)

+ (delivered over)

IP (Internet Protocol)

= "IPTV"

Well, the current IPTV offering is characterized by a two-way digital broadcast signal, broadband and is set-top based, coming over switched telephone or cable networks. Because we already have streaming Internet video, what would change? And will the promise of increased user control or MPEG quality force the telecoms, ISPs and portal sites to build out this new platform in the next year?[2]

Speaking in more detail about the two types of IP video, Vincent Dureau, former CTO of OpenTV, (at Google during the time of this writing) says, "There are two markets: one is embryonic, TV content through Internet to PC." However, until recently, the TV audience has been limited because quality of service—the video experience—was poor. "When we take DSL through the Internet—even at 5 Mbps between the edge of network and the home—there are multiple hops between routers and so forth, typically yielding low quality."

This might suffice for some short newscast on demand, or BBC catch-up channels, but not for live broadcast. "What's more," Dureau adds, "there are rights issues to consider—but regardless, it's a marginal market, I think. The second offering is live content through a set top box via a dedicated backbone that goes direct to the network. Telecom operators are building these backbones," he says.[3]

But companies are benefiting from many other technologies and methods that offer highly effective ways to deliver video over the Web. Just because you have video packets flowing over an IP network doesn't make it IPTV. IPTV is a fully managed multichannel service, a replacement or direct substitute for cable or satellite, while Internet streaming comes in many forms such as Webcasting, video-blogging, and podcasting, and it plays an increasingly more dynamic communications role.

Internet streaming is the generic process of delivering video content to a browser for immediate display. Though different in nature from true IPTV, the many methods of streaming audio and video over IP networks represent important applications. Table 11.1 highlights some of the distinctions between streaming and IPTV. It provides a summary checklist that builds on what we've talked about in Chapter 2 and creates the reference point for a closer look we will take at Web streaming technologies now.

Users encounter video streaming more and more while surfing popular Web sites, such as YouTube and MySpace, for personalized clips and references to

2. From "The Changing Face of Video on the Internet", Euromedia Magazine, by Howard Greenfield, *Euromedia Magazine*, August, 2005

3. "The New European Broadband," *TVB Europe Magazine*, By Howard Greenfield, March 17, 2005

| | IPTV | STREAMING |
|---|---|---|
| Viewing | Primarily through television via STB | Through computer monitor (or television connected to PC) |
| Programming | Predominantly scheduled, linear programming, some on-demand options | Mainly on-demand programming access |
| Copyright | Most material copyright protected by production studios (e.g., "Friends," BBC News) | Most material is not copyright protected: user-generated or short prime time segments tolerated by broadcast networks for exposure |
| Main Networks (CBS, ITV, TF1) | Strong presence, influence in new channels and territory | Emerging presence |
| Delivery Network | Delivered over purpose-built IP network (bundled with cost of programming) | Provided over previously existing "bring your own" IP network |
| Payment | Convention and history of paying for content (subscription and advertising) | Tradition of "free stuff," strong reluctance to pay (smaller, but growing penetration of subscription or advertising) |
| Audience | Larger niche and mass audiences | Individual access–most viewers are watching different clips and features |
| Resolution | All video is full standard definition (480i/575i) or better; delivered in real time | Most video is below standard definition; if it is above SD, it is not usually delivered in real time |

**TABLE 11.1** *IPTV and Streaming Compared and Contrasted*

mainstream media. Other sites include CNN.com for news stories; sonypictures.com, warnerbros.com, and Disney.com for trailers of upcoming movies; and mtv.com or music.yahoo.com for music videos. In addition, a growing number of Web destinations offer actual television programming over the Internet, including researchchannel.com and Bloomberg television (at www.bloomberg.com/streams/video/LiveBTV200.asxx). These sites all provide users with full-motion and synchronized audio that can be played on a normal PC equipped with a suitable-speed Internet connection and the software necessary to receive, decode and display the video streams. The quality and variety of available Internet Video just keeps improving.

Web video streams are used increasingly for marketing, entertainment, training and communications. Its powerful visual capacity to engage new business audiences, educate and train, and also to provide multimedia social networking environments, is riveting. Let's look at some of the tools for deployment, and some of the practices for integrating video into Web sites.

# Types of Internet Streaming

There are several forms of video streaming. First, there is *true streaming,* in which the video signal arrives in real time and is displayed to the viewer immediately. With true streaming, a two-minute video takes two minutes to deliver to the viewer—not more, not less.

In *download and play,* a file containing compressed video/audio data is downloaded onto the user's device before playback begins. With download and play, a two-minute video could take 10 seconds to download on a fast network, or 10 minutes to download on a slow network.

Finally, *progressive download and play* is a hybrid of the two preceding technologies that tries to capture the benefits of both. Using this technique, the video program is broken up into small files, each of which is downloaded to the user's device during playback. With progressive download and play, a two-minute video might be broken up into 20 files, each six seconds long, that would be successively downloaded to the viewer's device before each file is scheduled to play.

## Streaming and Downloading

Another industry observer compares the uses of Internet streaming and downloading:'

> Streaming offers an instant experience to consumers used to immediate gratification and is ideal for promotional material. But because some broadband networks are not yet fast enough to stream full-screen quality video without periodic buffering and dropped connections, all content can't be delivered in this way.

CONTINUED ▶

CONTINUED ▶

Downloading content means that operators need to deploy software to users' PCs to manage the download process. These download managers also offer other useful functionality such as the ability to pre-book content for download or be able to view content when the user is offline.

All the platforms will emerge with a hybrid combination of streaming for shorts and promotional materials and live and simulcast, scheduled ahead of transmission; download for news programming and series; and download for high quality movies and other high value content.[4]

We'll look further at some of the respective advantages and disadvantages later in this chapter.

To understand the principles better, consider a simple analogy for true streaming versus download and play: the two options available for the supply of fuel used for home heating. One alternative is natural gas, which is piped by means of a distribution network that runs into each customer's home. Another alternative is fuel oil, which is delivered on a periodic basis to each customer's home.

A true streaming system is somewhat like the natural gas system—the fuel (content) is delivered at exactly the rate in which it is consumed, and no storage is present inside the consumer's home. A download and play system is like the fuel oil delivery system since each user must own and operate a large tank (disk drive) in which the fuel (content) is loaded periodically by a fuel supplier. If the natural gas supply becomes inadequate, the rate of gas delivery to each consumer can slow down, possibly causing difficulty in heating some customers' homes. With the fuel oil tank, once the delivery has taken place, customers have control over that fuel oil and can use it however they wish.

Another technology issue that can arise in attempting to deliver streaming video to a mass Internet audience is ensuring that nothing impedes or blocks stream transmission between the provider and the user. The many pros and cons of technical transport trade-offs that systems architects grapple with are important for

---

4. Fearghal Kelly, IBC Daily, October, 2006, http://www.ibc.org/cgi-bin/ibc_dailynews_cms.cgi?db_id=23291&issue=3

executives and decision-makers on the business side because they highlight the terrain in setting up a content business for primetime or Web time.

For instance, true streaming often uses *UDP* (User Datagram Protocol), a standard IP protocol, for sending a sequence of data packets. But firewalls tend to block UDP because it has security risks (packet sequences are not numbered, so packets can be maliciously inserted). Many network administrators therefore block UDP on their firewalls, which makes it difficult to get UDP streams consistently.

*TCP* (Transmission Control Protocol), which is utilized in most day-to-day Web surfing, makes it extremely difficult to insert malicious data into a stream. However, even TCP has some built-in behaviors that, while very effective for data transfer, are not well suited for real-time video transport.

Another important protocol designed for real-time multimedia applications, *RTP* (Real-time Transport Protocol), monitors packet delivery rates and critical thresholds and contains time-stamping and synchronization features. RTP operates in conjunction with UDP and can have similar problems with firewalls and system administrators.

## Webcasting: Going Live or Real-Time

During Webcasting, an entire audience accesses a linear stream at the same time, which may be live, or may come from a previously produced and stored file. That viewing audience can consist of a handful of people or thousands. Often used in sports, entertainment and marketing, Webcasting can also play a central role in a training or Webinar event.

Highly viewed Webcast events that are streamed, or *simulcast* live over the Web, such as Apple Computer's annual meetings, have always been the acid test for how well streaming video scales. User demand for a particular event has crashed the servers more than once. Victoria's Secret's live Webcast (1.5 million viewers in 1999) has become a legendary case study in viewer demand overwhelming capacity. Such a spike in simultaneous Webcast viewers online and streams required exposes whether the server's stream replication is robust enough to serve everyone. But technologies and strategies are improving.

Streaming service providers distinguish themselves in their ability to foresee and overcome these obstacles, providing server load balancing as well as security and live broadcast simulation to customers before the event.[5] We'll delve deeper into the dynamics of live Webcasting in the Content Workflow section later in this chapter.

---

5. Grateful acknowledgement to Rick Kolow, audiovideoWeb.com, November, 2006

# Streaming System Architecture

Streaming technologies have specific objectives, one of which is to deliver video over the Internet to a viewer through their PC Web browser or specific player application. Producing and deploying direct Internet streaming requires an infrastructure that includes a media server, network and media player application, as well as a content preparation process (see Figure 11.1). We'll examine the latter two aspects later in the chapter. Let's first review the role of the streaming server, which has the responsibility to reliably deliver the video for smooth, steady display as it is needed.

## The Streaming Server

The streaming server is responsible for distributing media streams to viewers. It takes media content that has been stored internally and creates a stream for each viewer request. This stream can be either *unicast* or *multicast* and can be controlled by a variety of mechanisms. Content storage and retrieval is one of the main functions of a streaming server. As we have mentioned before, when content is prepared, it is normally produced in a variety of compression ratios so users with different network connection speeds can select the video rate that they require.

For example, on many Web sites, the user is given a choice between playback speeds that are suitable for a dial-up connection (56 Kbps, sometimes called "low speed"), a medium-speed connection (100 Kbps, sometimes called "ISDN" speed), and

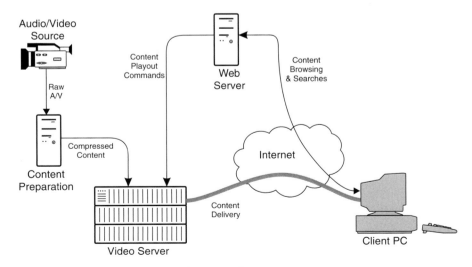

**FIGURE 11.1** *Architecture of a Typical Streaming System*

a high-speed connection (300 Kbps and up, sometimes called "broadband" or "ADSL/cable modem" speed). Each of these different playback speeds requires a different version of the content file to be created during the compression process. This means that one piece of content may be contained in many different files inside the server—one for each of the playback speed choices, and often others to handle different media player formats, which we'll discuss later in the chapter.

Other responsibilities of the server are to encrypt the packets in the outgoing stream, if required, and create well-behaved streams, meaning that the pace of the packets should be consistent. Finally, the server must be capable of accepting media player commands and changing the outbound stream appropriately, as well as be able to support hundreds or thousands of users by being part of a matrix of multiple load-balanced servers placed at different physical locations around the Internet. Needless to say, the ultimate maintenance and operational costs of the server networks and bandwidth charges are charged back to the content provider.

## Transport Network

Next there is the transport network between the server and the viewing device. Without delving extensively into network architecture, a few key points are good to keep in mind. Streaming servers supplying a number of simultaneous viewers require high-speed storage and network connections. For instance, a 2 GHz Pentium server could easily source enough simultaneous video streams to overwhelm a 1.5 Mbps T1 line several times over or put a serious dent in a 10BaseT Ethernet link. For large servers handling broadband streams, Gigabit Ethernet network interfaces are becoming common.

Typically, a streaming system will function better if some of the key IP network performance variables are controlled. One of the main parameters that affects streaming is the Packet Loss Ratio because if too many packets are lost, streaming performance will suffer. Another example includes delays such as Packet Delay Variation—critical because if a packet arrives too late, it can't be used in the playback, and End-to-End Delay, mostly important to ensure reliability in two-way conversation links.

As stated, the final key pieces are the media player application and content preparation, or workflow, which we'll look at further in a later section of this chapter.

## Streaming Applications: Media Players

What is a media player and why do we always have to be downloading some new software application or version update simply to play streaming media over the Web? Is it really that important? One historical answer to that question is the European Union's decision in 2004 to levy a 500-million Euro fine to one of the world's largest technology companies. The European Union's issue was with the company's "near monopoly" in bundling the media player with its ubiquitous operating system.

Even at that time, it was understood how big an influence media players would have on the future digital experience. In a contentious international lawsuit that pitted some of the world's largest software vendors against each other, one of the prevailing companies declared "a victory for consumers and the digital media industry [and] an opportunity for companies like RealNetworks to work more closely with PC manufacturers and OEMs."[6]

Why such a big deal about a commonplace PC application? First, the controversy stems from the media player application being the de facto interface to video and audio content at the junction of the three powerful, merging commercial domains of the PC, Internet and broadcast. Then there is the money factor: People are increasingly making credit card and PayPal purchases of music subscriptions, PPV videos and other e-commerce transactions through a media player interface or influence.

In a sense, the media player provider gains a measure of control over future commercial choices of the user (e.g., downloading music, subscribing to video services) by being the first to grab the user's attention with a rich interface displaying myriad content guides and subscription options. Media players are an important part of the user experience and gain commercial influence through first mover, ground floor sway over the user's choice of Internet content. The following applications are the dominant gatekeepers of Web surfer media content access.

## Player Software

Player software is responsible for accepting the incoming stream and converting it into an image that can be shown on the viewer's display. The performance of this software can have a major influence on how satisfied the user is with the streaming system overall.

Before streaming can begin, the user must select the content. This can be a complex process, because maintaining an accurate, up-to-date list of the available content can be a dynamic, daunting task. Unlike commercial broadcast networks, for most private streaming applications, the content supplier must maintain this list.

---

6. Dan Sheeran, RealNetworks' Senior Vice President, International, "From Technology to Content: The Real (Networks) Story", *Advanced Television*, by Howard Greenfield, September 2004

Typically, the list is presented to the user inside a Web page hosted on the streaming server, and the user simply clicks the appropriate link to begin content playback.

If the streaming server has encrypted the content, the player software needs to decrypt the incoming packets. This is a fairly simple process once the key is known. The keys can be obtained by communicating with the server or by connecting to a third-party authentication service.

The player software is also responsible for managing correct packet timing and a buffer that receives the incoming packets. Buffer underflows (too little data) and overflows (too much data) can severely impact the display of the stream, so the buffers need to be sized appropriately for the application. Overall, careful buffer design is a key factor in player success.

Since some streaming protocols, such as RTP, separate the audio and the video signals into two different streams, the player software is responsible for re-synchronizing the incoming streams. This is accomplished by looking at the time-stamp data contained in each stream and comparing it to the time-stamp data contained in the associated RTP overhead packets.

One of the most intensive jobs of the player software is to decompress the incoming signal and create an image for display. The amount of processing required varies depending on the size of the image and on the compression method. Older compression systems (such as MPEG–1) tend to be easier to decode than newer systems (such as MPEG–4) and therefore place less of a burden on the decoding device. Smaller images, with fewer pixels to process, are also easier to decode. Stand-alone devices, such as STBs, usually have hardware-based decoders and are generally restricted to a limited range of compression methods (primarily in the MPEG family).

Most recent-vintage PCs are also capable of running player software. This category includes desktop and laptop machines, as well as Windows-, Macintosh-, and Linux-based systems. It is also increasingly common to purchase hand-held devices capable of running player software.

# Commercial Players

A number of companies have developed video and audio player software that operates on personal computer platforms. All the major players will play content that has been encoded using standards such as MPEG and MP3, along with a variety of other proprietary and non-proprietary formats.

In these sections, we will discuss the three most popular players supplied by Apple Computer, Microsoft and RealNetworks and see how their technology works.

# Apple Computer

Apple Computer has been very active in developing a number of industry standards for streaming media and has made significant contributions to the realm of intellectual property in streaming standards. Many of these innovations center on *QuickTime*, which is Apple's name for its media streaming system. Apple provides free movie editing software (iMovie) as part of some software releases and sells a highly respected professional tool for editing movies called Final Cut Pro. The company has also actively embraced international standards, including MPEG–4.

QuickTime was originally created to support video clips that were stored on CDs and played back on personal computers. It has become a widely used format, with hundreds of millions of copies downloaded for both Windows and Macintosh PCs. Some of the best uses of QuickTime combine video, audio, animation and still images into a virtually seamless presentation to the viewer. A great many computer games and multimedia titles have been produced using QuickTime tools.

As in the other cases described previously, several different pieces of technology are used together to support QuickTime streaming. There are components for content preparation, streaming server management and various versions of player software. Like some of the other systems, content can be prepared and streamed on the same physical device, although system performance needs to be watched carefully to ensure that users will have their streams delivered smoothly.

For content owners and creators, Apple's use of standards can be a big positive. The QuickTime file format is the foundation for the MPEG–4 file format. The latest versions of QuickTime also use MPEG–4 compression technology. Apple provides players that work on both Windows and Macintosh PCs, and a version has even been designed for some Linux installations.

# Microsoft

Microsoft developed Windows Media Player to enable playback of video and audio files on PCs running Microsoft operating systems. Movie Maker is a free utility that enables users to capture video from camcorders and other devices and create finished movies that can be viewed with Windows Media Player. In addition, Microsoft has developed a number of file formats specifically to support streaming.

Several different file formats are commonly used for Windows Media content, including:

- Windows Advanced Systems Format File (.asf): A file format designed specifically for transport and storage of content intended for streaming applications.

- Windows Media Audio File (.wma): A file that contains audio signals encoded using the Windows Media Audio compression system and is in the ASF file format.

- Windows Media Video File (.wmv): A file that contains video and audio signals encoded using the Windows Media Video and Windows Media Audio compression system and is in the ASF file format.

Let's take a closer look at the ASF file format. Microsoft developed ASF and controls its destiny, in part due to patents on the fundamental stream format. ASF files can contain video, audio, text, Web pages and other types of data. Both live and pre-recorded streaming signals are supported. ASF can support image streams, which are still images intended to be presented at a specific time during play. ASF provides support for industry-standard time stamps and enables streams to be played beginning at times other than the start of the media file. Non-Microsoft encoders and decoders are supported inside ASF files; however, their data is treated as pure data and not supported by some of the nifty features that allow skipping forward and back in a stream—this task needs to be handled by specific user applications.

In addition to seeking standardization, Microsoft actively solicits hardware developers to create designs that support Windows Media at the chipset level. Presumably, this is to enable the creation of low-cost Windows Media players for embedded or cost-sensitive applications, such as STBs. Developers of hardware-based encoders are also active so real-time encoding can be performed on live video content. Moreover, attention is being paid to portable device manufacturers who would be able to install WM video and audio decoder functions in handheld devices once the costs are sufficiently reduced.

## RealNetworks

RealNetworks has long been a major innovator in multimedia players and servers. The company has developed a number of innovative compression techniques and has had its software deployed worldwide. RealNetworks offers a number of streaming-related products, including:

- RealPlayer: A version of player software for content encoded in RealAudio and RealVideo formats. A second version, caller RealOne Player, also has an integrated media browser and a provision for managing premium (paid subscription) content.

- Helix Servers: Server-side software that comes in a variety of models to handle streaming functions for hardware servers ranging from small, private streaming sites to large, professional sites that provide massive amounts of public content.

- RealProducer and Helix Producer: These take video and audio content and convert it into RealAudio and RealVideo formats for storage and playback to streaming clients. Note that these file formats support encryption so files can be protected when they are stored and while they are being transported over the Internet.

RealNetworks encoders and decoders employ advanced encoding techniques that compare favorably to other compression schemes such as MPEG–4 and Microsoft's Windows Media, at least according to test results provided by RealNetworks.[7]

Among the hallmarks of RealNetworks' advanced technology have been motion compensation and patented techniques for delivering compressed video streams using the following file format and extension naming conventions[8]:

- RealAudio clip (.ra): A clip that contains content audio encoded using the RealAudio format.

- RealMedia clip (.rm): A clip that contains audio and video content encoded with the RealVideo encoder. This type of clip can contain multiple streams, including both audio and video.

- RealVideo metafile (.ram or .rpm): The file that connects a Web page to one or more RealVideo or RealAudio clips. The metafile contains the address of one or more clips located on a server.

The fact that RealNetworks compression algorithms are private delivers both benefits and drawbacks to users. One benefit is the rapid pace of innovation for these products. While standards bodies serve an extremely critical function for the network as a whole, the due process rules can extend approval times for new compression methods into periods lasting several years. RealNetworks can develop and deploy new encoder/decoder technology more rapidly because standards bodies are not involved. This also drives another benefit, in that one company is responsible for both encoder (producer) and decoder (player) functions, so compatibility is assured.

One drawback of RealNetworks' proprietary stance is that the algorithms the company deploys are not accessible to third parties, so users are restricted to using

---

7. "RealVideo 10 Technical Overview" Version 1.0 by Neelesh Gokhale, RealNetworks 2003

8. Adapted from "Overview of RealVideo" located at http://service.real.com/help/videoccg/overview.html on April 12, 2004

software tools supplied by RealNetworks. Users who have operating systems less popular than those supplied by Microsoft and Apple can have trouble using these products. Also, since one company has to bear all of the development costs, the resources available for innovation might be smaller than what would be available if multiple firms were all developing products.

Finally, users with large libraries of content to encode may have some concerns about relying on a single company for all future support. Third-party editing and encoding software is available from a number of sources, but it is not at all unusual for these packages to be quite expensive, particularly for those that handle multiple users and have a rich feature set. On the other hand, it is good to note that RealNetworks offers free copies of limited-feature versions of its Producer software.

## Selecting a Streaming Format

All three of the streaming solutions discussed in this chapter (Real, Windows Media and QuickTime) deliver high-quality video and audio streams to the desktop. Because the market is competitive, these different formats are constantly being updated and upgraded to deliver more pleasing visual and audio results that require fewer and fewer bits.

When you are selecting a streaming format, popularity and previous adoption are important. It will pay off to prepare content for a platform that the target audience will have available. This does not necessarily mean the player that came with the operating system for the PC; all the three leading players have versions that work on both Windows and Macintosh PCs. The players are not interchangeable; a RealVideo stream needs to be played using a RealNetworks player, a Windows Media 10 stream needs to be played with a Windows Media player, etc.

Another important consideration is the version of the player that viewers will be using. If the video stream is created using the latest version of an encoder, but the viewer's player has not been upgraded, the video stream might not play. (This is true for some upgrades, but not all.) Of course, this can be remedied by having a user download and install a new version of the player. However, this may not please dial-up network users, who could face the daunting prospect of downloading a 5 to 10 MB file containing a player software update.

Many third-party content-processing solutions will produce output in multiple formats and at multiple stream speeds. These tools, including offerings from Adobe, Discreet, Avid's Pinnacle Division and others, enable the creation of a group of output files from a single source stream. One tool can be used to produce content simultaneously for, say, QuickTime and RealVideo, or all three different formats (plus many others, such as MPEG).

When you consider the number of different stream rates that might be required, it is easy to see a dozen or more different output files being created, each with a different combination of stream rate and player format. Many Web sites will list several combinations of stream format and bit rate, allowing users to select one that is compatible with their installed viewer software and network connection speed.

## Alternate Players and Plug-ins

At first glance, the difference between players and plug-ins seems straightforward enough. Whereas the media player is a separate application residing on the viewer's PC (as we discussed in Chapter 4), *plug-ins* are software stored on the viewer's PC that give additional functionality to their Web browser. Plug-ins enable the user to interact with more content types and perform transactions which the browser or HTML feature set do not inherently support. For example, an Adobe Acrobat Reader plug-in enables you to read PDF files within your browser. Software vendors supply plug-ins to enable users to access multimedia on the Web over their browser.

The twist is that media players themselves support their own plug-ins. For instance, WinAmp and MediaPlayer plug-ins can add local language menu support, sound effects, alarm clocks and other functions to a media player. Other important media player features include DRM to combat piracy and a tiered licensing model (free version with basic play/display and a premium version with additional features such as QuickTime Pro's full-screen display, editing and export capabilities.)

If most of the player software market to date has been dominated by the entrenched providers, there are alternatives. One example is WinAmp, freeware with a large user base (52 million monthly users in 2005). Many users develop new features for the product that are in turn made available to other WinAmp users.

At the time of writing, other media player offerings are in development. For example, SongBird is a free, multi-platform application built from Mozilla. One advantage is that it benefits from open-source community contributions. As one open community enthusiast gushes, "It's like taking iTunes, ripping out the music store, and replacing it with the rest of the Internet."[9]

---

9. Ross Karchner, http://rossnotes.com/archives/2006/10/01/playing-with-songbird/ – 2006

| | ADVANTAGES | DISADVANTAGES |
|---|---|---|
| True Streaming | Low delay; can support live content and doesn't require storage in display device. Supports true interactivity with server. | Trouble getting through firewalls, hard to do fast-forward and rewind (requires sophisticated interaction between client and server). Must remain connected to network for full duration of stream. |
| Download and Play | With a fast network, expedient way to obtain content; will work with most firewalls and standard settings (because video data appears as a file). | Doesn't support true interactivity with server; need to wait for all content to be delivered before you can start watching. Need enough storage to hold entire file. Can take a while for all content to arrive before playing. Content must be resident on user device before playback—potential security concern. |
| Progressive Download | Playback starts quicker. Avoids firewall problems (TCP/IP). Video file cached on user's PC for greater user control and management (fast-forward, rewind, etc.). | Content segmentation may not be supported by all media players. Can take up significant storage on end-user device. |
| Podcasting | Reaches mobile audience. Enables content to be played on device not connected to network. Doesn't require PC for playback. Excellent audio quality; can be delivered automatically upon subscription. | Limited screen size. Cannot interact with Web or PC content. |
| Video Blogging | Combines aspects of the above categories; flexible for powerful, personalized visual communications. | Production values often take second priority to real-time output; can have problems with firewalls, operational standards. |

**TABLE 11.2** *Streaming Summary Advantages and Disadvantages*

# Content Creation Workflows

Whether it's the summer family reunion at the coast, a European rugby match, or the new Jungle Bird primetime nature series, as the producer, what do you need to do to get content ready for Internet playout?

You've got to compress it, tag it so people can find it, and get it hosted on a server. You might also need to prepare the file for different formats, media players and download/resolution qualities. However, the more complete answer is that many different steps go into successful deployment. Although there is a difference between the types of video services that can be deployed over IP, there is a similarity in how most content must be created, managed and deployed for successful technical and commercial results.

Raw video generated by a camera or video recorded to tape is generally not well suited for streaming applications. Normally, the content needs to be processed to make it ready for streaming. To be utilized in a network production setting, video content must be digitized and compressed in various formats, indexed, tagged and distributed to meet various technical standards and performance requirements. There are benefits to getting this process right: 1) valuable, time-sensitive content is more available to internal and external audiences and 2) the content lifecycle is likely extended.

Scenarios for capturing and preparing content for viewing can be simple or intensive, depending on the goals of the users, their time constraints and budget allocations. The first step of this process involves aggregating the video from a contribution network that may consist of satellite, tape, live feed, VPN or Internet, and then ingesting, or digitizing, video that may include segmentation, metadata and storyboarding for later editing or preview. Figure 11.2 shows the content development process.

Along the way, storage, security and disaster recovery functions are implemented, after which a systems operator assigns user group access permissions to various internal production, marketing or advertising teams, as well as to the public. After any appropriate editing and formatting, the content is pushed to a server for download, streaming or playout.

As time goes by, production processes are increasingly influenced by new online video techniques and viewer expectations. Likewise, in addition to bandwidth aspects discussed in Chapter 9, content must be protected at each stage, from source to market, and tailored to evolving channels and distribution forms.

Moreover, many telcos and ISPs will need to build a network operations culture. Content programming networks are a brave, new world. As one executive put it, "Applying enterprise principles to carrier class problems is a recipe for disaster."

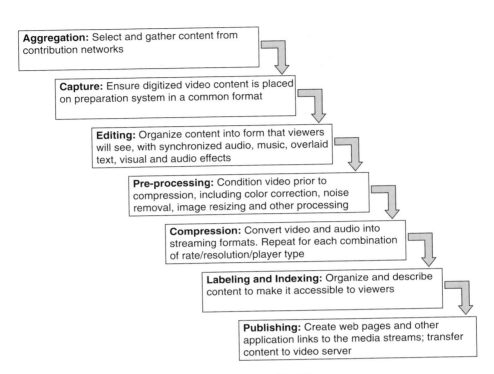

**FIGURE 11.2** *Streaming Content Creation Workflows*

Perhaps the most demanding instance of streaming is live Webcasting where media production and distribution must be fully reliable and fault-tolerant. Webcasting in real-time exposes the nitty-gritty audio-visual production issues, as discussed in *Webcasting* by Steve Mack and Dan Rayburn (Focal Press, 2006):

> Producing a Webcast is basically the same process as creating an on-demand streaming media file. Webcasting, however, is a little trickier because there is no room for error. Webcasts are produced in real-time; this affects each stage of the streaming media process. But with a little forethought and a lot of planning, a successful Webcast is well within your reach.

The Webcasting process is the same as creating on-demand streaming media files, with the important addition of a planning phase:

- Planning: Justifying the costs, securing the location, tools, and crew

- Production: Capturing the raw audio and video feeds, any other data types

- Encoding: Converting the raw media into formats that can be streamed

- Authoring: Connecting the audience to the Webcast via a link on a Web page

- Distribution: Securing the infrastructure to distribute the streams

Each phase has unique requirements during a Webcast. The most important thing to remember is that you only get one shot at a Webcast. If something goes wrong, the Webcast may grind to a halt if you haven't planned appropriately. Bearing this in mind, the planning phase becomes paramount, and the key to all other phases can be summed up in a single word: redundancy.

# User Scenarios: Turning Streams into Dollars and Influence

After analyzing the workflow, successfully applying the technology to the real world is what really counts. Whereas IPTV, as we have described it, pertains to professional broadcasting channels with budget and infrastructure to rival commercial television broadcasting, the versatility and effectiveness of streaming to niche audiences offers great advantages to smaller organizations. Some application examples are considered in the following section.

Video streaming is an ideal way to leverage the global reach of the Internet to *narrowcast*, that is, to broadcast to a specialized audience. These may be fly fishermen, digital signage point-of-purchase shoppers or clients of the new restaurant in town. Narrowcasting can potentially more easily, affordably and thoroughly reach these specific audiences. Let's take a brief look at some of the ways in which streaming video is being used today.

## Entertainment

Video over the Internet got a jump-start in the late 1990s with the availability of Hollywood movie previews on Web sites. No longer constrained to showing their wares on expensive television commercials or as coming attractions in theaters, movie studios began to reach out to the online community. At first, much of this content was set up for download and play, because very few home users had access to broadband connections that were suitable for high-quality streaming. One of the classics was the *Star Wars Episode I* trailer at a hefty 10.4 MB. It was released in March 1999, and, according to a press release, was downloaded 3.5 million times in its first five days of availability.[10]

---

10. A good source of movie information and trailers can be found at www.imdb.com, the Internet Movie Database

By the 2006, 68 percent of U.S. homes subscribed to a broadband service (cable modem, DSL, wireless or similar).[11] As a result, more and more content is available in streaming form. Today, a user can find a great deal of online movie trailers, music videos, animated shorts and adult content. A substantial portion of these are freely available, while many increasingly require payment of subscription fees.

## Corporate Video

Corporate video consists of content intended to improve the performance of an organization. We'll use the term "corporate" loosely here, because we want this term to apply to all types of public and private organizations, including government agencies, not-for-profit organizations and true private corporations.

Corporate video tends to focus on two areas: employee education and information sharing. Education can cover a wide range of topics, including training for new employees, instruction on new work procedures and equipment, job enrichment training and personal skills development, to name a few. Corporate executives use information sharing to make employees aware of corporate or organizational performance, to improve communication with employees and to deal with unusual challenges or opportunities. Sometimes the corporation produces this content strictly for internal consumption; other times, content is acquired from outside parties.

Live streaming is normally used for time-critical corporate video applications, such as company news distribution or executive speeches. Before streaming video became feasible, companies had gone to the expense of renting satellite time and deploying portable satellite receivers for special events. Permanent satellite systems have become popular with retail chains that have a large number of fixed locations with heavy needs for live video transmission, but this tends to be the exception rather than the rule. Today, high-quality streaming has made it possible to use corporate IP networks for this same function.

Many other forms of content are well suited to storage and subsequent on-demand streaming playback. For example, recorded training video material is very effective because it allows students to watch at their own pace; they can review material or skip ahead without disturbing other students.

Material can also be stored and played back at different times to meet the schedules of employees who work on different shifts or in different time zones, or those

---

11. Nielsen//NetRatings, March 14, 2006

who may have missed the original presentation. The server can also keep track of the number of times that each piece of content is viewed for royalty payment tracking. Contrast this with a download and play environment, where content gets dispatched to users around the network, thereby making accurate usage accounting difficult.

## Investor Relations

Since a wave of corporate scandals in the U.S. after 2000, treating investors equally has become a priority. Many companies decided to give both large and small investors the ability to participate in major corporate events. An increasingly popular way of accomplishing this is by using streaming video to transmit live meetings over the Internet. The content can also be recorded and played back on demand for users who were not able to watch the original live broadcast, or for those who wish to review what had transpired.

During live corporate video coverage, it is not unusual for several hundred simultaneous users or more to be connected. Multicasting (see Chapter 5) can be used to reach viewers located on properly equipped network segments. Typically, this applies only to private networks where multicasting can be enabled on the IP networking equipment. For users who are not connected to a suitable network, simulated multicasting can be used. With this technique, special servers are used to take a single incoming stream and produce multiple outgoing streams. This technology is particularly useful for investor relations uses, because it can scale up as more viewers connect by adding new server capacity as it is needed.

## Internet Radio and TV

A number of free and subscription services have appeared on the Internet to provide both audio and video content. There are literally thousands of Internet radio stations, due in part to the relatively low cost of equipment and the low bandwidth required. Internet television stations are much less common, but they are becoming more feasible as the number of users with broadband connections increases.

Video and audio streaming sites have been developed for a number of purposes, including corporate branding (free sites), advertising-supported (also free) and subs-cription (monthly or other periodic payment system). A huge variety of content is available, including newscasts, music, adult programming and entertainment. Because this material is organized similarly to a traditional radio or television broadcast, users are restricted to viewing the content in the order in which it is presented. It is not a content-on-demand service, where each user can watch in any order any content he or she chooses.

Much of this content is pre-recorded, so download and play technology is perfectly adequate. However, this can be somewhat disruptive to the flow of the broadcast, because each file must be downloaded before play can begin. (This technology is much more disruptive for video files than audio files, simply because video files are much larger and take much longer to download.) Progressive download greatly alleviates this problem, because playback of each new file of content can begin as soon as the first segment is downloaded to the PC. Of course, for live broadcasts, only streaming will do.

# Reality Check

Because there is a great attention being drawn to the use and impact of podcasting and independent video blogs, or *vlogs*, to reach niche audiences, we turn to those subjects for the focus of this chapter's Reality Check.

Some schools of industry thought consider podcasting and video blogging new, separate worlds of digital publishing unto themselves. For the focus of this book, because they both pertain directly to the IP video communications process, they are vital developments to consider in analyzing IP video transport.

## Podcasting

Content providers and audiences are being wooed in new ways. For example, podcasting has captivated listeners around the world in an emerging on-demand audio exchange—even though it's not yet clear exactly how it will be operated or monetized. Podcasting is online media publishing that enables producers to upload their content and listeners to download or subscribe to regular feeds that retrieve new files as they become available. The technique and terminology were validated when, in response to podcasting's sudden prevalence, the New Oxford American Dictionary named it *Word of the Year* in 2005.

Podcasting's power of syndication means you can upload your podcast with an XML Web publication file using RSS (Really Simple Syndication) which enables other Web users to subscribe to content feeds of their choice. The RSS reader in the subscriber's application (e.g., browser) looks on the Web for new publications and automatically downloads them to subscribers.

Thanks to podcasting's low cost of entry, anyone aspiring to produce and host their DJ radio talk show, broadcast garage band music demos or issue new corporate

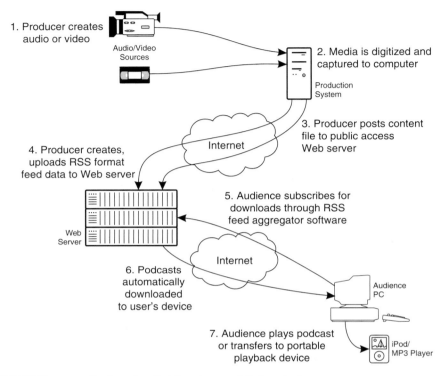

**FIGURE 11.3**  *Podcasting Publication and Subscription*

communications can post files of their recordings and make them available to a world audience on the Web. But when the technical team presents online strategies to the CEO, eager to launch to the world over IPTV, should podcasting be included in that evaluation? The criteria should be whether it will generate results—which makes podcasting a contender. So, here are some podcasting characteristics to consider for push or pull publication of audio and video:

- Subscriber or download based options

- Syndication feed compliance

- Supports user interface for interaction other Web content and e-commerce

- To date, typically audio-centric, but as MP3 players and other mobile devices increasingly gain ability to support video file standards and display, also becoming a video medium

A newsworthy 2006 case study is the decision by the CEO of chip manufacturing giant National Semiconductor to equip all 1,600 of its employees with 30 GB iPods. As corporate training and communications tools, they believe there will be benefits from the investment that will "create more value for customers."

## Video Blogging

Video blogging (vlogging) is not so much about technology as it is about the powerful reach of a new video publishing medium. Aggregation portals serve as video blog vehicles, but the pioneers creating the buzz are the independent blogosphere portals bringing news and viewpoint. Video blogging employs video documentary, interview, podcasting, journalism, diary, and streaming. Its reason for being is immediacy: getting a point of view out to the world quickly and emphatically—maybe even scooping the press establishment.

A video blog is recognizable by attributes such as:

- Timely, video-based information or reporting
- Interactive features for audience comment/contribution
- Commentary/point of view
- Relevant, associated links
- Syndication and aggregator friendly

The future of vlogging is bound up with that of grass roots media journalism. As non-news-professionals continue to contribute as sources of fuller, more varied news coverage, what we see today is a "pale imitation of what we'll be able to do as the tools become more sophisticated" says veteran journalist and ground-breaking blog pioneer, Dan Gilmore, author of *We the Media*.

Gilmore sees the addition of audio, video and animation to text blogs as a no-brainer. "But it's taken some time for these mediums to become part of the blogging toolkit. Bandwidth (or lack thereof) is the main reason," he says (as we discussed in Chapter 9). However, "As networks improve," concludes Gilmore, "we can take for granted that what technologists call 'rich media' formats will infiltrate."

The future shape of podcasting and vlogging is yet to be determined. But with the popular adoption of cheaper, easier content production tools for Web, broadcast and portable devices, people's media and news-gathering is guaranteed to figure significantly into IP video publishing.

# Summary

In this chapter, we have taken a much closer look at the variety of Internet Video technologies that offer a public universe of content delivery as an alternative to managed, billable, broadcast quality IPTV networks under development around the world. In addition to discussing varying views on the contrasts between IPTV and Internet Video streaming, we have looked at the basic end-to-end topology of streaming architectures that can be developed and deployed by enterprises or individuals that don't have the budget, staff or motivation to launch a full scale broadcast quality channel.

Of the many ways to stream over the Internet, there are significant variations in the respective benefits to true streaming, download, and progressive download and play. Though this book is designed as an executive briefing, it has taken the initiative to delve into some of the technology layers, such as RTP, TCP and UDP transport to expose why the investment of time and resources in streaming applications require skillful planning by technical and marketing teams to ensure the best end results.

We have also looked at media players offered by the mainstream industry software vendors and alternatives from the open source community, as well as detailed the primary elements or steps in the capture and preparation of video content for audiences. Lastly, we examined some of the main application domains where Internet Video is being applied, and some of the experiences of organizations seeking to exploit the power of visual interactive narrowcasting to their respective constituencies.

# 12 The Future of IP Video

We just want to get to the point where you will put video on your Web site as a default behavior.

—Peter Chane, Google Video

## The IPTV Story So Far

Communications networks are on the move. This final chapter highlights important trends for managers and business leaders navigating the emerging environment. The focus will be on an array of global technical and business developments forging a path for video transport over IP. We begin by reviewing advanced technologies that are steadily becoming mainstream offerings.

Throughout this book we have examined technical and business drivers behind IP Video that are sparking new service delivery models around the world. Perhaps this chapter might be better titled after IBM's report proclaiming that it's "the end of TV as we know it".[1] End or beginning, the changing IP landscape is rapidly becoming a more versatile framework for TV programming over both the public Internet and privately managed networks.

## The Corner Office View

"[Apple is] going to make the concept of connecting the TV to your PC a desirable concept. They are going to do wonderfully in creating this marketplace. People don't know you can do this today and even if they do know, it's too complicated . . . [Apple] will

CONTINUED ▶

---

1. www-935.ibm.com/services/us/index.wss/ibvstudy/imc/a1023172? cntxt=a1000062

CONTINUED ▶

deliver the best optimized and user-friendly solution within their closed environment . . . What we're trying to do is to go beyond that."
—Eric Kim, Intel's SVP and GM, Digital Home Group, "Intel IPTV exec sounds off"[2]

IP is an enabler. Its powerful abilities to control packets and manage services over the network, as we explored in Chapter 5, is why it serves as the foundation for so many streams, channels and devices rapidly evolving into end-to-end businesses. Examining the mechanics of video transport in earlier chapters, we have seen how the union of adequate bandwidth, DSL to the consumer and STB functionality is combining to stream video to viewers in a manner that could not be achieved until this time.

Like the social, collaborative Web 2.0 environment, other breakthroughs in compression, security and server scalability are contributing to next generation video. Call it Video 2.0 (or 3.0) or call it what you will—it means quadruple play offerings, ubiquitous access and interactivity ahead.

True, today your computer helps you google for information while your TV just sits there displaying channels. But video consumers operate increasingly at the heart of their own content kingdom, with home-page-like EPGs and timeless PVR storage access on its way.

Nonetheless, don't be deceived that sweeping change automatically generates winning products and market traction. "Early adopters may want to play around with new services" as one analyst puts it, "but most users just want to turn on the TV and sit back and be entertained." Will they ultimately pay more for *sit back* or *lean forward* modes of consumption?[3]

Ultimately, it will require creativity to combine the new narrowcast and traditional broadcast models, and it will take business acumen to convert existing voice/data customer relationships to new services while reducing customer churn. In the wake, revenues and capex will increase into multi-billion dollar markets.[4] We next look at this and other business drivers behind these expectations.

---

2. www.bit-tech.net, September 12, 2006

3. Deepa Iyer from "IPTV promise meets reality," C/NET, 2006

4. Infonetics, www.iptv-news.com/content/view/833/64/

# Business Drivers

The impact of more IPTV technology advancements on new service offerings shows no signs of slowing down. Exhilarating and bewildering at the same time, the myriad new features, devices, standards and initiatives are not easy to track. There is so much hype surrounding the next killer app that it brings to mind W.C. Fields' remark that "a thing worth having is a thing worth cheating for."

We spoke about business models in Chapter 3. Distinguishing the attention-grabbers from the money-makers will be key. "It may be cool, but is it a business?" asked Hearst-Argyle Television EVP Terry Mackin at NAB 2006. "The test becomes how do I turn this into a complete business, and what is the revenue strategy?" addressing the issues around turning content into cash. In this respect, other matters to address are:

- Settling licensing and distribution rights

- Solving piracy and copyright infringement

- Monetizing new, unproven services

There are many signs that analysts and trend watchers focus on when it comes to products and revenue. Two chief indicators are infrastructure commitment (investment) by operators and large, strategic acquisitions.

The proof that IP video business transformation is gaining momentum is the massive multi-billion dollar investment by telcos world wide in new networks and infrastructure. The daily business headlines are indicative of the change—and the risk/reward: "Phone Carriers Set Sights on Cable Television's Turf," declares the *Los Angeles Times* in December 2005. "The competitive landscape is shifting," according to Theodore Henderson, cable industry analyst with Stifel, Nicolaus Co. "That's why folks are cautious about telephone, cable and satellite stocks," Henderson goes on to say. "If you look at them, Wall Street is saying there isn't going to be a winner."

In addition to the financial outlay telcos boast about pouring into DSL and fiber networks to the home, other growth evidence is in the form of deals. This second business driver is a surge in large organizations financially angling for industry position. Among them, several come to mind, also referenced briefly in previous chapters. The first, eBay's $2.6 billion acquisition of VoIP leader Skype was a shot across the bow of telcos declaring change afoot: cash cow phone line and long distance revenues are going into decline. This one transaction set the stage for many new applications, including click-to-talk e-commerce sales functionality. It also represented a new alignment of two entrenched economic forces: retailing and telephony.

Other business driver events signaling the same changing of the guard are:

- News Corp's purchase of Intermix Media for $580 million, which included social media networking icon MySpace, a giant step for old guard broadcast into next wave Internet business.

- Adobe Systems' acquisition of Web development giant Macromedia in 2005 for $3.6 billion may have seemed like a software play. However, as an IP video business driver, bringing star products Flash, Dreamweaver and Adobe production under one roof, the union created further critical mass development focus on new HTML, video and animation production tools that cross the traditional boundary between broadcast and data networks. Winner of the 2006 Technical and Engineering Emmy Award from the National Academy of Television Arts and Sciences for its Flash® video technology, the company emphasized their role in how broadcasters deliver content and reach new audiences.[5]

- Google's impressive, if not over-reported acquisition of user-generated video portal YouTube. "This may sound like heresy for Google" says Google co-founder Sergey Brin explaining $1.65 billion outlay to gain higher ground in online video portals, "but search isn't always the best way to learn things. If you want to learn a sport or learn how to build a house, video is the best way to do that."[6]

To some, a new media market is opening up, while to others, gains from the next generation of video technology are merely today's revenues in tomorrow's wrapper. But leading analysts and integrators are doing the math and talking bullish about momentum ahead. Projecting a trillion dollar IP market may seem a little overboard. But consider some trends, starting with the fact that a billion people are already connected to the Internet world-wide.

In the U.S. alone, one-third of all households are online and that number is expected to double by 2010. By early 2006, Apple Computer had reported more than a billion legal iTunes downloads and more than 15 million video downloads (projected to grow to a $5 billion business in the next eight years). Likewise, according to Deloitte, IPTV subscribers will grow from 1.9 million in 2004 to more than 25 million by 2008. Finally, of two billion cell phones in use worldwide, 236 million already contain 3G video-enabled playback. Online advertising will reach $26 billion by 2010, and VoIP revenues are projected to reach nearly $7 billion by 2009.[7]

---

5. Adobe Systems, www.adobe.com/aboutadobe/pressroom/pressreleases/200611/110206 Emmy.html

6. www.lightreading.com/document.asp?doc_id=107860

7. "Trillion Dollar Challenge/Bounty", Deloitte, April 2006

That's enough statistics. By most accounts, this is a clear high-growth outlook. Other business drivers already discussed include increasingly commonplace time-shifting PVRs that make custom content more widely available and attractive. Viewers get their video when they want and can also have portable media to go, as we'll examine later in this chapter.

The future of television is about participation, as many of today's broadcast executives are beginning to understand and impart. Programming is becoming increasingly controllable through links to Web content—sport stats, cooking tips, election analyses and so on. But are we there yet? As one blogger recently put it, "There is no doubt in my mind that IPTV will prevail. I just hope it follows a shorter, faster path than VoIP to my living room."[8]

## Advanced Technology

If you had to pick the hottest 21st century innovation to date, it would be hard to find a better case in point than IPTV and Internet Video. The new service standard may be years in the unfolding, but industry executives around the world believe we have embarked on one of the most complex, exciting periods for the industry "When you move into the wired phase, the on-demand phase, what actually happens?" asks John Varney, former BBC chief technical officer. "We're not seeing a set of behaviors that would suggest we understand this yet—which makes it possibly the most fascinating phase in broadcasting history."[9]

But distinguishing the next breakthrough from the next red herring means sifting through design questions and benchmarking everything from network speed to market coverage, from device compatibility to quality of service. Part project management, part futurology, devising a strategy and executing successfully is a combination of calculated risk and smart investment of resources and budget.

For the present, assessments of an industry taking steps forward and backward are common:

> With some notable exceptions like France, Italy and parts of Asia, IPTV has been stalled by a combination of slow-to-arrive chipsets and STBs and delays to Microsoft's IPTV solution at several of the biggest telcos, including AT&T, BT and Swisscom. However, Ed Allfrey, senior solutions architect at Tandberg Television, reminded the audience that IPTV is not "just a telco thing," citing BSkyB's recent move to buy an ISP in the UK.

---

8. TekTidbits, www.tektidbits.com/2006/11/iptv_the_future.html, November 2006

9. "Broadcast's New Media Course," TVB-Europe, July 2005, Greenfield

IPTV subscribers will continue to grow from about 6.5 million subscribers at the end of this year to nearly 37 million by 2010. But there will be wild differences among countries depending on their competitive landscape, said Graeme Packman, principal consultant at Understanding Solutions, who predicted it will be a "long time" before financial success comes to most IPTV rollouts. By 2010, he predicted IPTV revenues will be $4 billion, or about 10 percent of total projected pay-TV revenues of $42 billion.[10]

Pressure on operators to increase DSL performance to the consumer will continue. Increasing network capacity and reducing channel change time to emulate conventional TV will put push providers to hit performance targets and eliminate latency. Some companies are already looking beyond ADSL2+ for added bandwidth to provide more services to each customer. There's no magic solution yet for HD to multiple televisions in a home, but VDSL2 is one promising standard, and innovation will continue in this area.

Today's operators seek the most advanced network that melds TV, PC and STB-based IPTV with zero latency access to everything: on-demand, primetime programming; user-generated Internet Video; DIY channels; interactive services; and portable, wireless access.

Will tomorrow's winning network architecture be hybrid IP, TV and mobile? The building blocks are improving: real-time H.264, MPEG–4 AVC Encoding, RTP and RTSP protocol, STB-on-a-chip, CPU+ DSP decoding, and 802.11g Wi-Fi. But are these sufficient to meet performance requirements and deliver economies of scale? Let's consider some of the anticipation surrounding what's ahead.

# Great Expectations

New ways to navigate, collaborate and interact with content are the hallmarks of tomorrow's television. That may be what's expected, but it will likely evolve and combine with today's conventions and viewing habits.

## Everything-On-Demand: Free and Billable

As we have discussed earlier, one vision of the future is EOD-oriented (everything-on-demand), delivered via VOD, PVRs, online access, DVDs, mobile devices and

---

10.  Bulkley, IBC Daily News, 2006.

more. TV is becoming a when-you-want-it experience. Or, as William Randolph Hearst III puts it, "Appointment-based television is dead."[11]

The consumer's history of getting content for free from broadcast TV, and perhaps even more so from the Internet, have created great expectations for whatever they want, whenever they want it, and eventually, wherever they want it. We looked at payment methods in Chapter 3 and some of the economics of the programming business. The effect of time-shifting, ad-zapping PVRs has not eluded the advertising industry anxious to protect a multi-billion dollar TV advertising revenue stream.

But "advertising change happens at the speed of molasses," says Rory Sutherland, Vice-Chairman OgilvyOne, who believes essentially nothing in advertising changed between the 50s and the advent of the Internet. However, new media makes possible a new kind of brand and requires a 21st century business model, according to Sutherland and other colleagues.[12] As a harbinger we have already begun to see advertising on the Web masquerading as entertainment, such as the 2006 Smirnoff Tea Partay ad campaign and Raw Tea Records (www.teapartay.com).

Internet TV ad spending is on an upward arc, with online video market poised for blistering growth over the next few years. Spending is expected to triple in the next few years. Media companies are reorganizing themselves around the concept of multi-platform content because video now reaches across television, computers, cell phones and iPods. This, according to others at Ogilvy, means "media companies must worry about how to monetize this content on multiple screens, while agencies only need ensure that our marketing messages reach consumers on these platforms."[13] The way forward therefore unites advertisers and content providers in creating new content for multiple devices.

Today, DVD mail rental services like Netflix and Blockbuster provide movie-watchers with unprecedented access and variety, but will they be superseded by next-generation IPTV delivery? In the traditional continuum of "rent, buy, subscribe" payment methods, watch for flexibility ahead: multi-tiered payment options, a broader range of niche content and interactive incentives (such as "buy this," "vote on that" or "get a free sample.").

Demographically targeted advertising is also the future. Custom advertising by new ad scientists will train its sights on fragmenting age, culture, economic and

---

11. William Randolph Hearst III, partner, Kleiner Perkins Caufield & Byers, *New York Times*, January 2, 2006

12. Rory Sutherland, Vice-Chairman OgilvyOne, BT Global Summit, September 2006

13. Maria Mandel, OgilvyInteractive, August 2006

geographic sub-groups, and viewing constituencies. Why? To learn more of what they want and to customize ads through the feedback loop: "On the Internet, marketers love their dashboards, their control panels, the ability to see results and to make changes based on those results" according to Seth Haberman, CEO Visible World. "When you look at offline advertising research, it's like going to the morgue," says Haberman. "They cut the guy open and tell you why he died. But that's worthless unless you can make a change. The real opportunity is in coordination and feedback."[14]

## Channels for All

"The next big thing is small."

—Seth Godin, Author, *Small is the New Big*

Is tomorrow's economy based on mass audiences or many niche markets? Because the Internet often surpasses the reach, effectiveness and budget benefits of traditional broadcast and marketing campaigns, aspiring content providers have spotted a new online TV opportunity to get their message out. Maybe you're an independent music video production company, a regional tourist board or a budding news and entertainment broadcaster trying to grow your audience without depleting next year's operating budget. More and more IP video solutions enable you to create your own channel without breaking the bank.

Streaming providers enable you to do what previously was only within reach of large corporate marketing budgets, by providing the technical talent and infrastructure to produce and deploy programming over the Web. Streaming media providers offer advantages such as:

- Global audience reach

- Live Webcasting

- Ability to create pay-per-view content options

- Podcast replication capability

- Load-balanced delivery for surges in audience size

- Archiving and DRM

- Advice on what works in the new Webcast medium

---

14. *Wired Magazine*, February 2006

This approach enables commercial companies and non-profits alike to operate in a new mode: "thinking vertically and interacting globally with people that really need to get the information".[15]

Some companies can host their own video portal, uploading content for streaming ad hoc, but most are novices at video and multimedia Web production and may lack the time, skills and talent to be successful. This is especially true as some seek improved broadcast quality—their own IPTV channel. IPTV channel services will let smaller enterprises or new product developers broadcast to the world.

The approach replicates what the consumer would experience at home using their remote control and TV—with similar quality to what you would expect from a satellite or cable provider. These end-to-end service providers run fully managed Internet channels with compression technologies that display on the television. Other services include billing and customer relationship management. Content companies reach a target audience and reach the world. Different from traditional cable services, users can plug their STB into the Internet from anywhere in the world and access their content.[16]

These and other broadband channel solutions continue to create new options for communicating through this medium. YouTube, Yahoo! and others offer even more user-friendly ways to click and upload videos for universal access. What, then, is a channel? ABC, BBC, NTV? Maybe it's just simpler to say that "a channel is a series of videos from the same source or user."[17]

# Portable Media: IPTV to Mobile Devices

ABI Research reported in 2006 that more than 250 million people worldwide will be watching mobile video by 2010, generating $27 billion in sales. But is portable streaming finally ready for prime time? The social debate continues over people's interest in watching TV on tiny two-inch screens. But there are more than two billion cell phones in use worldwide, hundreds of millions already equipped with 3G and other technologies enabling video playback, and there are expanding wireless content portals and production improvements.

---

15. Dave Gardy, www.tvworldwide.com

16. www.neulion.com/—example custom IPTV provider

17. video.yahoo.com/video/

The world's leading broadcasters are entering the fray as mobile phone and PDA providers ready new video-enabled hand-held devices. Start-ups are springing up to deliver a variety of mobile video programming, search, audio, radio and advertising models. MobiTV, which received a $100 million investment to continue its momentum in aggregating programming and operating mobile broadcast service, is already looking ahead to strengthening its market lead and research and development in areas such as WiMAX.

When the CEO of MobiTV is asked what's attracting an audience to the small screen, there's little hesitation that it's across the board interest:

CNBC *On The Money*: "What's the thing that people most want to see on their phone right now?"

MobiTV: "We're seeing broad usage across entertainment content, the 'time fillers,' as well as the breaking news events and sports scores. So, really there's something for everybody."

The attraction of portable media is individual access to watch or listen to your choice of content. "You may be on the east coast and want to watch the [San Francisco] Giants game that's not available to you when you're out and about" says Matt Crowley, Senior Manager Multimedia Products, Palm, Inc. "It's really about getting access to the content you care about when and where you want to."[18]

## Valuation of a New Network

Networks have a reputation for becoming increasingly valuable as more customers join the service. This is particularly true for wireless services where the more customers on the network, the more people there are to talk to and reach for business, personal, medical, educational purposes, etc. The Metcalfe Law of increasing returns to scale captures this very well. It posits that the value of a network increases exponentially with the number of nodes. Just as fax machines became a business necessity once most companies used them, broadcast networks are more valuable to broadcasters when there are more viewers: advertisers will pay more to sponsor highly viewed content. The same holds for portable video devices, but issues remain for creating a viable service.

---

18. Streaming Media 2006, San Jose, California

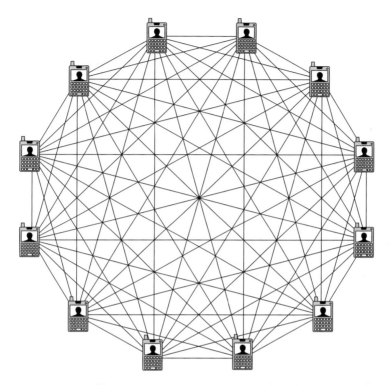

**FIGURE 12.1** *Metcalfe's Law: Increasing Returns Of Scale As Networks Grow*

## Mobile: Crossing the Technical Chasm

To date, monetizing small-screen, walk-about video has been slow to go mainstream because of technical issues such as rights-management, billing and interactivity (such as sharing videos and collaboration). Then there are human factor design issues in creating a new user interface, EPG, input-output control and so on. Finally, custom creation of effective mini-screen content, real-time and multi-platform version production requirements must also be tackled.

Some of the technology issues are:

- Finding the most viable model for content consumption (e.g., incentives to adopting a new medium and interface, and "downloads or streams?")

- Tradeoffs between 4G, WiMax and Wi-Fi network deployments

- Standards such as DVB-H (Digital Video Broadcasting-Handheld)

- Integration with GPS and with Bluetooth for control of home security, services, devices, etc.

- Battery charging (screen display, potential WiMAX demands)

Another technical issue that will be key to mobile media profitability is finding intelligent ways to provide and manage adequate broadcast bandwidth—and then price services attractively enough to attract consumers.

The mobile chasm is not just a technical one. "We're still learning how people are consuming [small screen mobile] video," says Kai Johansson, CTO, MobiTV. The biggest industry mistake could be believing that you can just move video from standard home display to small screen mobile device and people will watch. "That's just not the case" says Johansson. "Everyone has a different idea of what the mobile killer application will be, but I don't think anyone really knows, because there isn't big penetration yet. But it's coming!"[19]

## 2021: Holding It All in Your Hand

Nonetheless, executives have scouts on the new market trail for portable, mobile media. This may be driven by a new generation of *millennials* born after 2000, more likely to embrace the convenience a new breed of mobile device and functionality.[20] Another way to put it, writes *IPTVi Magazine* publisher Nick Snow regarding next generation media adoption, "Success will rest on the outcome of that other never-ending debate: is successful TV a passive pursuit or an active engagement. I'm guessing it's a generation thing."[21]

In addition to providing hand-held sports, news and dramatic mobisodes, the fruits of data storage will also be driven by an extraordinary continued price/performance improvement arc. Like *Dick Tracy* or *Star Wars* science fiction déjà vu, we will have visual content and communications wherever we go. With disk drive storage capacity doubling approximately every 18 months, current 3.5 inch drive capacity is projected to reach a terabyte by 2009. It is foreseeable that by 2015, that will grow to 16 TB (all the music that was ever recorded), and by 2021, to 256 TB (640,000 hours of video, or all the video and audio ever created up until now for movies and television— 73 years of continuous viewing).

---

19. Streaming Media 2006, San Jose, California

20. Anne Sweeney, Disney-ABC, "Monetizing New Distribution Platforms", April 2006

21. *IPTVi Magazine,* September 2006

The business potential is convincing. Will there be time for a strategy, given the speed of product and market change? In typical ready, fire, aim fashion, the technology industry answer seems to be experimenting our way into the future. "We're basically 'trying everything,'" says Larry Kramer, president of CBS Digital Media. "We're trying to put all our entertainment content on as many platforms as we can, to see how consumers accept it."[22]

# Final Reflections

For our final reflections on IP Video, we will consider how the myth of the blind men and the elephant provides an analogy for how today's thought leaders, soothsayers and technical experts (or geeks) envision the world influenced by IPTV and Internet Video technologies.

Whether your pulse on the industry originates from news feeds, analyst reports or the buzz at the office, most agree that today's IPTV baby steps are steadily building into awesome strides. From development through deployment and adoption, we are on our way to places only seen in part by the early visionaries.

We will continue to see an online, Amazon.com-like marketplace for video distribution. Studios and video bloggers alike will have a bigger and better platform for TV-grade, full-screen delivery to consumers—often without the financial, geographical or regulatory limitations imposed by conventional broadcast systems. The post-broadband era not long from today will drive wider Internet video consumption.

In the words of one lofty start-up, this "democratization of television broadcasting" is as profound as the arrival of the Internet itself. Strongly stated, but there's no doubt video is propagating in all directions. The transition might be parsed into old and new media characteristics something like Table 12.1.

Many readers are familiar with the tale of the blind men who had heard of, but had never seen, an elephant. When an elephant passed through their village one day, each man felt it. Upon inspection, the first blind man determined it was like a wall, the second man a spear, and another blind man was sure it was a rope, having respectively felt the elephant's side, its tusk and its tail. Each man called the other a fool.

As armchair futurists, we all speculate about the IPTV space, but here's what some of most qualified people are telling us about the elephant.

---

22. "Turning Content into Revenue," NAB, April 2006

| OLD MEDIA | NEW MEDIA |
|---|---|
| 20th Century | 21st Century |
| Analog Broadcast | Digital/IP Format |
| Centralized | Distributed: Personal/Portable |
| Daily-Weekly | On-Demand 24/7 |
| Secure, Authorized Installments | Time-shifted, with Piracy Issues |

**TABLE 12.1** *Media Empire Building Blocks*

# What the Business Leaders Say

Whether it's new broadband sites offering prime-time television, movies or user-generated video content, the power of Internet Video portals is a growing force this year, next year and beyond.

Many business executives leading the charge are confident that problems with IPTV technology will soon be resolved. "To me, it's more about ergonomic user experience and uniqueness of the service; this is the real challenge in the IPTV space," says Mario Mariani, CEO of Tiscali, Italy.[23] Companies transitioning to new IPTV service offerings seek to protect and increase RPU (revenue per user) by filling their end-to-end network.

So, filling the network with several services to increase RPU is an important goal. "Another IPTV/PC-TV challenge is the content availability," says Mariani. "The content industry is used to working with television broadcasters and is not yet well enough organized to have relationships, at least not in Europe, with ISPs and telco providers."

One of the assumptions by IPTV business leaders in Europe is that "the European customer wants a better TV experience, which means a better TV environment with HD content using an IPTV environment," says Carl Rijsbrack, vice president, marketing and communications at Alcatel Bell. Because you can use the platform to create individual TV environments that connect subscribers together in buddy lists and consume at any time, "IPTV is here and happening—the train has already pulled out of the station," believes Rijsbrack. "TV becomes way better TV. It becomes personalized and it's a true triple-play experience."[24]

---

23. Interview with Greenfield, August 2006

24. September 11, 2006, IBC

For others, there will be a variety of devices that will keep consumers in touch with an expanding media experience. "The near-term is about additive media," says ABC-Disney executive Anne Sweeney, adding that "Disney's bet is that the new technology allows content to follow you—and your money."[25]

Among others, Showtime has announced a 3G content portal, calling mobile broadcasting "increasingly important ... offering an excellent subscriber acquisition and program sampling opportunity," according to Robert Hayes, Showtime's senior vice president and general manager of digital media.[26]

The ability to become a producer is falling into the hands of amateurs everywhere. Some industry veterans maintain this type of video has a long way to go before really competing with television. Ricky Gervais, co-creator of "The Office" television comedy series argues that "you can't knock-up [create] an episode of *The Sopranos* or *24* on a little handheld digital camera".[27] But other insiders maintain we need to take a serious look at best practices and reconsider where it's all headed. "This is a fascinating new production and sharing of stuff, a phenomenon I find truly astounding," says Nick De Martino, Director of the American Film Institute (AFI) New Media Ventures. "With a $500 computer, a $500 camera and a $300 a year broadband connection, you're in business. You have the pieces in place for phenomenal change in what an individual voice can become," believes De Martino. "It's epic-making change in what the Internet can do."

The advent of people's video is a new force shaping things to come. "Initially there was a lot of viral growth in terms of people sharing links and embedding videos," explained YouTube CEO Chad Hurley about his Web site's growing popularity. "There's still a lot of that going on, but we've primarily become a destination zone on video," says Hurley. "Our idea is that everyone exists on the same level; we're just creating a stage. Even with NBC [U.S. network broadcaster], we're not pushing NBC on our users. They just exist on our system like everyone else."

According to NAB President and CEO David K. Rehr, we finally have built a strong foundation for digital TV and "are about to reinvent our industry." Rehr says, "We are about to ride a new wave of technology that will take us places that we have never been before."

---

25. Anne Sweeney, Disney-ABC, "Monetizing New Distribution Platforms", April 2006

26. www.prwebdirect.com/releases/2006/10/prweb448357.htm

27. Interview with Greenfield, November 2006, London

# What the Pundits Say

Adding to the momentum of new technologies and business models, the most influential industry players are voting with their feet. "AOL, Google, Yahoo!, MSN, Apple, major broadcast TV networks, pay-TV services and local TV stations are all working on ways to blend their video assets with personalized TV services," says Gerry Kaufhold, In-Stat analyst (2006). He adds, "The future of television is slowly being defined online, where the big Internet portals are finding ways to blend professional video with their high-touch services that follow consumers from screen to screen during the course of a typical day."

But how do we really get there from here? IPTV is already making waves in the broadcast sector, but according to many industry analysts, it will accelerate only after a few more pieces of the puzzle fall into place:

- Web and TV programming must be better and more seamlessly joined together through a more singular format

- In many countries, including the U.S., higher speed broadband to distribute a competitive IPTV offering must become more prevalent—particularly when it comes to HDTV bandwidth requirements

- There must be a more uniform architecture uniting PC, STB, cable and telcos

Another issue is service assurance. "If something goes wrong or it doesn't work, how is it reported and who's going to fix it?" asks Mark Weiss, IBM's IPTV/Triple Play Solutions Executive. To be successful, it will be essential to synchronize back office systems to log, monitor and respond cohesively. "If somebody says they didn't get a movie," says Weiss, "you've got the ability to verify it."

Some would call it a new TV culture. The next-generation video combination of social networking, buddy-lists and community PVRs shared between viewers is a market driver. So is user-generated video, such as the YouTube portal where you can share video, as well as interact with friends in real-time through Instant Messaging (IM) that delivers user-controlled content.

Whether it's a BBC documentary or political debate, NBC running the latest episode of "Lost," or a Chinese broadcaster covering the Beijing Olympics, IPTV and communications layers are interweaving. You may be watching at the same time with a friend in your community—or on another continent—and commenting to one another through IM, or another video interface layer, just as if you were together in the same place watching the same show.

Dedicated IPTV and Web streaming both confront the same user-interface challenge in the transition from browse to search. The PC filters Internet content with increasing elegance, but same cannot be said for the TV's ability to glean what viewers seek. "Where today you browse through channel grids and you channel surf, in the future you're going to interact with your TV set like you do with Google" according to Craig Moffett, vice president and senior analyst at Bernstein Research. Moffett believes that, "At least some of the time, you will be actively searching for what you want to watch and you'll be searching through content libraries of movies, old shows and entertainment from the Web".[28]

# What the Geeks Say

We all stand on the shoulders of giants, the forerunners who dream big and then manage to make the technologies that make a difference happen. We respectfully salute the geeks—counting ourselves among them—and turn to them next for an outlook on what is moving the IP Video culture forward.

In Chapter 9, we talked about the vital role bandwidth plays in any practical service provider offering, especially as viewers will not tolerate picture jitters or sluggish channel surfing. Imagine a world where throughput is no longer an issue, where there is enough speed and volume for all. Advances between now and 2020 are so inevitable that, by then, we'll look back at today's devices and interfaces and laugh at how primitive they were. Hossein Eslambolchi, former head of AT&T Labs says,

> The average of all the bandwidth speeds of all the 150 million DSL and cable customers globally is 3 Mbps. My projection is that 3 Mbps is going to expand to 40 Mbps by the end of the decade and over 1 Gbs by 2020. How do you know it's going to expand to that level by the end of the decade? Well it's a very simple formula that you can apply to any type of computing processing.
>
> If you assume Moore's Law—that price/performance improves by a factor of two every 18 months, that's a factor of 60 every 10 years, then you end up in the year 2010 at the speed of 40 Mbps—it's just a simple mathematical calculation. So, as long as Moore's Law holds, there's nothing there stopping us until at least the end of the decade.[29]

---

28. "Streaming vs. IPTV," Greenfield, Advanced Television, 2005

29. "2020 Technology Vision," Churchill Club, June 6, 2006

Another observer, veteran *New York Times* Silicon Valley correspondent, John Markoff interprets tomorrow's multimedia developments and IPTV in *Coming Soon to TV Land: The Internet, Actually*:

> At the onset of the dot-com era, large online service companies like AOL, Compuserve and MSN tried to lock customers into electronic walled gardens of digital information.
>
> But it quickly became apparent that no single company could compete with the vast variety of information and entertainment sources provided on the Web.
>
> The same phenomenon may well overtake traditional TV providers. Potentially, IPTV could replace the 100- or 500-channel world of the cable and satellite companies with millions of hybrid combinations that increasingly blend video, text from the Web and even video-game-style interactivity.[30]

Simply summarized, many close to the action know what Bradley Horowitz, Yahoo Director of Media Search, told us in 2005: "Convergence is not about smashing the TV and PC together, it's more about … making it 'my media' as opposed to 'mass media.' "

## IPTV: Meat Grinder or Metamorphosis?

The ground floor of a global 21st century broadband network is nearing completion and bandwidth is increasing. Like Metcalfe's Law of networks discussed earlier in this chapter, the result will be greater than the sum of its parts. Just as the fax machine or the newly connected 19th century railroad created new forms of commerce and communication that developed over subsequent decades, many projects will pound in the golden spike in the near future.

Telecoms around the world will begin operating at a new level: AT&T on ADSL2+ in the U.S., France Telecom on ADSL2+, T-Com, in Germany, on 50 Mbps VDSL. This will be an infrastructure for yet-to-be-invented services beyond IPTV or triple play offerings as we know them.

Last but not least, don't underestimate the impact of consumer design and communications innovators—companies pushing forward on the buzz and revenues of multimedia devices and service markets. Of the many examples of additional new products and services being developed and perfected, several come to mind, disruptors that will create a place for themselves in this emerging marketplace.

---

30. "Coming Soon to TV Land: The Internet, Actually", John Markoff, *New York Times*, January 7, 2006

*Placeshifting* sounded like sci-fi jargon until a commercially successful product came along that lets your video world travel with you around the globe. It might sound like tech-speak, but it describes what *Slingbox* does: brings the TV signal from the user's home TV, cable and PVR devices to user over the Internet anywhere in the world. With the HDTV and mobile compatibilities (including 3G) to deliver content over PDA and smart phones, an improved value proposition for portable media is providing access to personal media anywhere any time.

Then there's Apple Computer who "could have the most important position," according to Tim Bajarin, principal analyst with Creative Strategies. Like many observers, he sees the company as a proactive force that's bringing the Mac or PC to the center of content distribution. In Apple's model, content flows into the PC and the Mac integrates "Web-based interactivity through the IPTV layer, with traditional cable, telco and satellite as a secondary layer," says Bajarin. "And in the short term, that may be the way that all these guys are gonna have to deal with it."

Managing a recent 27 percent jump for Apple Computer quarterly profits (largely iPOD-based), CEO Steve Jobs, stated that this is "likely to be one of the most exciting new-product years in Apple's history." Will that be spelled I-P-T-V?

Bajarin says the main achievement will be "one, to make it much simpler to move the content from the TV to the PC—whether in the living room or upstairs ['Den, living room, car, pocket,' as Jobs puts it]; and, two, typical of Apple, I expect them to do it in the most elegant way, not only technologically, but from the standpoint of user interface."

A final apropos innovation example comes from the founders of Kazaa and Skype and builds on their prior runaway successes in music sharing and VoIP: another P2P media application, a video sharing service. In the words of former Skype CEO Niklas Zennström, "We're fixing TV, removing artificial limits such as the number of channels that your cable or the airwaves can carry, and then bringing it into the Internet age, adding community features, interactivity, etc." Designed to take the best from the new Web 2.0 culture of sharing and collaboration and combine it with legitimate rights and professional broadcast culture, it "could threaten the viability of network television" according to *USA Today*.[31] As one .tv provider states (stretching the point), "Television programming is so 1999."

Vendors are also inventing evermore powerful, cost-effective tools, and facilitating content production, storage and distribution at a new level. Crowd-pleasing benefits of storage, compression, ingest and playout advances are carrying us toward a

---

31. "Disrupter Man goes after TV this time," *USA Today*, December 6, 2006

"fully connected tomorrow," as Thomson Chairman & CEO Frank Dangeard put it, "where the consumer is in charge of the content they watch." We will no doubt continue to see greater proficiencies for collaborative content creation and rolling out on-demand services, new mobile platforms, and commonplace HDTV presence.

Some viewpoints included in this final chapter emphasize disruption. We, however, envision remarkable opportunity in change. The fully connected tomorrow may still be somewhere over the rainbow, continuing to keep us guessing about its final features. But the next phase belongs to those organizations—large or small, startup or incumbent—willing to embrace the future by mastering the processes and markets that emerge with any new technology. We leave it for you to exploit these viewpoints and fuel the next period in this extraordinary series of events that will continue to evolve and impact the industry for years to come.

# Summary

We have seen during this book's journey through the high-growth world of IPTV and Internet Video that new services, business practices and economic models are springing up. As an executive briefing, we have endeavored to provide sound perspective on the state of the industry, inspecting technology more deeply when it seemed valuable and appropriate for the reader.

In this chapter, we re-visited the IPTV story so far, then explored the business drivers and advanced technology on the horizon that are shaping this emerging world of interactive media. We then considered the expectations surrounding these new, often over-hyped developments. We considered the increasing availability of more and more types of content and programming in an everything-on-demand media universe.

We also took stock of services enabling personal and enterprise producers to create their own custom channels or programming networks. In the world of portable media, we saw how all content is going mobile, as consumers continue to hold more and more information in the palm of their hands and as devices get smaller, smarter and more connected.

In our final reflections on IP Video, we looked at how the myth of the blind men and the elephant provides an analogy for how today's thought leaders, soothsayers and technical wizards, envision the world influenced by IPTV and Internet Video technologies.

# Glossary

3G—Third generation mobile communications technology. Technology promises increased bandwidth, up to 128 Kbps in a moving automobile, up to 384 Kbps when a device is moving at less than walking speed, and up 2 Mbps in stationary locations. Subject of a multi-billion dollar radio spectrum auction at the dawn of the 21st century.

AAC (Advance Audio Coding)—Audio coding system for MPEG–2 and MPEG–4 signals that provides up to 48 channels of audio. Frequently used at 192 kbps for 5.1 surround sound.

ADSL (Asymmetric Digital Subscriber Line)—Technology that enables a standard telephone line to carry high-speed data in addition to normal voice telephony. Operates by using very high frequencies to carry data; requires DSL modem devices to be installed at customer premises and in provider facilities. Technology is termed "asymmetric" because the data rate from the service provider to the end user is higher than the data rate from the user back to the provider.

ATM (Asynchronous Transfer Mode)—Digital multiplexing and networking standard that transports information in uniform size packets called "cells." Each cell contains 48 bytes of user data and a 5-byte header. Popularized in the 1990s for video and data transport.

ATSC (Advanced Television Systems Committee)—Industry consortium originally formed in 1982 to coordinate television standards across different media. ATSC was instrumental in developing standards for digital and high definition television broadcasts in the U.S. Current standards cover many areas of digital broadcasting, including compression profiles, RF modulation techniques and other areas needed to ensure compatibility between broadcaster and viewer equipment.

Avail—Timeslot in linear programming feed that is available to a system operator for local advertisement insertion.

AVC (Advanced Video Coding)—Video compression system standardized in 2003 that provides significant improvement in coding efficiency over earlier algorithms. Also known as H.264 and MPEG–4 Part 10.

Bandwidth—A measurement of the network capacity or throughput, usually expressed in Mbps or kbps.

B Frame—The most highly compressed type of MPEG–2 video frame; uses data of the preceding and following I or P frames.

Broadband—Term used to describe signals or systems that carry a high bandwidth signal, at a speed of at least 256 kbps.

CA (Conditional Access)—Policies for controlling the access to video, audio or other data files. User access, such as viewing or recording of video files, can be limited to specific categories of viewers that meet specific conditions, such as only those viewers who subscribe to a premium movie service.

Cache—Short-term, temporary storage location. Commonly used in conjunction with disk drives and microprocessors to speed up data transfer by allowing larger blocks of data to be transferred in each read or write operation. Can also be used to simplify the connection between high-speed devices and low-speed networks.

CAS (Conditional Access System)—Hardware and/or software system that enforces conditional access policies. Typically includes mechanism for scrambling or encrypting content prior to transmission, a mechanism to permit authorized user devices to descramble or decrypt content at the user's location, and a mechanism to securely distribute the required descrambling or decryption keys to authorized users.

Capture—Process of converting raw audio and video content into files that can be manipulated by computer-based editing, production and streaming systems.

CAT5 (Category 5 Unshielded Twisted Pair Cable)—Type of data communication cable certified for use in 10BaseT and 100BaseT (Ethernet) network connections.

CAT6 (Category 6 Unshielded Twisted Pair Cable)—Type of data communication cable certified for use in 1000BaseT (Gigabit Ethernet) network connections.

CATV (Cable Television or Community Antenna Television)—System that distributes video programming to subscribers through the use of broadband fiber and coaxial cables. Modern systems offer several hundred channels of broadcast and on-demand video programming as well as data and voice services.

CDN (Content Delivery Network)—Network of distributed servers used to deliver content such as Web pages or video/audio files to users in multiple geographic areas.

Closed Captioning—Process that adds text captions to video images that can be displayed on suitably equipped televisions. These captions are called "closed" because they are not visible on-screen unless the viewer chooses to display them. In many cases these captions will include descriptions of sound effects in addition to a text rendition of any spoken dialog.

CO (Central Office)—Facility used by a telephone company or other service provider to deliver signals to subscribers. Normally, a telephone CO will contain equipment that is used to process user telephone calls, and it may also contain data or video transport and processing equipment.

Coaxial—Cable or connector that contains two conductors, one in the center of the cable, and another that completely surrounds it, separated by an insulating layer. Coaxial cables are frequently used for video applications, because of their superior performance with both analog and digital video signals.

Codec—Device or software that encodes (compresses) and decodes (decompresses) digital stream or data.

CSS (Content Scramble System)—Method used to scramble the content of DVDs and thereby prevent them from being duplicated or played on unauthorized playback devices.

Decoder—Device used to convert compressed audio and/or video content into original form, using technologies such as MPEG, JPEG, etc.

Digital Turnaround—Process of taking video and audio signals that are encoded in one format and converting them into another format.

Domain Name System—Translation system that takes easy to remember names (i.e., "elsevier.com") and converts them into IP addresses required for Internet communication.

Download and Play—Internet Video delivery technique where the entire content file is downloaded to the player device before playback begins. Contrast with streaming and progressive download and play.

DRM (Digital Rights Management)—A generic term used to describe various mechanisms for controlling users' access to digital content. This can include a variety of functions, including encryption, scrambling and copy protection, which are commonly applied to copyrighted or other proprietary works.

DSL (Digital Subscriber Line)—Popular mechanism for providing high-speed data connections to users over existing telephone wiring. Several different generations of technology have come to market, with varying combinations of speed and useful distance.

DSLAM—Digital Subscriber Line Access Multiplexer (DSLAM) provides a high-speed data conduit between multiple DSLs and the high bandwidth network backbone.

DTH (Direct-To-Home)—Satellite television broadcasting system in which programming is transmitted directly to antennas mounted on subscribers' premises. Differs from other satellite-based services that deliver programming to CATV, IPTV, and terrestrial service providers who then distribute programming to viewers.

DTV (Digital Television)—System for broadcasting video using compressed digital signals. Can be either standard definition or high definition video images. Employs analog 6 MHz television channel that has been converted into a digital transmission channel capable of carrying 19 Mbps or more of data traffic.

DVB (Digital Video Broadcasting)—Organization formed in Europe to create standards for broadcasting digital television signals. Includes a variety of distribution methods (see DVB-H) and formats that can be used in the content-creation process.

DVB-H (Digital Video Broadcasting – Handheld)—One standard for delivering live television to handheld devices competing with other standards such as DMB/DAB and FLO (Forward Link Only).

DVD (Digital Versatile Disc)—High-density, removable storage medium commonly used for recording high-quality digital video and audio signals. Widely used for movie and other video content sales/rentals to consumers; has displaced VHS tapes as most popular format for new consumer purchases.

DVI (Digital Visual Interface)—Connector used to carry digital video signals between signal sources (PCs, DVD players, STBs) and displays of various types. Supports High-bandwidth Digital Content Protection protocol that can be used to ensure that content is distributed only to proper display devices and not to recording equipment that could be used to pirate video content. This 24-pin connector can now be found on many high-performance video displays.

DVR (Digital Video Recorder)—See PVR.

EAS (Emergency Alert System)—Government-mandated system for broadcasters in the U.S. that is used for transmitting emergency alerts to the public in the event of a natural or man-made disaster or other emergency.

Encoder—Device used to convert raw audio and/or video content into compressed form, using technologies such as MPEG, JPEG, etc.

Encryption—Technique used to make data unreadable to parties other than the sender and intended recipients. Normally accomplished through the use of a mathematical operation performed on raw data in conjunction with a key known only to the sender and the recipients. Encryption algorithms are considered strong when third parties that do not have access to the key are unable to recover the original data.

EOD (Everything On Demand)—Potential future video content delivery concept where all content is delivered to users at the time of their choosing; the complete elimination of linear programming and scheduling.

EPG (Electronic Program Guide)—An on-screen display that allows viewer navigation of television programs scheduled for broadcast and available for VOD playback.

ES (Elementary Stream)—Term used in MPEG systems to describe the raw compressed data that is fed into a video or into an audio decoder. These streams can also be converted into other forms for recording (see PS, Program Stream) or transport (see TS, Transport Stream).

Feeder Plant—Portion of a telephone network that transports signals between local central offices and remote terminals. Remote terminals are in turn connected by means of local loops to individual houses over twisted pair copper or other technology.

Firewall—Device used at junction point between two networks to ensure that certain types of data on one network do not get transmitted to the other network. Commonly used when connecting private LANs to the Internet to protect the local users from harmful data or unwanted probes.

Forward Error Correction (FEC)—Technology used to identify and correct transmission errors in digital network feeds. Adds variable amount of overhead to content streams.

FTTH (Fiber To The Home)—System for distributing high-speed data and video services directly to customer premises using optical fiber for the entire link. Also known as Fiber To The Premises (FTTP). Contrast with DSL and HFC networks, both of which typically employ fiber in portions of the network but use electrical cables for connection to customers.

GB (Gigabyte)—Storage capacity equal to 1024 Megabytes of computer memory. Also defined as 1 billion bytes on a hard disk drive.

Gbps (Gigabit per second)—Data transmission speed of 1 billion bits per second.

GigE (Gigabit Ethernet)—LAN data transmission standard operating at 1Gbps, standardized in IEEE 802.3.

Group of Pictures (GOP)—A series of frames in an MPEG system consisting of a single I frame and zero or more P and B frames.

HD (High Definition)—Video image with resolution greater than standard definition. Typical formats include 720-line progressively scanned images, 1080-line interlaced images, and many other formats. Many HD signals have an aspect ratio of 16:9.

HDCP (High-Bandwidth Digital Content Protection)—DRM technology used between HD receivers and digital displays to prevent unauthorized copying of digital content files.

HDMI (High-Definition Multimedia Interface)—High performance digital audio and video connector system used to connect STB, HD-DVD players and HD displays.

HDTV (High Definition Television)—Broadcast version of HD signal, typically compressed to 18 Mbps or lower to fit into single DTV broadcast channel.

Head End—In a CATV or IPTV system, the source of video and other programming that is distributed to numerous subscribers.

HFC (Hybrid Fiber Coax)—Architecture commonly used in CATV distribution systems, in which fiber optic cable is used for long-distance connections from the head end into local areas and coaxial cables are used to distribute the signals into subscriber premises. This has the benefit of providing high-bandwidth, low-loss fiber optic transport for analog and digital signals over long distances without the expense of having to install fiber optic receivers in every customer's location.

Home Gateway—Connects the networked devices in the house with any server storage and the Internet through a high-speed DSL modem and communications ports.

HPNA (Home Phoneline Networking Alliance)—An industry organization with technology members such AT&T, HP, IBM and Intel that explores ways to establish home networking standards that drive innovation and interoperability between telecom and IT data, device and service providers.

HTTP (HyperText Transfer Protocol)—The primary protocol used on the World Wide Web to provide communications between clients and servers. Much of the information transported by HTTP consists of Web pages and related data. HTTP is stateless, meaning that each transaction is self-contained and that there is no built-in mechanism to connect a server to a particular client. To get around this limitation, many servers issue "cookies" to clients to enable the server to keep track of the status of different clients.

Hub—Data communications device used in twisted pair Ethernet networks to connect multiple circuits within the same domain.

IETF (Internet Engineering Task Force)—Group of engineers that develop solutions and specifications needed to provide a common framework for the operation of the Internet. The IETF is responsible for creating the technical content of the RFCs that make up the standards that govern the operation of the Internet.

I Frame—Type of MPEG frame that is intra-coded, i.e., does not depend on data from any other frames. These frames typically require the most amount of data to encode, but are required by the decoder whenever a new stream is presented, such as during a channel change.

Impulse PPV—Method used by consumers to order Video on Demand (VOD) services that are offered on a pay-per-view (PPV) basis. With Impulse PPV, subscribers can simply use their remote control to order VOD content, with the charges normally being deducted from a pre-arranged account. This contrasts with the method used on many traditional PPV systems in which viewers call a telephone number displayed on their screen to order VOD content by speaking with a customer service agent.

Interactive TV—Video programming style that allows viewers to participate in various ways through a user-interface with content that is being furnished to them.

Internet—Global network that provides interconnection among a large community of data providers and users. The Internet is used on a daily basis by millions of users for communication, reference and entertainment; it provides a common medium for a diverse set of applications that allow many modern business, government and personal activities.

Internet Video—Video content delivered in discrete pieces selected by individual Web viewers for viewing on a display connected to a personal computer or other Internet-enabled device.

IP (Internet Protocol)—Standard set of rules for formatting and transporting data across the Internet and other networks that use packetized datagrams for communication. These rules include a standard format for headers that appear on each packet and a mechanism for addressing packets so that they can be sent from a source to a destination. The standard that we call IP today was defined in RFC 791 in September 1981 for the Defense Advanced Research Projects Agency of the U.S. government; it is now part of the set of standards maintained by the IETF.

IP Address—A 32-bit number that provides unique identification of each data transmitter and receiver on an IP network. Often represented in dotted decimal form, such as 129.35.76.177.

IPTV—A two-way digital broadcast signal over broadband that uses STBs and is delivered over switched telephone or cable networks. Similar to traditional CATV, satellite and broadcast television, where continuous channels of programming are delivered to consumers for viewing on traditional television sets.

IRD (Integrated Receiver/Decoder)—Device used in satellite television systems to receive an incoming signal and decode it for display on a consumer television set. Often includes circuits necessary to descramble protected content and to convert digital satellite signals into analog video signals that are compatible with a consumer television set.

ISO (International Organization for Standardization)—International body made up of member organizations from around the world that defines and establishes international standards in a wide variety of areas.

ISO/IEC—The International Organization for Standardization and the International Electrotechnical Commission have a joint committee for developing standards on information and communications technology. Many of the MPEG standards have been approved by this committee, and so carry the designation ISO/IEC before their number.

ISP (Internet Service Provider)—Company or group that provides network access to the Internet for business and individuals, generally on a fee-for-service basis.

JPEG—A standard method of compression for digital images established by the Joint Photographic Experts Group.

kbps (kilobit per second)—Data transmission rate equal to 1,000 bits per second.

Kbyte (Kilobyte)—1,024 bytes of data.

Key (Encryption Key)—Secret digital value that is manipulated along with user data by an encryption algorithm to produce an encoded message. Because only the sender and the receiver possess the key to an encoded message, other parties cannot understand the message, provided the encryption algorithm has not been compromised.

LAN (Local Area Network)—Data communications network that covers a local area, such as a house, a business office or a small building. Most LAN technologies are limited to transmission distances on the order of hundreds of meters.

LEO (Local End Office)—Portion of an IPTV network closest to viewer where video signals are converted into the form that will be delivered to each individual household.

Lip-sync—Property of video and audio signals in which both are aligned in time so that on-screen images of lip motions match the voice sounds. When lip-sync is not present, video programming can be annoying to watch.

Macroblock—Fundamental working unit of the MPEG compression system that contains a 16 × 16 pixel portion of one frame or field of a video sequence. Macroblocking is often used to describe a deteriorated MPEG image in which portions of the image have been replaced with single color blocks that occupy a 16 × 16 pixel portion of the displayed image; this is normally caused by missing or corrupt data in a compressed video stream that is being processed by an MPEG decoder.

MB (Megabyte)— Storage capacity equal to 1024 Kilobytes of computer memory.

Mbps (Megabit per second)—Data transmission rate equal to 1 million bits per second.

Metadata—Literally, "data about data." Metadata is used to describe the contents of digital files, with the goal of making the files easier to locate and work with. Metadata about video content might include information such as the title of the work, the duration, the format and other useful information. Often, some metadata is inserted into the video stream itself to allow automatic identification of the content of the video. An analogy for metadata would be a label on the outside of a videotape cassette, which allows a person to find a specific piece of material without needing to view the actual content of each tape.

Metcalfe's Law—States that a network's value is related to the square of the number of users of the system. Robert Metcalfe formulated the axiom in regard to Ethernet; it helps explain the additive effects and value of Internet and wireless communication networks.

MhP (Multimedia Home Platform)—Middleware standard developed by DVB that defines the interfaces between operating system software and user applications on set top boxes. Used to simplify the tasks of software developers and STB designers and to provide a common platform for development and deployment.

Middleware—A series of software functions or services that links specific components (such as application servers, VOD servers and STBs) and application software (such as conditional access control, billing systems and interactive services).

Moore's Law—A prediction about transistor density as applied to processors that has come to apply to a doubling of information technology price-performance every 18 months.

Motion Estimation—A key part of the compression process used in MPEG. Successive frames of video are analyzed and compared to determine if any portions of the image have moved. If so, the MPEG decoder can be instructed to simply move one or more macroblocks from one location in the image to another location in the following frame.

Motion Vectors—These describe the motion of a macroblock from one position to another between two successive frames of a video image, including both direction and magnitude of the motion.

MPEG (Moving Pictures Experts Group)—A committee first formed in 1988 to develop international standards for video and encoding for digital storage. Numerous standards have been produced by this group and given international approval by ISO/IEC. Today, the MPEG acronym is used to describe a wide range of compression formats.

MPEG LA (MPEG Licensing Authority)—Providers of consolidated patent licenses for MPEG technology.

MPLS (Multi-Protocol Label Switching)—Technology used in a variety of pocket transport networks to simplify the functions performed by core routers and improve the flow of many different types of data.

Multicast—Data transmission from a single source to multiple, simultaneous destinations. Contrast with unicast.

Musicam—Another name for MPEG Layer 2 audio. This is used in DAB (Digital Audio Broadcasting) and DVB (Digital Video Broadcasting) systems in Europe.

NTSC (National Television System Committee)—Committee that in the early 1950s selected the color television broadcast standard for the U.S. NTSC is often used as an abbreviation for the 525-line, 29.97 frames per second, interlaced video standard used in North America, Japan and a number of other countries.

NVOD (Near Video On Demand)—Video delivery system that simulates some of the attributes of a Video on Demand system without the individual video stream control capabilities. One common form of NVOD is sometimes called staggercasting, in which multiple copies of a program are played starting at five-minute intervals, thereby limiting any individual viewer to no more than a five-minute wait before his or her program begins to play.

OCAP (OpenCable Application Platform)—Middleware interface standard developed by CableLabs to permit portability of software applications and STBs for cable operators in the U.S. Based in part on MhP standards.

OTA (Over the Air)—Television broadcast technique that uses standard RF transmission to aerials on receiving televisions, also called terrestrial broadcast.

Packet—A variable length data container that can be transported over an IP network.

PAL (Phase Alternating Line)—Color video signal that is commonly used in Europe, where the individual lines alternate in phase from one line to the next. Also used as shorthand for the 625-line, 25 frames per second interlaced video standard used extensively in Europe and other countries around the world.

PC (Personal Computer)—Generic term used to describe desktop and portable computers, often those based on Intel/AMD processors and running an operating system supplied by Microsoft. Can also be used to describe Macintosh- and Linux-based computers in some contexts.

PES (Packetized Elementary Stream)—Term used in MPEG to describe an elementary stream that has been divided into packets, prior to further processing. PES packets can be hundreds of kilobytes long, so they typically need further processing into transport stream packets before they are sent over an IP network.

P Frame—Type of MPEG video frame that uses data from a prior I frame. Typically contains more data than a B frame but less than an I frame.

PID (Packet Identifier)—Method used to identify each of the different video and audio content streams contained in an MPEG Transport Stream. Each packet contained in a transport stream can have data from only one elementary stream, such as a video or an audio ES, and each packet has a single PID. A demultiplexer can easily locate the streams it desires by sorting the incoming packets by their PID.

Placeshifting—Delivering video programming from a user's home TV, cable, PVR, etc. to user's PC or wireless device over the Internet anyplace in the world.

Podcasting—Online media publishing that enables producers to upload their content and audience to download or subscribe to regular feeds that retrieve new files as they become available.

Portable Media—General term referring to the growing mobility of audio, video and image content to be accessed wirelessly and compactly carried on ever more powerful, streamlined devices with greater disk drive capacity, and downloaded or streamed through. New terms such as mobisode are used to describe shorter, smaller video.

PPV (Pay-Per-View)—Method for charging viewers for the right to watch or listen to a specific piece of content for a specific time. Rights may be limited to a single showing of the content or may expire after a designated period of time (such as 24 hours).

Progressive Download and Play—Internet Video delivery technique where the video content is broken up into a series of small files, each of which is downloaded in turn to the user's device during playback. Contrast with streaming and download and play.

PS (Program Stream)—An MPEG stream that contains one or more packetized elementary streams that have a common clock source. These streams can be different types (such as video and audio), and they can be played in synchronization. Program streams are not well-suited for transport, but do work well for recording purposes and disk storage, including DVDs.

Push VOD (Push Video on Demand)—Technique for storing VOD content in user STBs for playback under user control. Removes need for high-speed video data connection to central servers used in normal VOD systems.

PVR (Personal Video Recorder)—Device that allows the recording and playback of content under the control of an end user; normally based on video compression and hard disk technology. TiVO was one of the first brand names for this technology.

QoS (Quality of Service)—Mechanism in IP and other data networks that allows some data flows to have higher priority over other flows that share the same communications line or device.

Quadruple play—A combined telecommunications service offering that consists of Internet, television, telephone and wireless services.

QuickTime—A software framework developed by Apple Computer to integrate the multimedia applications and functionality that handle video, audio, image, animation, music and text.

Remote Terminal—Portion of traditional telephone network where digital telephony signals are converted into standard two-wire analog telephony signals. Often used to provide physical space, power, etc., for installing DSLAM devices.

Return Path—Communications channel flowing in the opposite direction to the principal flow of information. Term popularized in cable television applications in which many networks were originally constructed to operate in one direction only (from cable TV provider to subscriber homes). A return path is required for two-way applications such as data or voice communication.

RF (Radio Frequency)—High-frequency electrical signals that are capable of radiating from or being received by an antenna. A huge variety of devices use RF signals, including AM/FM radios, televisions, cellular phones, satellite receivers and all modern computing devices.

RJ-45—Standard connector for 10BaseT and subsequent data communication standards that are commonly used for Ethernet communication. The RJ-45 connector is a small plastic clip with up to eight wires that is very similar in appearance to the four- or six-wire connectors that are widely used for connecting telephone sets to wall plugs. "RJ" stands for "Registered Jack."

Router—(1) In IP networks, a device that is responsible for processing the headers on IP packets and forwarding them toward their ultimate destination. (2) In video networks, a device that provides switching of connections between video sources and their destinations.

RTCP (Real Time Control Protocol)—Data transport control protocol that works in conjunction with RTP for transporting real-time media streams. Includes functions to support synchronization between different media types (e.g., audio and video) and to provide information to streaming applications about network quality, number of viewers, identity of viewers, etc.

RTP (Real Time Protocol or Real-time Transport Protocol)—Data transport protocol that is specifically designed for transporting real-time signals such as streaming video and audio. RTP is often used in conjunction with UDP and provides important functions such as packet sequence numbering and packet time stamping. RTP is used in conjunction with RTCP.

RTSP (Real Time Streaming Protocol)—Protocol used to set up and control real-time streams. Commonly used to create links on Web sites that point to streaming media files.

SAP (Session Announcement Protocol)—Broadcast IP packets used to send out information about each of the multicast streams available on a network, along with information that user devices need in order to connect to a multicast.

SD (Standard Definition)—Video image with a resolution defined in standards popularized in the 1950s and widely used for television around the world. For 60Hz NTSC systems, the video image is composed of 525 interlaced horizontal lines, of which 485 represent the actual image. For 50Hz PAL systems, the video image is composed of 625 interlaced horizontal lines, of which 576 represent the actual image. Both of these standards use a 4:3 aspect ratio.

SHE (Super Head End)—In a CATV or large IPTV system, a SHE is commonly used to receive signals from various sources and distribute them to head ends or VSOs located within an MSO's territory. It is not uncommon for one SHE to provide service to several hundred thousand subscribers.

SLA (Service Level Agreement)—A contractual agreement between a carrier and a customer that specifies the level of network performance that the carrier will deliver to the customer. This often includes a set of network performance guarantees (minimum availability, maximum error rate, etc.) and a set of remedies (such as billing credits) if these minimums are not met.

Smart Card—Small plastic card or chip that contains a microprocessor and memory. Often used for storing and transporting decryption and authorization codes for devices such as set top boxes or mobile phones.

SMPTE (Society of Motion Picture and Television Engineers)—U.S.-based organization that, among other things, develops standards for movie and video technology. For more information, go to www.smpte.org.

Slingbox—Brand name for one of the first commercially successful TV devices that delivers the TV signal from the user's home TV, cable and PVR devices to the user over the Internet anywhere in the world. See placeshifting.

Social Networking—Web interaction between users facilitated by voice, chat (IM), Web pages, sharing of videos, buddy-lists in a collaborative manner – often described as the nature of Web 2.0.

Soft Real Time—Video transport application in which the video signals are transported in the same amount of time as it takes to display them. Video signals may be live or pre-recorded for soft real time, and significant end-to-end delays are acceptable.

S/PDIF (Sony/Philips Digital Interface Format)—Digital audio format commonly used in consumer audio playback equipment.

STB (Set Top Box)—Device used in conjunction with video delivery systems that performs a variety of tasks, including signal processing, demodulation, decryption and digital-to-analog conversion. STBs are normally required for DSL–based IPTV and DTH satellite television systems and are frequently required on CATV systems.

Streaming—Method for delivering video or other content over a network in a continuous flow at a rate that matches the speed at which data is consumed by the display device.

Subtitles—Text that is added to motion picture and television content for many purposes, including content display in another language. When content is subtitled, the text becomes part of the video image and is displayed to all viewers. Contrast this with closed captioning in the U.S., which can be displayed or hidden upon viewer command.

Supertrunk—High-performance link commonly used in CATV applications to transmit multi-channel signals from one head end to another. These signals can be either analog or digital, depending on the distances and the application.

S-video—Analog video signal in which the chroma and luma signals are carried over separate signal paths. This can improve video quality in comparison to a composite signal by eliminating the need to separate the chroma and luma signals in the television display.

Switch—In Ethernet networks, a device that provides multiple ports that each has a separate logical and physical network interface. This feature eliminates the possibility of packet collisions between devices on separate ports of the switch, thereby improving overall system performance.

TB (Terabyte)—Storage capacity equal to 1024 GB.

TCP (Transmission Control Protocol)—Reliable data transfer protocol used in IP networks that offers connection-oriented data transport, along with automatic data transfer rate control and re-transmission of corrupted packets. One of the most widely used data transport protocols, TCP is used throughout the public Internet. However, for live or streaming media signals, RTP over UDP is often a better choice.

Timeshifting—Practice of recording a broadcast television program at one time using a PVR or other device and viewing the program at a later, more convenient time.

TiVo—Brand name for one of the pioneering types of PVR (See PVR).

Transcoding—process of converting a video signal that is encoded in one technology (say MPEG-2) into another technology (say MPEG-4).

Transrating—Process of changing the bit rate of a compressed video stream.

Triple Play—A combined telecommunications service offering that consists of Internet, television and telephone services.

True Streaming—Internet Video delivery technique where a video signal is delivered to viewing device in real time and is displayed to the viewer immediately. Contrast with download and play.

TS (Transport Stream)—Standard method used in MPEG for converting PES streams into a stream of packets that can easily be transported, say, over an IP network, a satellite link, or over a digital television broadcast to a home. Each TS packet is a fixed 188 bytes long, although FEC data can be added, bringing the TS packet size up to 204 or 208 bytes. Note that MPEG IP packets generally contain multiple transport stream packets.

UDP (User Datagram Protocol)—Data transfer protocol used on IP networks that offers connectionless, stateless data transport. It is often used in video transport applications (along with RTP) because it offers low overhead and does not provide automatic rate reductions and packet re-transmissions (supplied by TCP) that can interfere with video transport.

Unicast—Data transmission from a single source to a single destination. Contrast with multicast.

Upconvert—Video processing technique used to convert an SD signal into an HD signal.

UTP (Unshielded Twisted Pair)—Form of electrical cable used to transmit data signals, including a variety of forms of Ethernet.

VC–1—Video compression technique standardized as SMPTE 421M. Formerly known as Windows Media 9.

VDSL (Very high-speed Digital Subscriber Line)—Digital Subscriber Line technology that is capable of delivering a large amount of bandwidth. First generation standard provides 52 Mbps up to 1000 ft. (300 m) from source. Speeds in this range are generally required to deliver multiple simultaneous HD video streams to multiple television sets over a single DSL circuit.

Video Blogging (also called vlogging)—Delivery of video stories, news or other coverage over the Web in the form of a log, report or updated communications series from amateurs or professionals. Like podcasting, often takes advantage of syndication which allows other Web users to subscribe to content feeds of their choice.

VOD (Video On Demand)—Process for delivering video programming to viewers when they want it. Commonly includes the ability to skip ahead (fast-forward) or rewind the video signal under user control. Contrast with NVOD.

VoIP (Voice over IP)—Method for voice telephony that uses IP (Internet Protocol) networks in place of the public switched telephone network.

VSO (Video Serving Office)—Portion of a large IPTV network where local programming is processed for distribution to CO/RT equipment for distribution to IPTV viewers.

Walled Garden—A Web browsing environment where user navigation is restricted to content and navigation offered by a service provider.

WAN (Wide Area Network)—Network that connects two or more network segments across a significant geographic distance—across a city, or around the world.

Web 2.0—Collaborative, content-sharing enhancement to the World Wide Web, seen as an evolutionary advance in information contribution by users.

Wi-Fi—Wireless local area data networking technology, also known as 802.11. Found on a wide variety of PCs, most new laptops, and a variety of handheld devices.

xDSL (Digital Subscriber Line)—In this abbreviation, "x" represents any one of a selection of words, including "A" for Asymmetric DSL, "H" for High Speed DSL and others. xDSL is a generic term intended to mean "any of a variety of forms of DSL."

(Ad) Zapping—The practice of skipping ads by the viewer through controlling program playback over PVR or VOD system.

# Index